RAKESH BANSAL, a post graduate in Business Management, grew interested in the stock market in 1998 and is now a full time market trader, mentor and advisor. Equally, he is a prominently featured market expert on top Indian business television channels.

With his vast repertoire of knowledge and rich experience of more than two decades, Mr. Bansal has been mentoring and advising large numbers of traders and investors through his seminars. He is an expert panellist with Zee Business television channel where he regularly shares his market outlook and trading picks. His equity advisory services focus on "Return OF Capital along with Return ON Capital."

Rakesh Bansal is the author of two other successful books on trading, *Profitable Short Term Trading Strategies* and *Profitable Elliott Wave Trading Strategies*, both published by Vision Books.

~

Also by
Rakesh Bansal

~

Profitable Short-Term Trading Strategies

~

Profitable Elliott Wave Trading Strategies

~

PROFITABLE TRADING WITH DOW THEORY

RAKESH BANSAL

www.visionbooksindia.com

www.vision**books**india.com

Disclaimer

The author and the publisher disclaim all legal or other responsibilities for any losses which investors may suffer by investing or trading using the methods described in this book. Readers are advised to seek professional guidance before making any specific investments. This book is meant purely for the purpose of investor and trader education.

Earlier Published as *Wealth Creation with Dow Theory*
This Revised Edition Published by Vision Books in 2020
Reprinted 2023

ISBN 10: 93-86268-43-4
ISBN 13: 978-93-86268-43-3

Published by
Vision Books Pvt. Ltd.
(Incorporating Orient Paperbacks and CARING imprints)
24 Feroze Gandhi Road, Lajpat Nagar 3
New Delhi 110024, India.
Phone: (+91-11) 2984 0821 / 22
e-mail: visionbooks@gmail.com

Printed at
Ashim Print Line
38/2, 35 & 36 Sahibabad, Industrial Area, Ghaziabad
Uttar Pradesh 201010, India.

Dedication

SHRI RADHA KRISHAN DHINGRA

I would like to take this opportunity to introduce to the readers someone very special. I am dedicating this book to my maternal grandfather, late Shri Radha Krishan Dhingra, to thank him from the bottom of my heart for everything he did for me.

He was a true Karma Yogi; he was sympathetic, tolerant, humble and free from hatred, jealousy, harshness, greed, anger and egoism. Above all, he never expected any kind of fruits for his actions.

Throughout his life, he always stood beside me in whatever I did.

Thank you, Nana ji, for everything. I love you — and miss you . . . .

Contents

Preface

THE BASICS OF TECHNICAL ANALYSIS ARE EASY TO LEARN but difficult to implement. This is because a majority of traders get distracted by seemingly new and more lucrative approaches or theories and fail to persist with their own strategy.

I have learnt from experience that Dow Theory can be used for trading the stock markets profitably. In the market, simple, straightforward approaches like Dow Theory help in wealth creation, while fancy, complex theories and structured products could cost you a fortune.

This book is all about profitable trading using Dow Theory.

Each chapter in this book is organized in a logically sequential manner. The reader should therefore read it chapter wise, from the beginning to the end, in order to grasp all the nuances of trading using the Dow Theory. Each topic is explained in sufficient detail and illustrated with real-life examples from the Indian stock market.

Through this book I have tried to explain Dow Theory and its implementation in a very simple yet comprehensive way.

All effort has been made to keep the book error-free; some errors may still have inadvertently crept in. I would welcome the reader's cooperation in bringing to my knowledge any errors that you may come across. Constructive criticism is always welcome and will be gratefully acknowledged.

RAKESH BANSAL

Chapter 1

~

Introduction to Technical Analysis

TECHNICAL ANALYSIS IS A STUDY OF THE PAST PRICE and volume data of an underlying security or financial instrument in order to ascertain its future price direction. In other words, technical analysis is primarily a systematic study of demand and supply. Thus, if the demand for a financial security is more than its supply, then the price rises and the trend is considered as up. On the other hand, if the supply is more than the demand, then the price falls and the trend is considered as down.

Assumptions of Technical Analysis

1. The market is always right.
2. At all times, the price of a security is the sum total of the following factors:
   - Hopes, fears and greed of market participants.
   - Domestic and global economic situation.
   - Corporate developments.
   - News, including insider news, etc.
3. The price of a financial security discounts everything, except for natural calamities, such as a tsunami, earthquake, corona virus, etc.
4. Market movements are not chaotic, though they may seem so. Rather, market movements are orderly, and the market moves in trends.

Advantages of Technical Analysis

1. Technical analysis helps in ascertaining the price trend.

2. Technical analysis helps in a quicker review of an investment decision as the price anticipates all relevant information well in advance.

3. Technical analysis is a systematic approach as the maximum risk is known at the time of initiating a trade.

Pitfalls of Technical Analysis

1. Technical analysis is not an exact science with perfectly predictable results. In fact, no method of market analysis is.

2. The basics of technical analysis are easy to learn but difficult to implement and master. This is because a majority of traders often get enticed mid-way with seemingly lucrative "new" theories and thus fail to continue with the approach they have started with.

~

Chapter 2

~

Dow Theory

Introduction

Dow Theory is named after Charles H Dow (1851-1902), who is widely regarded as the Father of Technical Analysis.

Interestingly, Charles Dow never wrote any book himself, nor published his complete theory. His followers and associates propounded and published his insights from the 255 editorials he wrote in *Wall Street Journal,* and christened these as Dow Theory.

Principles of Dow Theory

First Principle — The Stock Market Discounts All Information

Dow Theory holds that the price of a stock discounts all information, except for natural calamities like earthquake, tsunami, Corona virus, etc. Basically this means that all factors, past, present and future, are priced into the market at all times.

Second Principle — The Stock Market Has Three Trends

Primary Trend

The primary trend is the main trend of the market. When the primary trend is up, the overall market trend is considered up. Conversely, when the primary trend is down, the overall market trend is considered down.

Secondary Trend

The secondary trend is a move in the direction opposite to that of the primary trend. In other words, the secondary trend is a shorter term correction, or counter move, within the primary trend. Thus, for instance, a secondary trend would be a downward price correction in an up trending market or, conversely, an upward price pull back in a down trending market.

Dow Theory suggests that one should be particularly careful when trading in the direction of the secondary trend as it has a tendency to change direction relatively quickly and that, too, without giving much of a warning signal.

Primary and secondary trends in up trending and down trending markets would become clearer from Figure 2.1 and Figure 2.2.

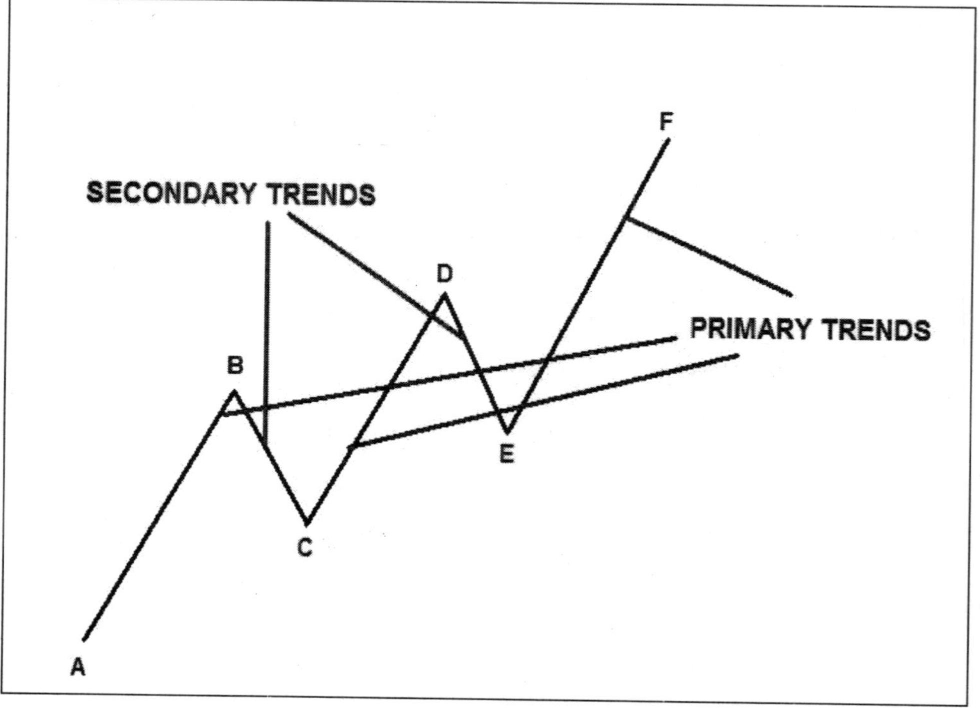

Figure 2.1: **Primary trends and secondary trends in an up trending market**

Figure 2.1 illustrates:

1. The primary trend is up as the stock price is moving ever higher.
2. A-B, C-D and E-F are moves in the direction of the primary trend.
3. B-C and D-E are moves in the direction of the secondary trend, as these are downward price corrections in the up trending market

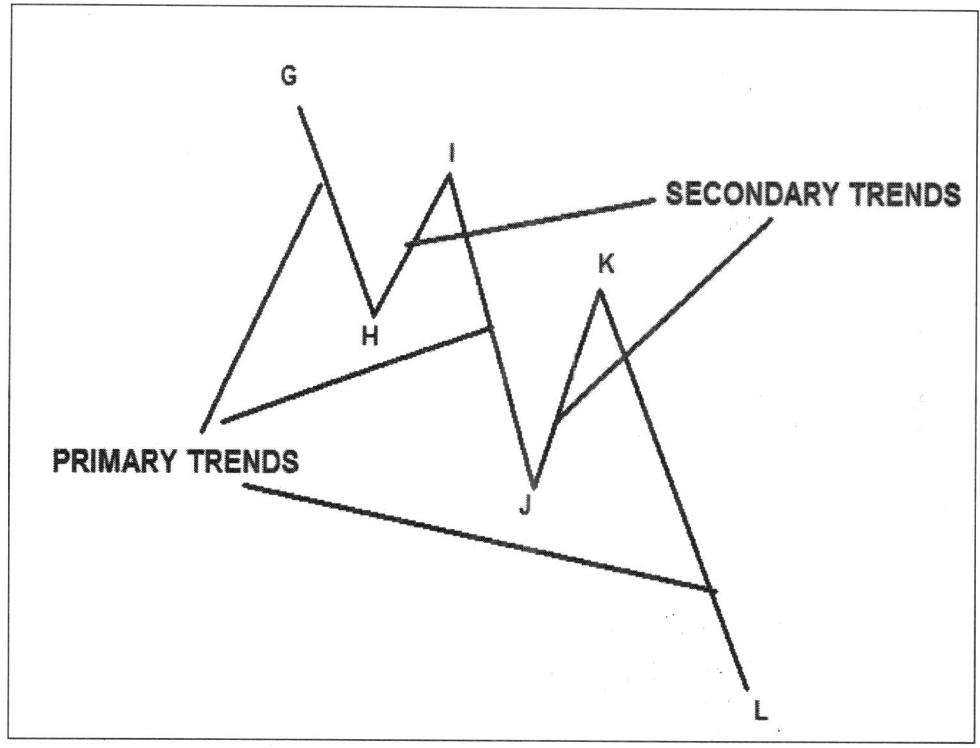

Figure 2.2: **Primary trends and secondary trends in a down trending market**

~

Figure 2.2 illustrates:

1. The primary trend is down since the stock price is declining.
2. G-H, I-J and K-L are moves in the direction of the primary trend.

3. H-I and J-K are moves in the direction of the secondary trend, as these are upward price pullbacks in a down trending market.

Minor Trend

A minor trend comprises minute to minute, even second to second price fluctuations. A minor trend is extremely short term in nature. Dow Theory trading focuses on the longer term; minor trends are not of much use for Dow Theory traders. A focus on minor trends leads to erratic trading which, in turn, creates losses and distracts a trader from trading with a clear perspective.

Dow Theory suggests one should never try to predict and trade minor trends.

Minor trends are illustrated in Figure 2.3.

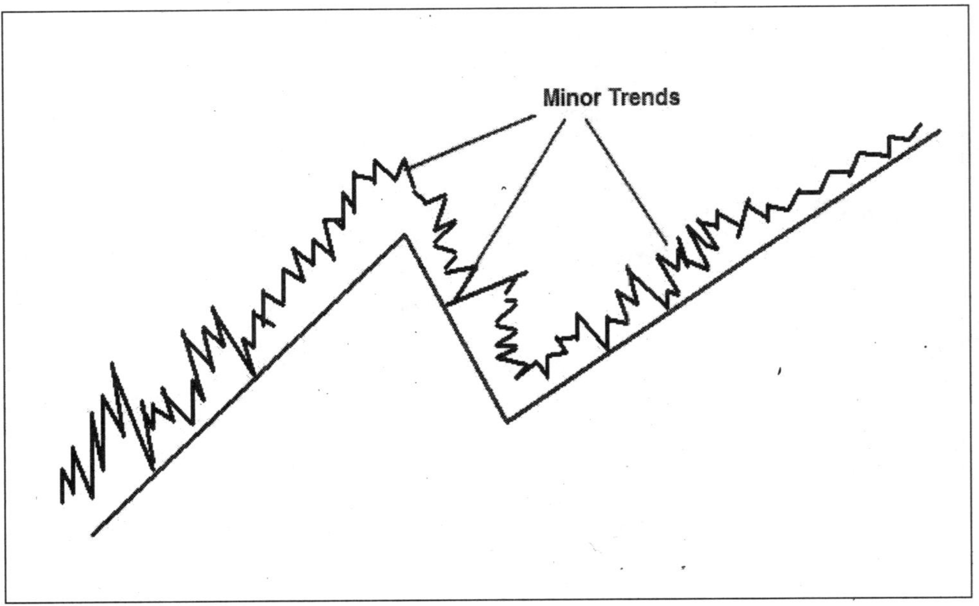

Figure 2.3: **Minor trends**

In practice, price never moves smoothly in a straight line. Rather, there is a day to day, hour to hour, minute to minute, even second to second price fluctuations. These price fluctuations are better known as minor trends and are displayed as black zig zag streaks in Figure 2.3.

Third Principle — Primary Trends Have Three Phases

Accumulation Phase

The first stage of a primary trend is referred to as accumulation phase, and it marks the start of an up trend. This is the time when typically the environment is pessimistic and most market participants are unwilling to buy. That's because the accumulation phase comes at the end of a downtrend, when the entire environment is pessimistic and everything seems to be at its worst. At such times, most market participants believe that things can only worsen.

Only informed investors and knowledgeable technical analysts and traders are buyers in this phase of the market.

Participation Phase

After the accumulation phase when the price starts to move up and pessimism starts fading, more and more market participants turn buyers. This is known as the participation phase.

As compared to the accumulation phase when only informed investor and savvy technical analysts and traders were buyers, in the participation phase the general public joins the bandwagon and starts buying as well.

Distribution Phase

The last stage of a primary up trend is known as the distribution phase. During this phase, informed investors and knowledgeable technical analysts and traders turn sellers whereas the general public remains a buyer as the overall market environment is optimistic and most market participants continue to believe that things would only get better from here.

Fourth Principle — Stock Market Indices Must Confirm Each Other

Charles Dow created two indices, namely the Dow Jones Industrial Index and the Dow Jones Transportation Index.

The industrial index reflected the state of manufacturing whereas the transportation index reflected the vigour of the manufactured goods being transported to retail stores from where good are sold.

This principle holds that the trend is considered up when both industrial and transportation indices are rising and, conversely, the trend is considered down once both industrial and transportation indices are declining. It follows that:

- Buying is suggested when both industrial and transportation indices are rising.
- Selling is suggested when both industrial and transportation indices are declining.
- Buying and selling should be avoided when there is disharmony between the two indices.

Now, this principle is more than a hundred years old. During Charles Dow's time, manufacturing was the core part of the U.S. economy. But today, technology and banking constitute a major part of the economy. For example, during 1997-1999 Nifty demonstrated a strong rally without any participation from industrial stocks. The rally was front-led by the technology sector. Had one waited for a buy confirmation from the industrial and transportation indices, one would have certainly missed the great bull run of technology stocks. Therefore, this fourth principle of Dow Theory should not be considered inviolable any more.

Fifth Principle — Volume Must Confirm the Trend

According to this principle, the volume of stocks traded should increase when the stock price moves in the direction of the primary trend and, conversely, the volume traded should reduce when the stock price moves in the direction of the secondary trend. Thus, in an up trending market, the volume should increase when stock price rises and shrink when stock price declines. Conversely, in a down trending market, the volume should increase whenever the stock price declines and volume should decline when the stock price rises.

Sixth Principle — A Trend Remains Intact Until and Unless a Clear Reversal Signal Occurs

As mentioned earlier, Charles Dow never wrote any book himself nor published his complete theory. However, his followers and associates published his ideas from 255 editorials written by him in the *Wall Street Journal* and christened it as Dow Theory.

Being one of his strong followers, I have interpreted his sixth principle in today's challenging and volatile stock market as follows:

1. Buy as and when the stock price makes the first higher top, higher bottom formation. Thereafter, hold the buy side, i.e. long, position until either the ongoing higher top, higher bottom pattern formation gets distorted, or the stock price enters a lower top, lower bottom pattern regime.

2. Sell as and when the stock price makes the first lower top, lower bottom pattern. Thereafter, hold the sell position until either the ongoing lower top, lower bottom pattern formation gets distorted, or the stock price enters a higher top, higher bottom pattern regime.

Trading higher top, higher bottom and lower top, lower bottom pattern formations requires a thorough understanding of up trends and down trends, which is tackled next in Chapter 3.

~

Chapter 3

~

How Dow Theory Defines Trends

Up Trend According to Dow Theory

Dow Theory holds that so long as each successive top is higher than the previous top, and each successive bottom is higher than the previous bottom, the trend is considered to be up, and we say that the markets are bullish. This is illustrated in Figure 3.1.

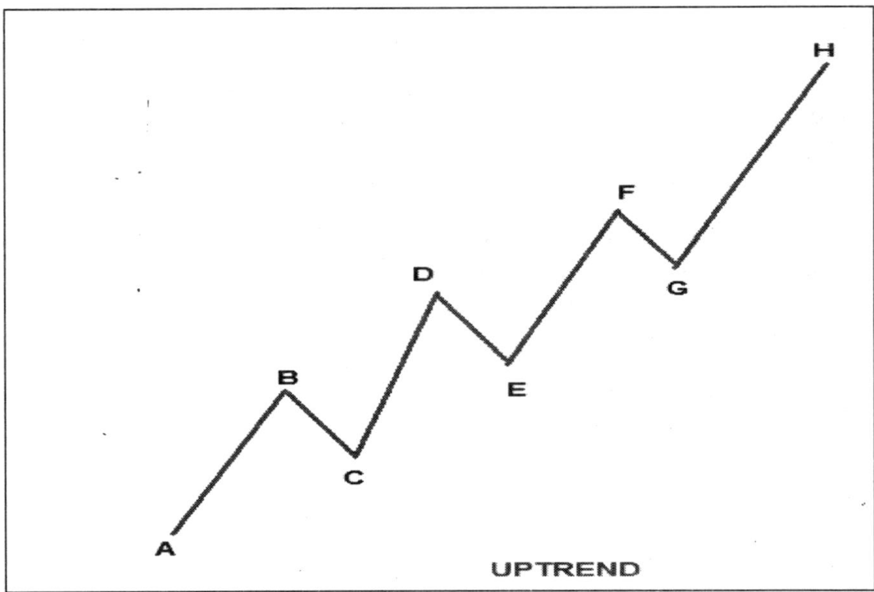

Figure 3.1: **Up trend — successive higher tops and higher bottoms characterize an up trend**

~

Figure 3.1 illustrates that each successive top, namely Point D, Point F and Point H, respectively, is higher than the previous top, and each successive bottom, namely Point E and Point G, respectively, is higher than the previous bottom. Accordingly, in this case the trend is considered up.

Down Trend According to Dow Theory

Dow Theory says that so long as each successive top is lower than the previous top, and each successive bottom is lower than the previous bottom, the trend is considered to be down and we say that the markets are bearish. This is illustrated in Figure 3.2.

Figure 3.2 highlights that each successive bottom, namely Point D, Point F and Point H, respectively, is lower than the previous bottom, and each successive top, namely Point E and Point G, respectively, is lower than the previous top. Accordingly, the trend is considered down.

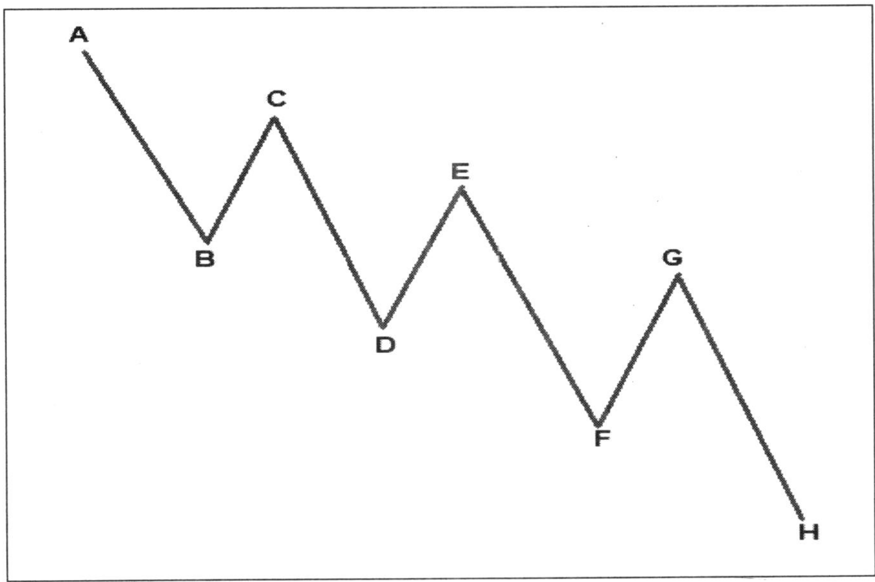

Figure 3.2: **Down trend — successive lower tops and lower bottoms characterize a down trend**

~

Chapter 4

~

How to Trade Dow Patterns

TRADING HIGHER TOP, HIGHER BOTTOM AND LOWER TOP, lower bottom patterns is the core part of this book. There can be three market scenarios as follows:

1. Up trend signalled by higher top, higher bottom patterns.
2. Down trend signalled by lower top, lower bottom patterns.
3. Sideways trend characterised by alternating higher top, higher bottom **and** lower top, lower bottom pattern formations.

Trading Higher Top, Higher Bottom Patterns (Up Trend)

In this scenario, you buy as and when the stock price makes the first higher top and higher bottom formation. Thereafter, hold the long position until either the ongoing higher top, higher bottom pattern gets distorted, or the stock price goes into a lower top, lower bottom pattern.

This is demonstrated in Figure 4.1.

In Figure 4.1, one buys as and when the level made earlier by Point B is cracked during the up move from Point C to Point D. At the time of buying, the stop loss is to be placed at Point C. Subsequently, when the level made earlier by Point D is cracked in the up move from Point E to Point F, the stop loss is shifted upward to Point E level. Again, when the level earlier made by Point F is cracked on the upside during the up move from Point G to Point H, the stop loss is shifted upward to Point G.

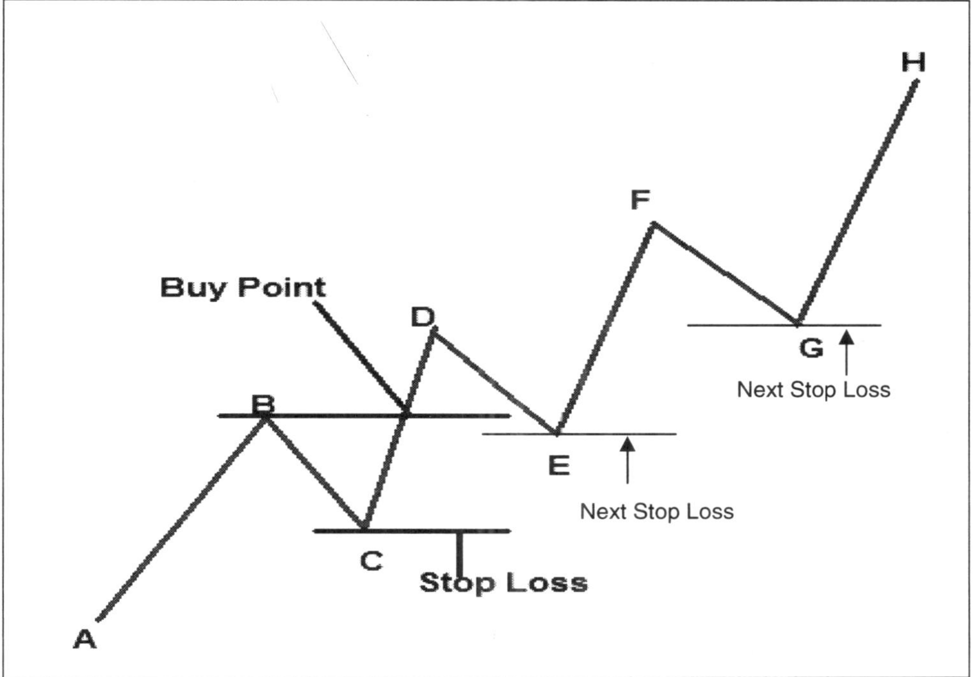

Figure 4.1: **Trading higher top, higher bottom pattern formations**

~

Now, we can clearly see that Point G is above the buying price, which was the level of Point B. Thus, once your stop loss reaches Point G, then your trade becomes loss-proof.

One should hold the long position until either the ongoing higher top, higher bottom pattern formation gets distorted, or the stock price forms a lower top, lower bottom pattern.

The distortion of a higher top, higher bottom pattern formation is illustrated in Figure 4.2.

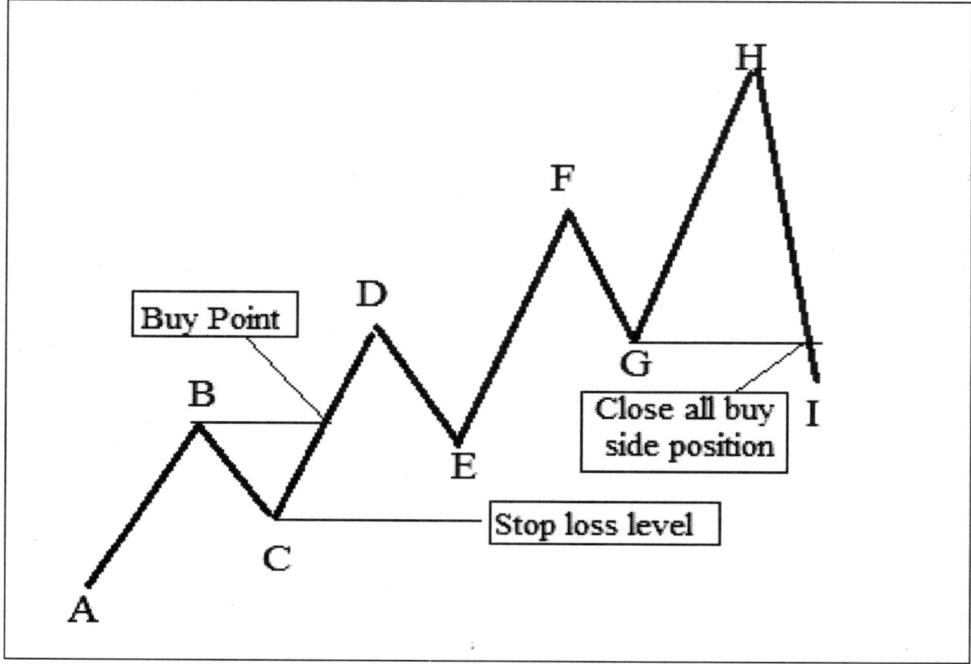

Figure 4.2: **Distortion of a higher top, higher bottom pattern formation**

~

Figure 4.2 shows that after forming a high at around Point H, the stock price declined and cracked on the downside the level earlier made by Point G in the down move from Point H to Point I. One should close the buy position as and when the level earlier made by Point G is cracked on the downside since that marks a distortion, namely a break, of the ongoing higher top, higher bottom pattern.

Trading Lower Top, Lower Bottom Patterns (Down Trend)

In this scenario, you sell as and when the stock price makes the first lower top, lower bottom pattern formation. Thereafter, you hold the sell / short position until either the ongoing lower top, lower bottom formation gets distorted, or the stock price enters a higher top, higher bottom pattern.

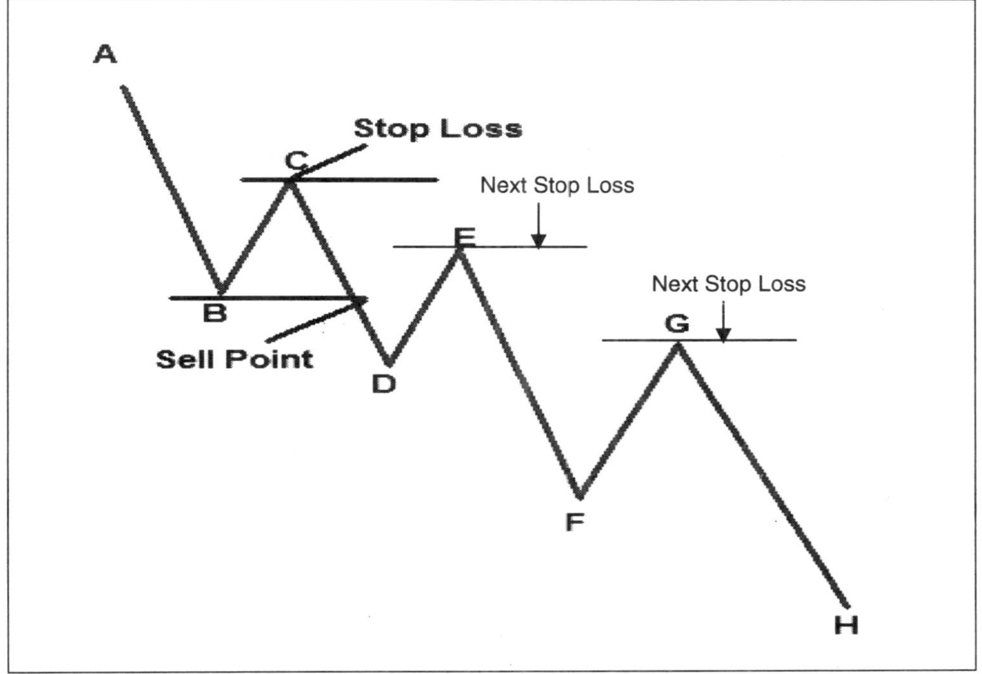

Figure 4.3: **How to trade lower top, lower bottoms**

~

Figure 4.3 illustrates the sell / short trade in a lower top, lower bottom pattern. One sells as and when the level made earlier by Point B is cracked in the down move from Point C to Point D. At the time of initiating the sell, the stop loss can be placed at Point C. Subsequently, when the level earlier made by Point D is cracked in the down move from Point E to Point F, the stop loss should be shifted downward to Point E. Similarly, when the level made earlier by Point F is cracked in the down move from Point G to Point H, the stop loss needs to be shifted downward to Point G. The level of Point G is clearly below the selling level at Point B. Thus, once your stop loss reaches Point G, the trade is then guaranteed against a loss.

One should hold the sell, or short, position until either the ongoing lower top, lower bottom pattern formation gets distorted, or the stock price starts a new higher top and higher bottom pattern.

This distortion of lower top, lower bottom pattern formation is demonstrated in Figure 4.4.

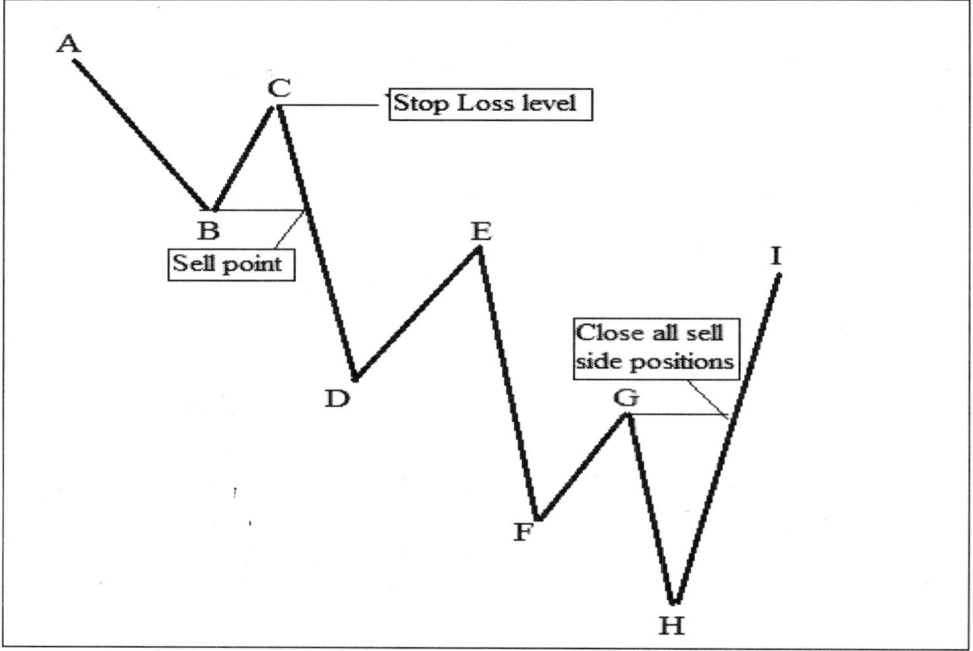

Figure 4.4: **Distortion of lower top, lower bottom pattern**

~

As you can see in Figure 4.4, from the lows of around Point H the stock price rallied strongly and cracked the level made earlier by Point G in the up move from Point H to Point I. This distorts the ongoing lower top, lower bottom pattern formation and one should thereafter close the sell position. This is because the stock's lower bottom at Point H was followed by a higher top when Point G is cracked on the upside.

Trading Higher Top, Higher Bottom and Lower Top, Lower Bottom Patterns (Sideways Trend)

Trading during a sideways trend requires trading higher top, higher bottom and lower top, lower bottom patterns. The strategy is illustrated in Figure 4.5 and Figure 4.6.

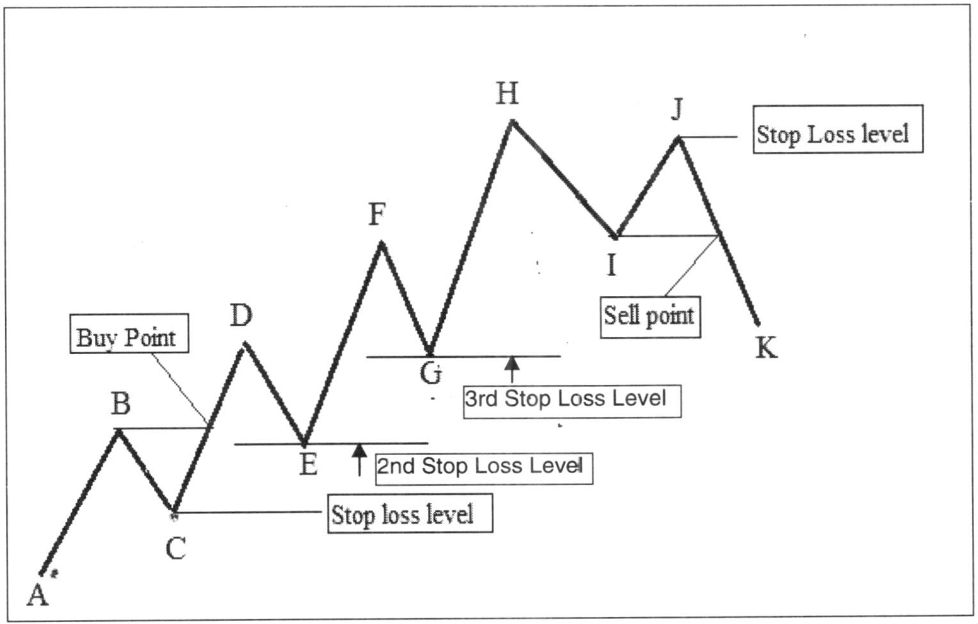

Figure 4.5: **Trading higher top, higher bottom and lower top, lower bottom patterns during a sideways trend**

~

In the example in Figure 4.5, one buys as and when the earlier level of Point B is cracked in the up move from Point C to Point D. At the time of buying, the stop loss can be placed at Point C. Subsequently when the level made earlier by Point D is cracked in the up move from Point E to Point F, the stop loss should be shifted upward to Point E. Similarly, when the level made earlier by Point F is cracked in the up move from Point G to Point H, the stop loss is to be shifted upward to Point G.

After reaching a higher Point H, the stock price began declining and cracked the level earlier made by Point I in the down move from Point J to Point K. One should close the buy position — and also initiate a fresh sell position — as and when the level made earlier by Point I is cracked on the downside as the higher top, higher bottom pattern thereupon stands distorted since the top at Point J is lower than the preceding top at Point H.

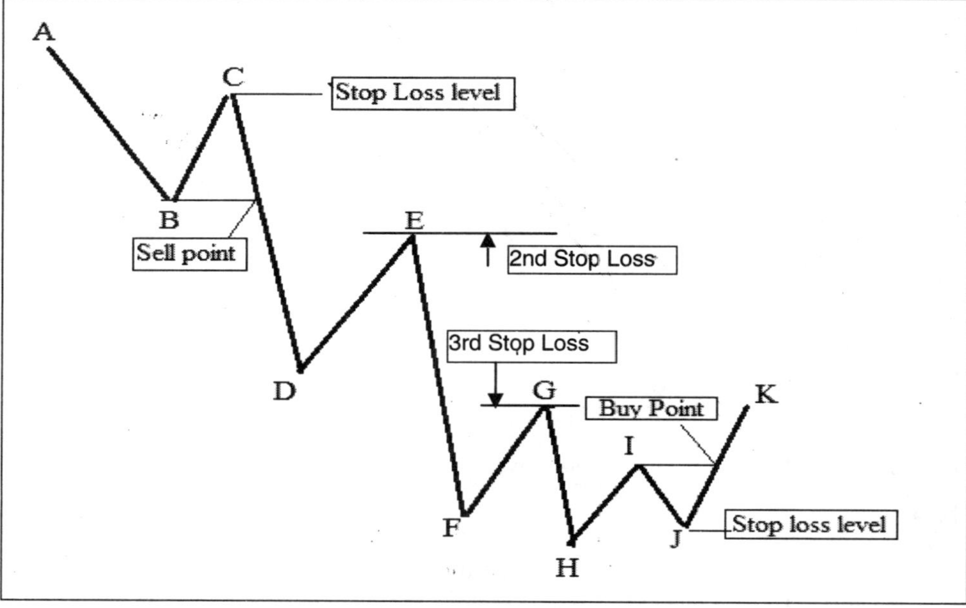

Figure 4.6: **Sell trade during a lower top, lower bottom pattern**

~

Figure 4.6 illustrates a sell / short trade as the pattern changes to one of lower tops and lower bottoms. One should sell as and when the level made earlier by Point B is cracked in the down move from Point C to Point D. At the time of selling, the stop loss is to be placed at Point C. Subsequently, when the level made earlier by Point D is cracked in the down move from Point E to Point F, the stop loss is to be shifted downward to Point E. Similarly, when the level made earlier by Point F is cracked in the down move from Point G to Point H, the stop loss is shifted downward to Point G.

From the lows of around Point J, the stock price then rallied up strongly and cracked the lower high made earlier at Point I in the up move from Point J to Point K. One should then close the sell position — and also initiate a fresh buy — as and when the Point I level is cracked on the upside as the stock price enters a higher top, higher bottom pattern regime at that time, when the bottom at Point J is higher than the bottom at Point H and, subsequently, the lower top at Point I is also cracked on the upside.

~

Chapter 5

~

50 Real-Life Profitable Dow Trades

IN CHAPTER 4 WE SAW HOW ONE CAN PROFIT by trading higher top, higher bottom and lower top, lower bottom pattern formations.

In this chapter we present 50 real life examples from the Indian stock market. These examples demonstrate the wealth creation possibilities of Dow trading, namely of trading higher top, higher bottom and lower top, lower bottom pattern formations.

Example 1: Asian Paints

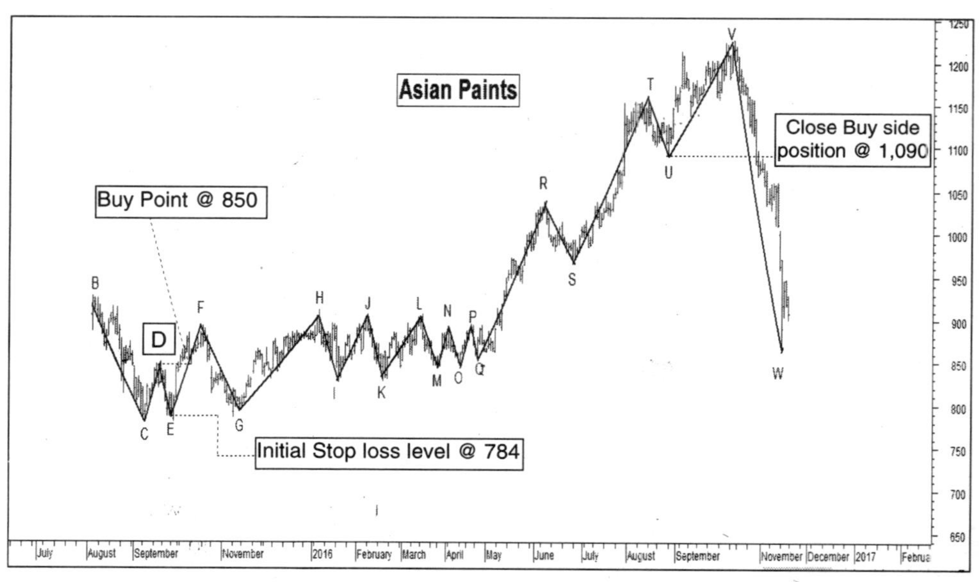

Figure 5.1: **Daily stock price chart of Asian Paints**

~

The higher top, higher bottom and lower top, lower bottom pattern formations in Figure 5.1 would first suggest buying as and when the level made earlier by Point D at about ₹850 levels is cracked in the up move from Point E to Point F. This is because the stock price thereupon initiates a higher top, higher bottom pattern. At the time of buying, the stop loss can be placed at the Point E levels of around ₹784.

Thereafter the stock price rallied up to the highs of around Point F, and then entered a consolidation phase making lower highs but higher lows.

The stock price then rallied strongly upward from Point Q and made successive higher tops at Point R, Point T and Point V, and successive higher bottoms at Point S and Point U. From the highs of around Point V, the stock price declined and cracked the level earlier made by Point U at ₹1,090 levels in the down move from Point V to Point W. One should close the buy positions when this occurs because the ongoing higher top, higher bottom pattern is distorted at that point.

The stock price fell further to ₹850 levels on the downside in a manner which does not comply with the lower top, lower bottom pattern regime. As a result, Dow Theory practitioners would not have been able to sell during this down move.

Trade Summary

1. Initiating a buy / long trade at ₹857 levels, i.e. buying after the price closes above the Point D levels of ₹850.
2. Closing the long positions at ₹1,085 levels, i.e. exiting after the price closes below Point U levels of about ₹1,090.
3. Trading higher top, higher bottom and lower top, lower bottom pattern formations would have resulted in a profit of 228 points in this instance.

~

Example 2: Infosys

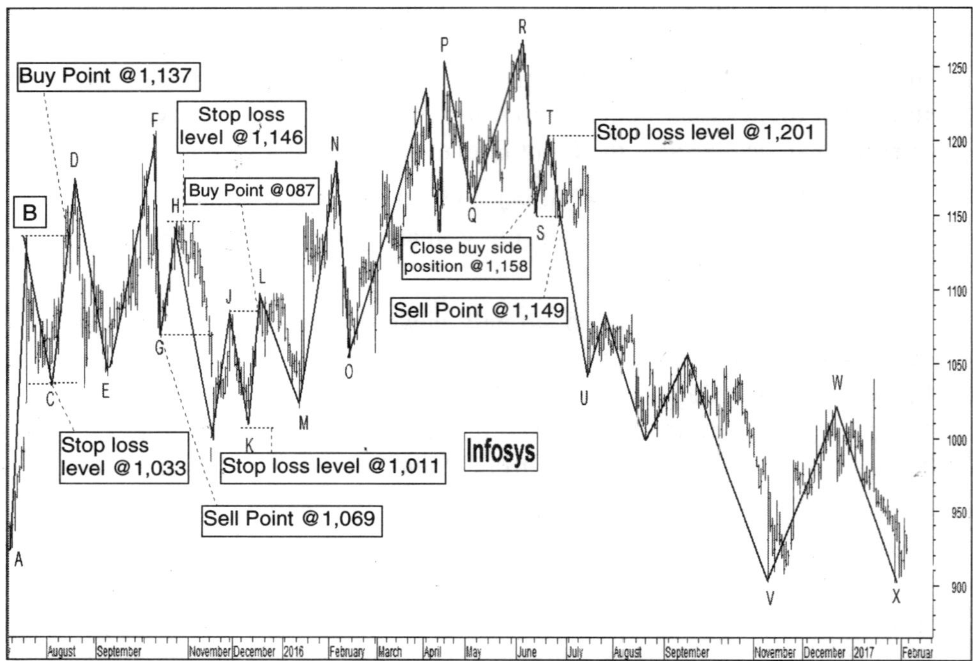

Figure 5.2: **Higher top, higher bottom and lower top, lower bottom formations in the daily price chart of Infosys**

~

Higher top, higher bottom and lower top, lower bottom pattern formations in the Infosys chart in Figure 5.2 would have suggested buying as and when the Point B level made earlier at about ₹1,137 levels is cracked during the up move from Point C to Point D because the stock price then enters a higher top, higher bottom pattern regime. At the time of buying, the stop loss can be placed at Point C, i.e. at about ₹1,033 levels.

The stock price declined sharply thereafter and cracked the level earlier made by Point G at around ₹1,069 levels during the down move from Point H to Point I. One should close the buy position — and instead initiate a fresh sell position at this time. From there on, the stock price enters a lower top, lower bottom pattern formation. At the time of selling, the stop loss can be placed at Point H, i.e. at about ₹1,146 levels.

The stock price subsequently rallied strongly and cracked the level made earlier by Point J, at around ₹1,087, in the up move from Point K to Point L. One should close the sell position — and instead initiate a fresh buy position at this point because thereafter the stock price enters a higher top, higher bottom pattern regime. At the time of buying, the stop loss could be placed at the Point K level, i.e. at around ₹1,011.

The stock price then rallied to the highs of around the level of Point R in a higher top, higher bottom pattern formation.

From the highs of around Point R, the stock price then began a sharp decline and cracked the level earlier made by Point Q at ₹1,158 in its down move from Point R to Point S. One should close the buy position here because this distorts the ongoing higher top, higher bottom pattern.

The stock price thereafter rallied from Point S to Point T. From the highs of around Point T, however, the stock price declined sharply and cracked the level earlier made by Point S in the down move from Point T to Point U. One should sell as and when this happens because the stock price then enters a lower top, lower bottom pattern. At the time of selling, the stop loss could be placed at the Point T level of around ₹1,201. The stock price declined to the lows of around Point X in a lower top and lower bottom pattern regime.

At the time of this writing, the stock price was trading around ₹935 levels.

Trade Summary

1. Initiate a buy trade at ₹1,146 levels, i.e. after the price closes above the Point B levels of around ₹1,137.

2. Initiate a sell trade at ₹1,068 levels, i.e. after the price closes below the Point G levels of ₹1,069.

3. Buy at ₹1,096 levels, i.e. after the price closes above the Point J levels at ₹1,087.

4. Closing buy positions at ₹1,157 levels, i.e. exiting after the price closes below the Point Q levels of ₹1,158.

5. Sell at ₹1,145 levels, i.e. after the price closes below the Point S levels of ₹1,149.

6. At the time of this writing, the stock price of Infosys was trading at around ₹935. If the price of ₹935 is taken into account to calculate the mark to market profit / loss account, then trading higher top, higher bottom and lower top, lower bottom pattern formations in this case would have resulted in a profit of 165 points.

~

Example 3: Datamatics Global Services

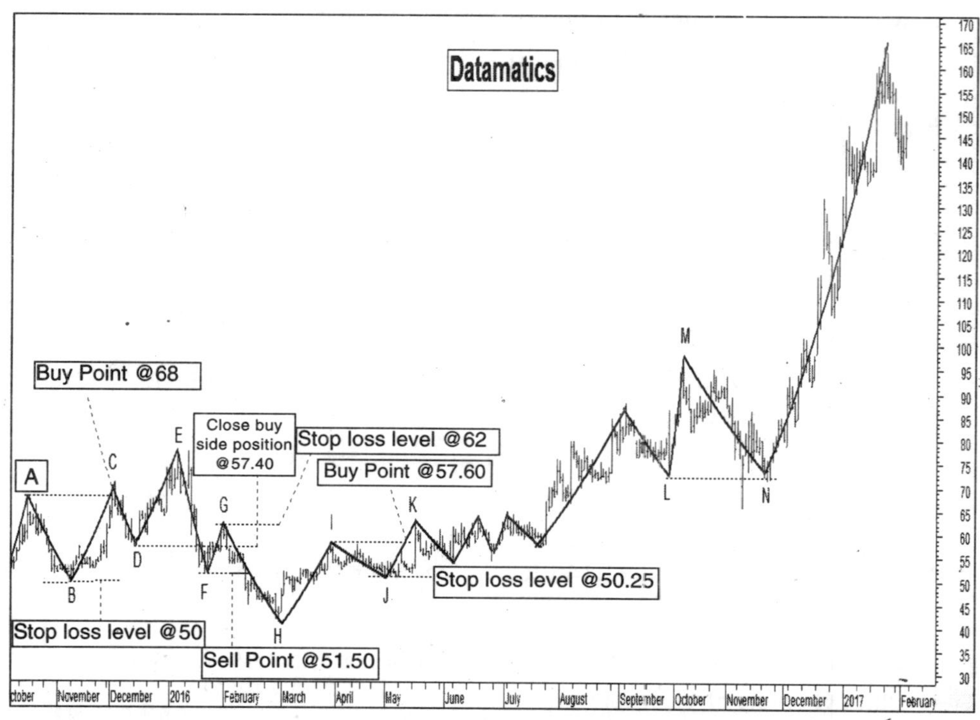

Figure 5.3: **Trading higher top, higher bottom and lower top, lower bottom patterns in the daily stock price chart of Datamatics**

~

Higher top, higher bottom and lower top, lower bottom pattern formations in Figure 5.3 would suggest buying as and when the level of Point A made earlier at about ₹68 levels is subsequently cracked in the up move from Point B to Point C. This is because the stock price then enters a higher top, higher bottom pattern. At the time of buying, the stop loss can be placed at the Point B levels of ₹50.

The stock price then duly rallied up to the highs of around Point E, but then declined sharply and cracked the level earlier made by Point D (₹57.40) during its down move from Point E to Point F. One should close the long position as and when the ₹57.40 level is cracked since this break distorts the ongoing higher top, higher bottom pattern formation.

The stock price then declined further and cracked the level earlier made by Point F at around ₹51.50 during the down move from Point G to Point H. One should initiate a sell trade as and when the ₹51.50 level is cracked on the downside because the stock price then enters a lower top, lower bottom pattern. At the time of selling, the stop loss can be placed at the level of Point G, i.e. at ₹62 levels.

From the lows of around the level of Point H, the stock price then rallied strongly upward and cracked the level earlier made by Point I at about ₹57.60 levels in the up move from Point J to Point K. One should close the sell position — and instead initiate a fresh buy position — when this occurs because the stock price then initiates a higher top, higher bottom pattern. At the time of buying, the stop loss can be placed at the Point J level of around ₹50.25.

The stock price then rallied higher to around ₹164 levels in a higher top, higher bottom pattern regime. During this up move, the level earlier made at Point L seemingly got cracked by Point N, whereas in reality Point N never closed below Point L on the downside.

At the time of this writing, the stock price was trading around ₹142 levels.

Trade Summary

1. Buying at ₹69 levels, i.e. when the price closes above the level of Point B.

2. Selling at ₹57 levels, i.e. when the price closes below the level of Point D at about ₹57.40.

3. Buying again at ₹61 levels, i.e. when the price closes above the Point I levels of ₹57.60.

At the time of this writing, the stock price was trading around ₹142 levels. Based on this price, the higher top, higher bottom and lower top, lower bottom pattern trades resulted in a profit of 65 points.

~

Example 4: Yes Bank

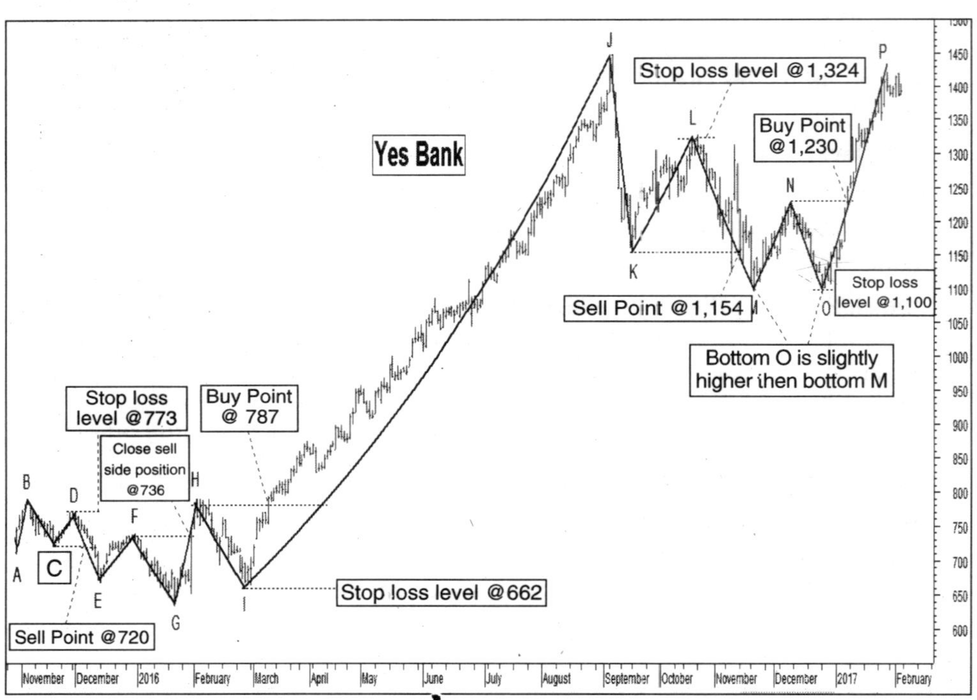

Figure 5.4: **Trading higher top, higher bottom and lower top, lower bottom patterns in the daily stock price chart of Yes Bank**

~

Trading higher top, higher bottom and lower top, lower bottom pattern formations in the chart of Yes Bank in Figure 5.4 would suggest initiating a sell / short trade as and when the level earlier made by Point C at around ₹720 is cracked in the down move from Point D to Point E. This is because the stock price then enters a lower top, lower bottom pattern. At the time of selling, the stop loss can be placed at Point D, i.e. at around ₹773 levels.

The stock price duly declined, forming a lower top, lower bottom pattern and made a lower top at Point F and lower bottoms at Point E and Point G.

From the lows of around ₹600 levels, i.e. from Point G, the stock price then rallied strongly upward and cracked the level earlier made by Point F at ₹736 levels in its move from Point G to Point H. One should close the sell position as and when the Point F level is cracked on the upside as the ongoing lower top, lower bottom pattern formation gets distorted at that time.

Thereafter the stock price rallied higher and cracked the earlier level of Point H in the up move from Point I to Point J. One should buy as and when the Point H level of ₹787 is cracked on the upside. This is because the stock price then enters a higher top, higher bottom pattern regime. At the time of buying, the stop loss can be placed at Point I, i.e. at ₹662 levels. The stock price then rallied to the highs of around ₹1,440 levels on the upside, i.e. to Point J, from where it declined sharply and cracked the Point K levels of ₹1,154, in its down move from Point L to Point M. One should close the buy position and, instead, initiate a fresh sell position as and when the Point K level is cracked on the downside because the stock price then enters a lower top, lower bottom pattern regime. At the time of selling, the stop loss can be placed at Point L, i.e. at about ₹1,324 levels.

The stock price then declined to a little below ₹1,100 levels, from where it rallied upward strongly and cracked the level earlier made by Point N at around ₹1,230 in an up move from Point O to Point P. One should close the sell position — and, instead, initiate a fresh buy position — as and when the Point N level of ₹1,230 is cracked on the upside since the stock price then enters a higher top, higher bottom pattern regime. At the time of buying, the stop loss can be placed at the Point O level at ₹1,100.

The stock price then rallied to the highs of around ₹1,414 levels on the upside. At the time of this writing, the stock price was trading around ₹1,400 levels.

Trade Summary

1. Selling at ₹717 levels, i.e. selling after the price closes below the Point C at ₹720 level.
2. Closing sell positions at ₹747 levels, i.e. exiting after the price closes above the Point F level of ₹736.
3. Initiating a buy trade at ₹799 levels, i.e. after the price closes above the Point H level of ₹787.
4. Selling at ₹1,112 levels, i.e. after the price closes below the Point K level of ₹1,154.
5. Buying at ₹1,247 levels, i.e. buying after the price closes above the Point N level of ₹1,230.
6. At the time of this writing, the stock price was trading around the ₹1,400 levels. If the price of ₹1,400 is taken into account to calculate mark to market profit / loss account, then trading higher top, higher bottom and lower top, lower bottom pattern formations in this case would have resulted in a profit of 301 points.

~

Example 5: Nifty

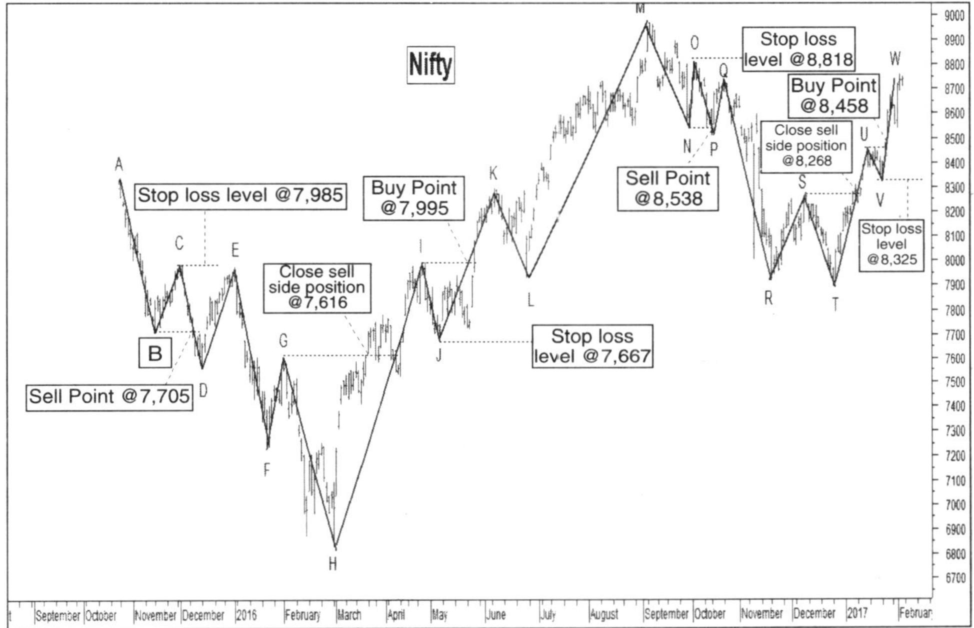

Figure 5.5: **Dow trades in the daily chart of Nifty**

~

The higher top, higher bottom and lower top, lower bottom patterns in Figure 5.5 would suggest selling Nifty as and when the level made earlier by Point B at about 7,705 level is cracked in the down move from Point C to Point D because when this happens Nifty enters a lower top, lower bottom pattern regime. At the time of selling, the stop loss could be placed at Point C, i.e. at about 7,985 levels.

Thereafter, Nifty made successive lower tops at points E and G, and successive lower bottoms, at points D, F and H.

From the lows of Point H around 6,850 levels, Nifty turned around and rallied upward strongly and cracked the level earlier made by Point G at around 7,616 levels in its up move from Point H to Point I. One should close the sell position as the ongoing lower top, lower bottom pattern formation gets distorted here.

Thereafter, Nifty rallied higher and cracked the level made earlier by Point I at 7,995 in its up move from Point J to Point K. One should go long as and when this level is cracked on the upside because Nifty then enters a higher top, higher bottom pattern regime. At the time of buying, the stop loss may be placed at Point J, i.e. at about 7,667 levels.

Nifty reached the highs of around 8,950 levels from where it began a sharp decline, cracking the level earlier made by Point N at about 8,538 in the down move from Point O to Point P. When this happens, one should close the buy positions and instead initiate a fresh sell position as and when the Point N level at 8,538 is cracked since Nifty then enters a lower top, lower bottom pattern regime. At the time of selling, the stop loss may be placed at Point O, i.e. at about 8,818 levels.

Thereafter Nifty declined to a little below the 7,900 levels, from where it then rallied strongly upward and cracked the Point S level of 8,268 in its up move from Point T to Point U. One should close the sell position as and when this happens because the ongoing lower top, lower bottom pattern regime then gets distorted.

Nifty then rallied higher and cracked the Point U level of 8,458 in its up move from Point V to Point W. One should buy when the Point U level is cracked as Nifty thereafter enters a higher top, higher bottom pattern regime. At the time of buying, the stop loss can be placed at Point V, i.e. at around 8,325 levels.

Nifty duly rallied to the highs of around 8,750 levels on the upside. At the time of this writing, Nifty was trading around 8,740.

Trade Summary

1. Selling at 7,701 levels, i.e. after the price closes below the Point B level of 7,705.
2. Exiting the sell / short positions at 7,704 levels, i.e. after the price closes above the Point G level of 7,616.
3. Initiate long trade at 8,070 levels, i.e. buying after the price closes above the Point I levels of 7,995.
4. Selling at 8,520 levels, i.e. going short after the price closes below the Point N level of 8,538.

5. Closing sell side positions at 8,274 levels, i.e. exiting the sell trade after the price closes above the Point S level of 8,268.
6. Buying at 8,476 levels, i.e. after the price closes above the Point U level of 8,458.

At the time of this writing, Nifty was trading around 8,740 levels. If 8,740 is taken into account to calculate the mark to market profit / loss account, then trading higher top, higher bottom and lower top, lower bottom pattern formations in this case would have resulted in a profit of 957 points.

~

Example 6: Mindtree

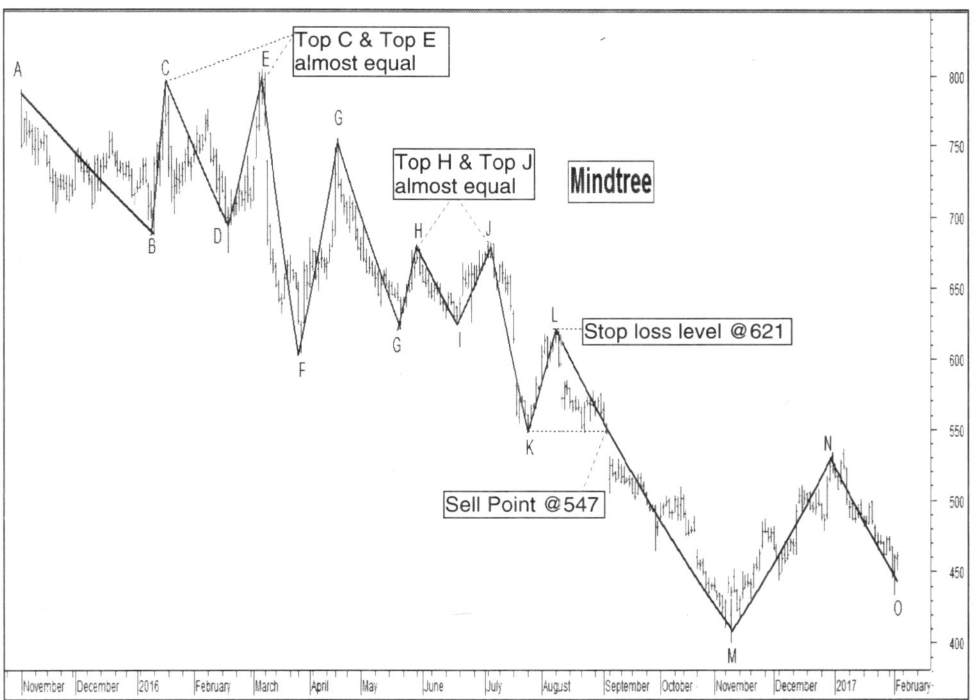

Figure 5.6: **Trading the daily stock price chart of Mindtree using Dow Theory**

~

In Figure 5.6, the stock price of Mindtree can be seen initially declining from Point A to Point K in a pattern which does not comply with a lower top, lower bottom formation because the top at Point E is almost equal to the top at Point C, and the top at Point J is almost equal to the top at Point H.

From Point L, the Mindtree price declined sharply and cracked the level made earlier by Point K at about ₹547 in its down move from Point L to Point M. One should sell as and when this happens because the price then enters a lower top, lower bottom pattern regime. At the time of selling, the stop loss can be placed at around the Point L level of ₹621. Thereafter, the stock price declined to the lows of around ₹415 levels.

At the time of this writing, the stock price was trading around ₹460 levels.

Trade Summary

1. Selling at ₹546 levels, i.e. selling after the price closes below the Point K level of ₹547.
2. At the time of this writing, the stock price was trading around ₹460 levels. If the price of ₹460 is taken into account to calculate the mark to market profit / loss account, then trading higher top, higher bottom and lower top, lower bottom pattern formations in this example would have resulted in a profit of 86 points.

~

Example 7: Zee Entertainment

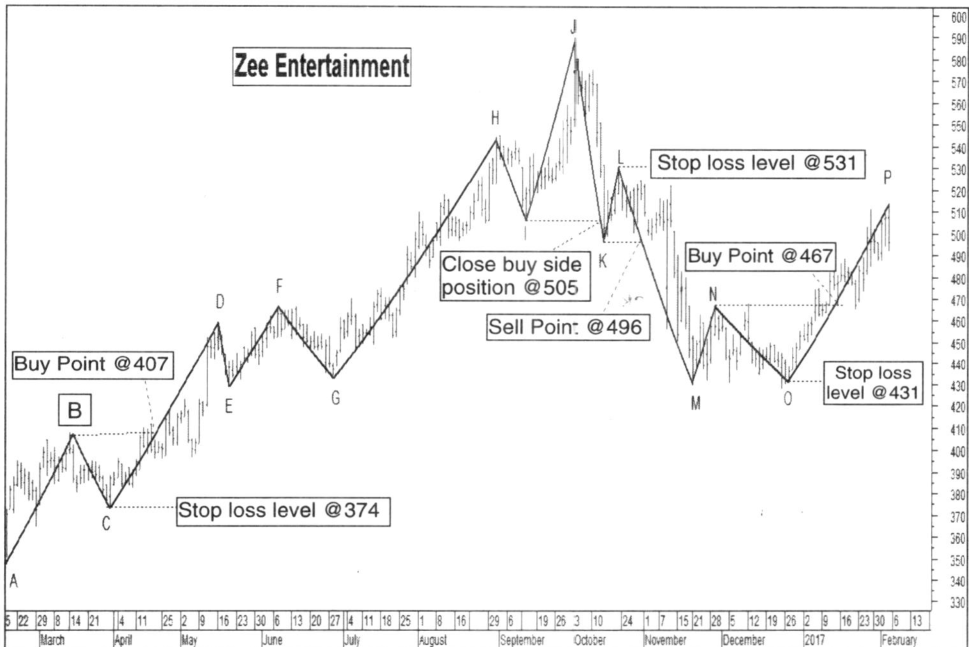

Figure 5.7: **Daily stock price chart of Zee Entertainment**

~

The higher top, higher bottom and lower top, lower bottom pattern formations in Figure 5.7 would suggest initiating a buy trade as and when the level of ₹407 made earlier at Point B is cracked in the up move from Point C to Point D. At that time, the stock price enters a higher top, higher bottom pattern regime. At the time of buying, the stop loss may be placed around the Point C level of ₹374.

The stock price then rallied forming a higher top, higher bottom pattern with higher tops at points D, F, H and J, and higher bottoms at points E, G and I.

From the highs of around ₹586 levels, i.e. from Point J, the stock price declined sharply and cracked the level made earlier by Point I at ₹505 during the down move from Point J to Point K. One should exit the buy position as and when the level of Point I at ₹505 is cracked on the downside as the ongoing higher top, higher bottom pattern formation then gets distorted.

Thereafter the stock price declined further and cracked the level of Point K around ₹496 levels in the down move from Point I to Point M. One should initiate a sell as and when the level of Point K at about ₹496 is cracked on the downside since the stock price then enters a lower top, lower bottom pattern regime. At the time of selling, the stop loss can be placed at Point L levels of ₹531.

The stock price then duly declined to the lows of around ₹430 levels, i.e. to around Point O, from where it then rallied upward strongly and cracked the Point N level of ₹467 in its up move from Point O to Point P. One should close all the sell positions — and instead initiate a fresh buy position — when this occurs because thereupon the stock price enters a higher top, higher bottom pattern regime. At the time of buying, the stop loss is placed at the Point O level of ₹431.

Thereafter the stock price rallied to the highs of around ₹509 levels. At the time of this writing, the stock price was trading around ₹495 levels.

Trade Summary

1. Buying at ₹414 levels, i.e. buying / going long after the price closes above the level earlier made by Point B at about ₹407.
2. Exiting the buy positions at around ₹502 levels, i.e. after the price falls below the level earlier made by Point I at ₹505.
3. Selling at ₹482 levels, i.e. after the price closes below the Point K level of ₹496.
4. Buying at ₹471 levels, i.e. after the price closes above the Point N levels of ₹467.

At the time of this writing, the stock price was trading around ₹495 levels. If the market price of ₹495 is taken into account to calculate the mark to market profit / loss account, then trading higher top, higher bottom and lower top, lower bottom pattern formations would have resulted in profit of 123 points in this case.

~

Example 8: Maruti

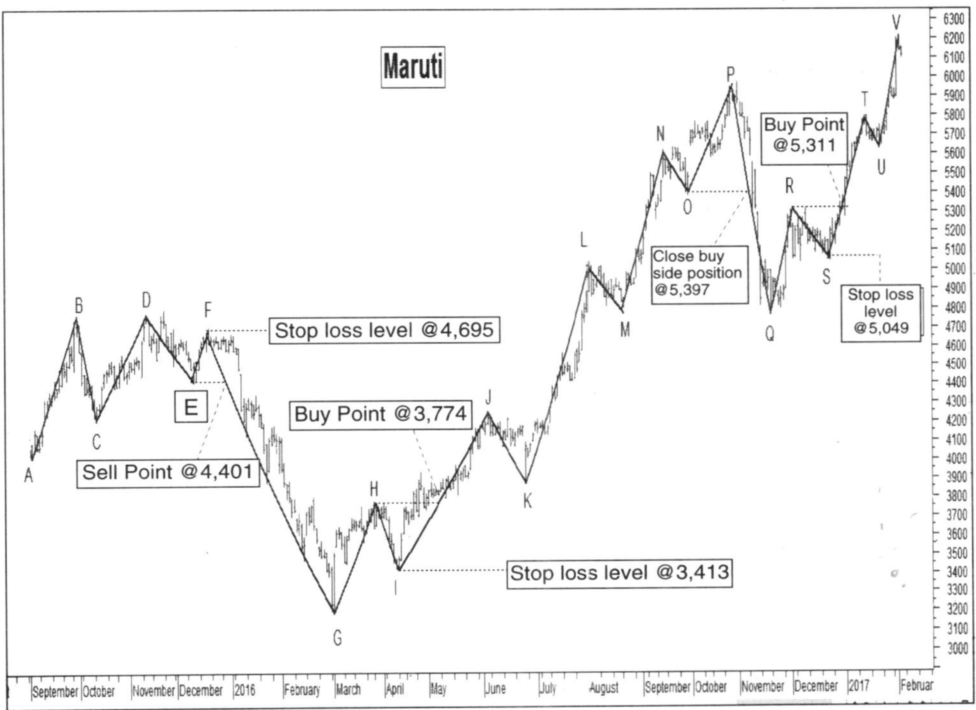

Figure 5.8: **Dow trades on the daily stock price chart of Maruti**

~

Higher top, higher bottom and lower top, lower bottom pattern formations in the case of Maruti in Figure 5.8 would suggest initiating a sell trade as and when the level made earlier by Point E at about ₹4,401 is cracked during the down move from Point F to Point G. This is because the stock price then enters a lower top, lower bottom pattern regime. At the time of selling, the stop loss can be placed at about the ₹4,695 level earlier made by Point F.

Thereafter the stock price declined sharply to the lows of Point G at around ₹3,230 levels, from where it then rallied up strongly and cracked the level earlier made by Point H at ₹3,774 in its up move from Point I to Point J. One should close the sell position and initiate a fresh buy position instead when the level earlier made by Point H at about ₹3,774 is subsequently cracked on the upside since the stock price then enters a higher top, higher bottom pattern regime. At the time of buying, the stop loss can be placed at the level earlier made by Point I, i.e. around ₹3,413 levels.

The stock price rallied thereafter, making a higher top, higher bottom pattern and made successive higher tops J, L, N and P, and successive higher bottoms K, M and O.

Then, from the highs of Point P at around ₹5,938 levels, the stock price declined sharply and cracked ₹5,387, the level earlier made by Point O in the down move from Point P to Point Q. One should close the buy position as and when this happens since that marks a distortion in the ongoing higher top, higher bottom pattern.

As the stock price declined almost vertically to Point Q at around ₹4,800 levels in a pattern which does not comply with the lower top, lower bottom pattern regime. Dow Theory practitioners would not have been able to sell in this down move.

Then, from the lows of around ₹4,800 levels at Point Q, the stock price rose strongly higher and cracked the earlier level made by Point R of ₹5,311 in its up move from Point S to Point T. One should close the sell position — and instead initiate a fresh buy position — as and when the Point R level of ₹5,311 is cracked on the upside as thereafter the stock price enters a higher top, higher bottom pattern regime. At the time of buying, the stop loss can be placed at ₹5,049, the level of Point S.

Thereafter the stock price rallied to the highs of around ₹6,200 level. At the time of this writing, the stock price was trading around ₹6,100 levels.

Trade Summary

1. Initiating a sell trade at ₹4,267 levels, i.e. after the price closes below the Point E level of ₹4,401.
2. Buying at ₹3,816 levels, i.e. after the price closes above the Point H level of ₹3,774.

3. Exiting the buy positions at ₹5,392 level, i.e. after the price closes below the Point O level at ₹5,397.
4. Buying at ₹5,314 levels, i.e. after the price closes above the Point R level of ₹5,311.

At the time of this writing, the stock price was trading around ₹6,100 levels. If the price of ₹6,100 is taken into account to calculate the mark to market profit / loss account, then trading higher top, higher bottom and lower top, lower bottom pattern formations would have resulted in a profit of 2,813 points in this case.

~

Example 9: Delta Corp

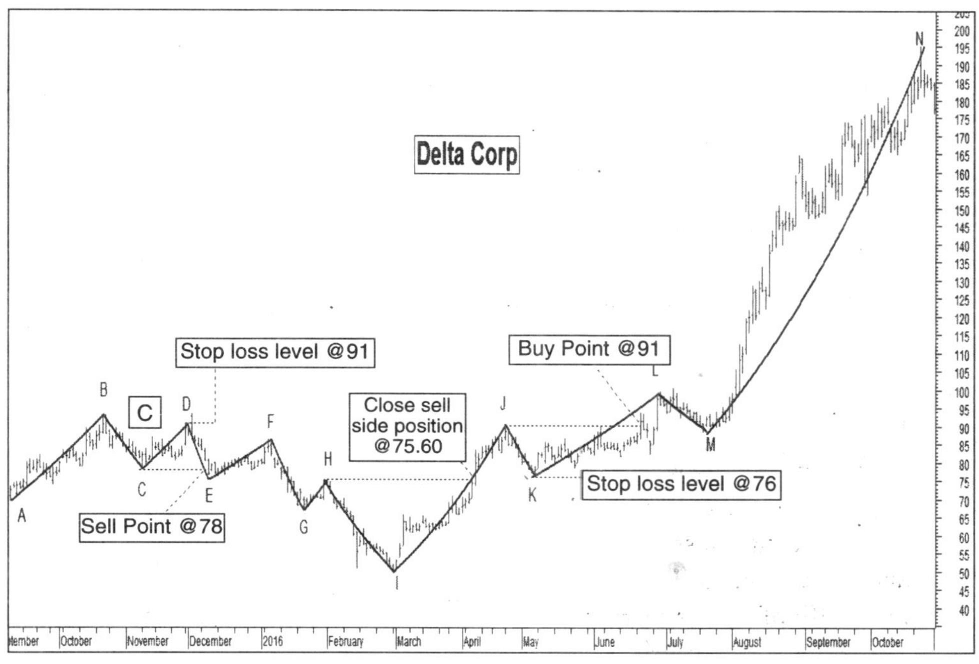

Figure 5.9: **Daily stock price chart of Delta with profitable Dow Trades highlighted**

~

The higher top, higher bottom and lower top, lower bottom pattern formations in the chart of Delta Corp in Figure 5.9 would require one to sell when the level made earlier by Point C at ₹78 is cracked in the subsequent down move from Point D to Point E because the stock price then enters a lower top, lower bottom pattern regime. At the time of selling, the stop loss can be placed at the Point D level of ₹91.

The stock price thereafter declined and made successive lower tops at points F and H, and successive lower bottoms at points E, G and I.

From the lows of around ₹52, i.e. from Point I, the stock price turned around and rose strongly higher and cracked the level made earlier by Point H at ₹75.60 in its up move from Point I to Point J. One should close the sell position as and when this happens since it marks a distortion in the ongoing lower top, lower bottom pattern formation.

The stock price rose further and cracked the Point J levels of ₹91 in its subsequent up move from Point K to Point L. One should buy as and when the level of Point J around ₹91, is cracked on the upside since the stock price thereafter enters a higher top, higher bottom pattern regime. At the time of buying, the stop loss can be placed at Point K at about ₹76 levels.

The price then rose to the highs of around ₹190 levels. At the time of this writing, the stock price was trading around ₹176 levels.

Trade Summary

1. Initiating a sell trade at ₹77 levels, i.e. selling after the price closes below the Point C level of ₹78.

2. Exiting sell positions at ₹79.85 levels, i.e. after the price closes above the Point H level of ₹75.60.

3. Buying at ₹91.50 levels, i.e. buying after the price closes above the Point J level of ₹91.

At the time of this writing, the stock price was trading around ₹176 levels. If the price of ₹176 is taken into account to calculate mark the market profit / loss account, trading higher top, higher bottom and lower top, lower bottom pattern formations would have resulted in a profit of 81.65 points in this case.

~

Example 10: Escorts

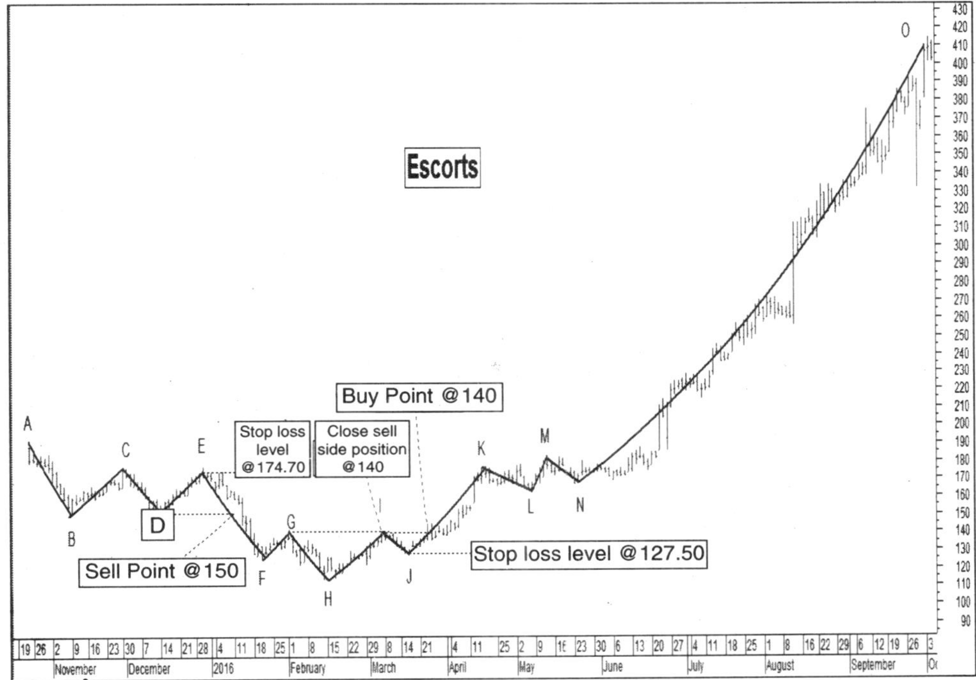

Figure 5.10: **Daily stock price chart of Escorts**

~

Trading higher top, higher bottom and lower top, lower bottom pattern formations in Figure 5.10 of Escorts would suggest initiating a sell trade as and when the level made earlier by Point D at ₹150 is cracked in the subsequent down move from Point E to Point F. This is because the stock price then enters a lower top, lower bottom pattern regime. At the time of selling, the stop loss can be placed at Point E, i.e. at around ₹174.70 levels.

The stock price thereafter declined in a lower top, lower bottom pattern regime and made a lower top G and lower bottoms at points F and H.

From around Point H, however, the stock price changed direction and rallied strongly upward and cracked the level made earlier by Point G at around ₹140 during its up move from Point H to Point I. One should close all sell positions as and when the Point G level is cracked on the upside because the ongoing lower top, lower bottom pattern formation is then distorted.

Thereafter the stock price rallied higher and cracked the earlier Point I level of ₹140 during its up move from Point J to Point K. One should buy as and when this happens because the stock price then enters a higher top, higher bottom pattern regime. At the time of buying, the stop loss can be placed at the Point J levels of ₹127.50.

The stock price went on to make successive higher tops at points K, M, and O, and successive higher bottoms at points L and N. At the time of writing, the last traded stock price in Chart 5.10 was ₹400.

Trade Summary

1. Initiating a sell trade at ₹148.85 levels, i.e. after the price closes below Point D level of ₹150.
2. Closing sell side positions at ₹140 levels, i.e. exiting after the price closes above the Point G level of ₹140.
3. Exiting a buy trade at ₹145.55 levels, i.e. after the price closes above the Point I level of ₹140.

The last traded price in Chart 5.10 is ₹400. If this price is taken into account to calculate the mark to market profit / loss account, then trading higher top, higher bottom and lower top, lower bottom pattern formations resulted in a profit of 263.30 points in this case.

~

Example 11: Cairn India

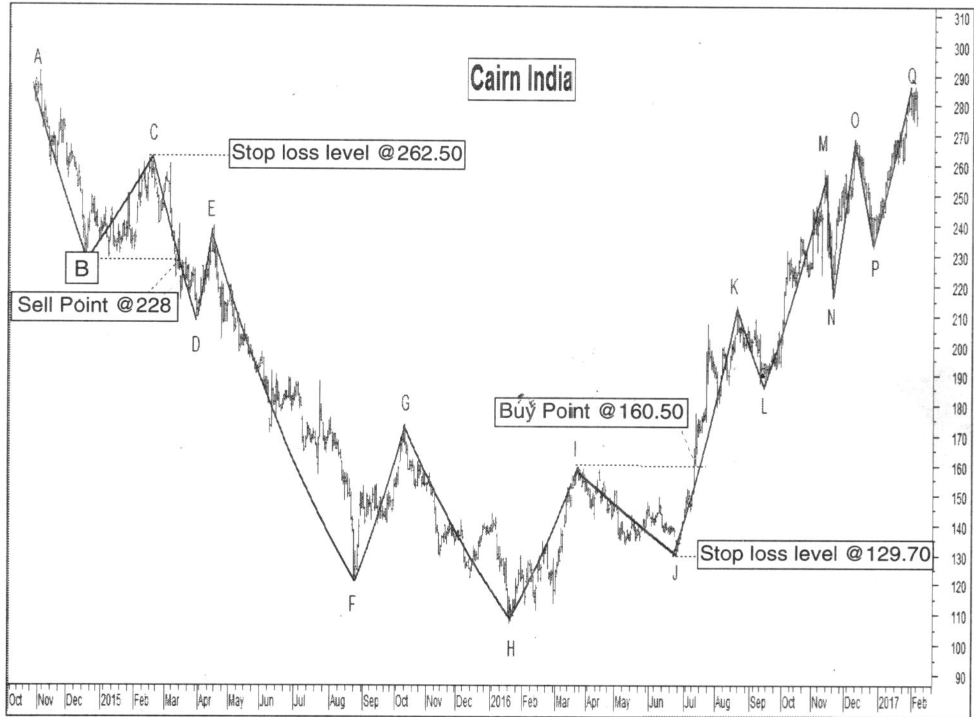

Figure 5.11: **Dow trades highlighted on the daily stock price chart of Cairn India**

~

Trading higher top, higher bottom and lower top, lower bottom pattern formations in Cairn India's chart depicted in Figure 5.11 would suggest initiating a sell / short trade as and when the level made earlier by Point B at about ₹228 is cracked in the down move from Point C to Point D because the stock price then enters a lower top, lower bottom pattern regime. At the time of selling, the stop loss can be placed at Point C, i.e. at about ₹262.50 levels.

The stock price then made successive lower tops at points E, G and I, and successive lower bottoms at points D, F and H. From the lows of around ₹110 levels, i.e. from around Point H, the stock price changed direction and rallied strongly upward and cracked the level made earlier by Point I, at about ₹160.50, during its up move from Point J to Point K. One should close all sell positions and initiate instead a fresh buy position as and when the ₹160.50 level is cracked on the upside because the stock price then enters a higher top, higher bottom pattern regime. At the time of buying, the stop loss can be placed at Point J, i.e. around ₹129.70 levels.

Thereafter the stock price made successive higher tops at points K, M, O, and Q and successive higher bottoms at points L, N and P.

At the time of this writing, the stock price was trading around Point Q, i.e. at about ₹277 levels.

Trade Summary

1. Sell trade at ₹223 levels, i.e. selling after the price closes below the Point B of ₹228 level.
2. Initiating a buy at ₹162 levels, i.e. after the price closes above the Point I levels of ₹160.50.

At the time of this writing, the stock price was trading around ₹277 levels. If the price of ₹277 is taken into account to calculate the mark to market profit / loss account, then trading higher top, higher bottom and lower top, lower bottom pattern formations resulted in a profit of 176 points in this case.

~

Example 12: Adani Transmission

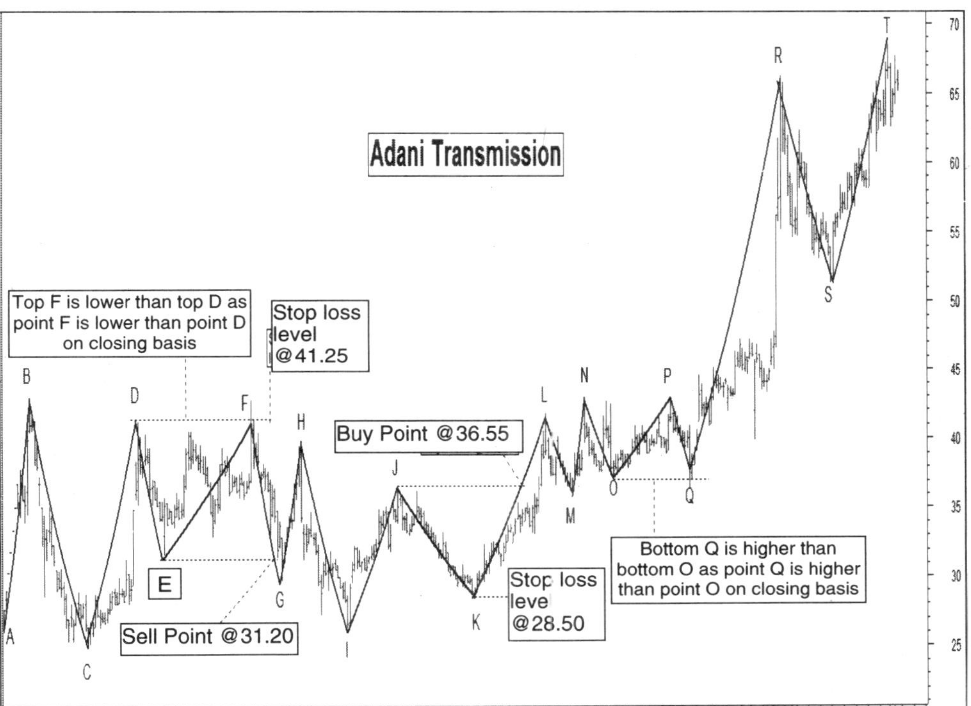

Figure 5.12: **Daily stock price chart of Adani Transmission with Dow trades highlighted**

~

Trading higher top, higher bottom and lower top, lower bottom pattern formations in the case of Adani Transmission in Figure 5.12 would suggest selling as and when the level made earlier by Point E at about ₹31.20 is cracked in the subsequent down move from Point F to Point G. This is because the stock price then enters a lower top, lower bottom pattern. At the time of selling, the stop loss can be placed at around the Point F level of ₹41.25.

Thereafter, the stock price made successive lower tops at points H and J, and successive lower bottoms at points G and I.

From the lows of around ₹27, i.e. from around the level made earlier at Point I, the stock price rallied upward strongly and cracked the Point J level of ₹36.55 in the up move from Point K to Point L. One should close the sell position — and initiate a fresh buy position — as and when the level made earlier by Point J at around ₹36.55 is cracked on the upside because the stock price thereafter enters a higher top, higher bottom pattern regime. At the time of buying, the stop loss can be placed at the Point K level of ₹28.50.

Thereafter the stock price rallied and made successive higher tops at points L, N, R, and T, and successive higher bottoms at points M, O, Q and S.

At the time of this writing, the stock price was trading around the Point T levels of ₹65.70.

Trade Summary

1. Initiating a sell trade at ₹31.15 levels, i.e. after the price closes below the Point E level of ₹31.20.
2. Buying at ₹38.85 levels, i.e. after the price closes above the Point J levels of ₹36.55.

At the time of this writing, the stock price was trading around ₹65.70 levels. If the price of ₹65.70 is taken into account to calculate the mark to market profit / loss account, then trading higher top, higher bottom and lower top, lower bottom pattern formations in this case resulted in a profit of 19.15 points.

~

Example 13: Bank Nifty

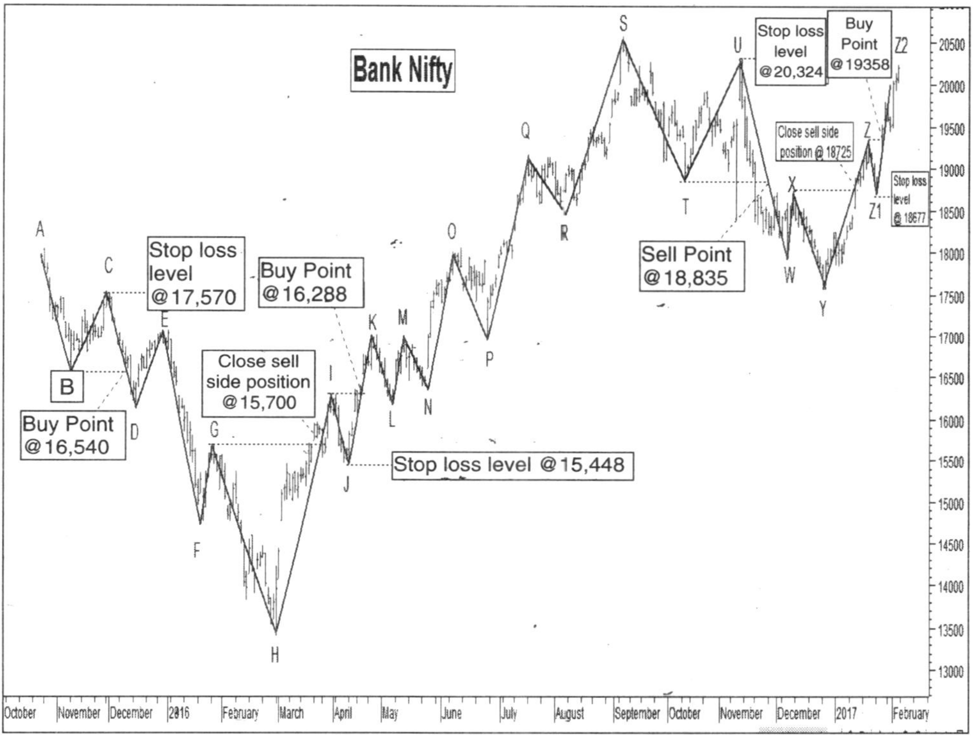

Figure 5.13: **Profitable Dow trades highlighted on the daily stock price chart of Bank Nifty**

~

The higher top, higher bottom and lower top, lower bottom pattern formations in Figure 5.13 would suggest initiating a sell trade as and when the level made earlier by Point B at about 16,540 is cracked in Bank Nifty's down move from Point C to Point D because Bank Nifty thereupon enters a lower top, lower bottom pattern regime. At the time of selling, the stop loss can be placed at Point C, i.e. at about 17,570 levels.

Bank Nifty thereafter made successive lower tops at points E and G, and successive lower bottoms at points D, F and H.

From the lows of around 13,570 levels, i.e. from around Point H, Bank Nifty rallied strongly and cracked the level made earlier by Point G at 15,700 in its up move from Point H to Point I. One should close all sell positions as and when the Point G level of 15,700 is cracked because the ongoing lower top, lower bottom pattern formation then gets distorted.

Bank Nifty thereafter climbed higher and cracked the level made earlier by Point I at about 16,288 levels in its up move from Point J to Point K. One should buy as and when the Point I level of 16,288 is cracked on the upside, whereupon Bank Nifty enters a higher top, higher bottom pattern regime. At the time of buying, the stop loss can be placed at the Point J level of around 15,448.

Bank Nifty then rallied to the highs of around 20,500 levels, from where it declined and cracked the level made earlier by Point T at around 18,835 in its down move from Point U to Point W. One should close all buy side positions and instead initiate a fresh sell position as and when the level made earlier by Point T at around 18,835 is cracked on the downside because Bank Nifty then enters a lower top, lower bottom pattern regime. At the time of selling, the stop loss can be placed at Point U, i.e. at around 20,324 levels.

Thereafter, Bank Nifty declined in a lower top, lower bottom pattern regime and made a lower top at Point X and lower bottoms at points W and Y.

From the low of around 17,650, i.e. from around the Point Y levels, Bank Nifty rallied strongly and cracked the level made earlier by Point X at 18,725 in its up move from Point Y to Point Z. One should close all sell position as and when this happens as the ongoing lower top, lower bottom pattern formation gets distorted at that time.

Bank Nifty thereafter rose further and cracked the level made earlier by Point Z at 19,358 in its up move from Point Z1 to Point Z2. One should buy as and when the Point Z level of 19,358 is cracked on the upside as Bank Nifty subsequently enters a higher top, higher bottom pattern regime. At the time of buying, the stop loss can be placed at the Point Z1 level of 18,677.

Bank Nifty thereafter rallied higher to around 20,200 levels. At the time of this writing, Bank Nifty was trading around 20,200.

Trade Summary

1. Initiating a short trade at 16,342 levels, i.e. selling after the price closes below the Point B level of 16,540.
2. Exiting short positions at 15,926 levels, i.e. after the price closes above the Point G level of 15,700.
3. Buying at 16,637 levels, i.e. buying after the price closes above the Point I level of 16,288.
4. Selling at 18,446 levels, i.e. after the price closes below the Point T level of 18,835.
5. Exiting sell positions at ₹18,830 levels, i.e. exiting after the price closes above the Point X level of 18,725.
6. Buying at ₹19,473 levels, i.e. after the price closes above the Point Z level ₹19,358.

At the time of this writing, Bank Nifty was trading around 20,200 levels. If the level of 20,200 is reckoned to calculate the mark to market profit / loss account, then trading higher top, higher bottom and lower top, lower bottom pattern formations would have resulted in a profit of 2,568 points.

~

Example 14: AIA Engineering

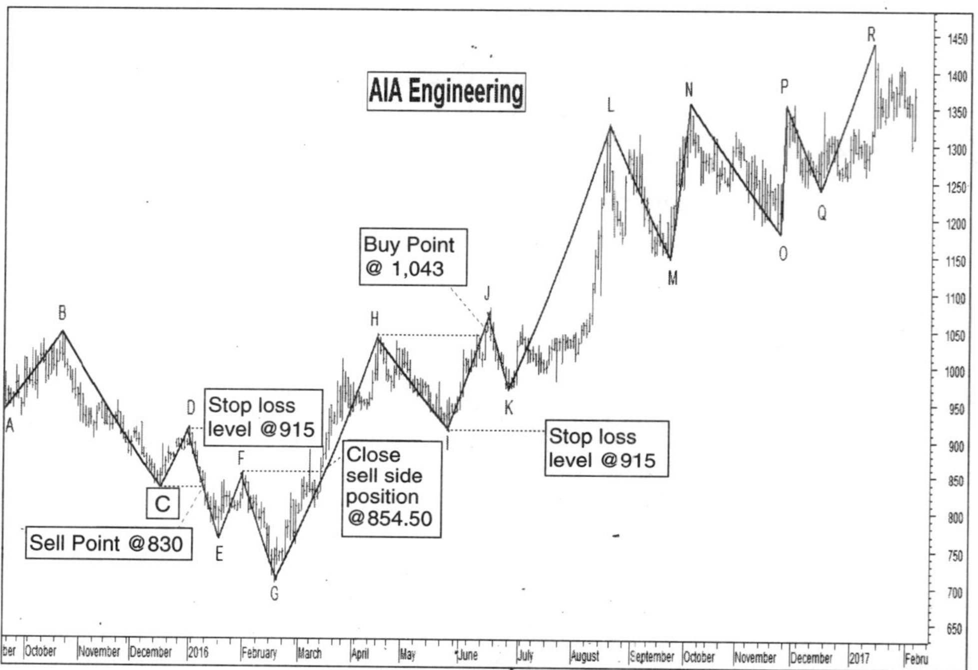

Figure 5.14: **Daily stock price chart of AIA Engineering with profitable Dow trades highlighted**

The higher top, higher bottom and lower top, lower bottom pattern formations in the chart of AIA Engineering in Figure 5.14 suggest initiating a sell trade as and when the level made earlier by Point C at around ₹830 is cracked in the down move from Point D to Point E, because at that time the stock price enters a lower top, lower bottom pattern regime. At the time of selling, the stop loss can be placed at the Point D levels of ₹915.

Thereafter the stock price made a lower top at Point F and lower bottoms at points E and G.

From the lows of around ₹720 levels, i.e. from around Point G, the stock price rose strongly upward and cracked the level made earlier by Point F at about ₹854.50 in its up move from Point G to Point H. One should close the sell position as and when the Point F level of ₹854.50 is cracked on the upside because as at that point, the ongoing lower top, lower bottom pattern formation is distorted.

The stock price thereafter climbed higher and cracked the level made earlier by Point H at ₹1,043 in the up move from Point I to Point J. When this occurs, the stock price enters a higher top, higher bottom pattern regime. At the time of buying, the stop loss can be placed at around the Point I level of ₹915.

The stock price rose further and made successive higher tops at points J, L, N, and R, and successive higher bottoms at points K, M, O and Q.

At the time of this writing, the stock price was trading around the Point R levels of ₹1,370.

Trade Summary

1. Selling at ₹814 levels, i.e. after the price closes below the Point C level of ₹830.
2. Exiting the sell positions at ₹860 levels, i.e. after the price closes above the Point F level of ₹854.50.
3. Buying at ₹1,047 levels, i.e. after the price closes above the Point H level of ₹1,043,

At the time of this writing, the stock price was trading around ₹1,370. If the price of ₹1,370 is taken into account to calculate mark to market profit / loss account, then trading higher top, higher bottom and lower top, lower bottom pattern formations would have resulted in a profit of 277 points in this case.

~

Example 15: Sutlej Textiles

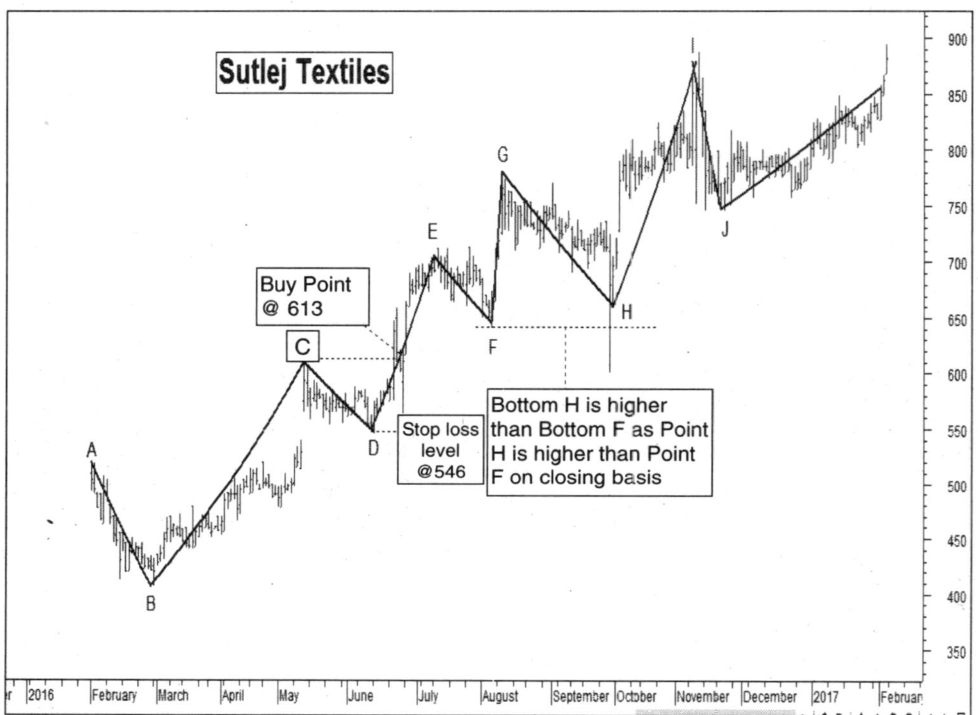

Figure 5.15: **Profitable Dow trades highlighted on the daily stock price chart of Sutlej Textiles**

~

Higher top, higher bottom and lower top, lower bottom pattern formations in the chart of Sutlej Textiles in Figure 5.15 would suggest buying as and when the level made earlier by Point C at around ₹613 is cracked in the up move from Point D to Point E because the stock price thereupon enters a higher top, higher bottom pattern regime. At the time of buying, the stop loss can be placed at Point D levels of ₹546.

Thereafter the stock price made successive higher tops at points E, G and I, and successive higher bottoms, at points F, H and J.

Trade Summary

Buying at ₹639 levels, i.e. buying after the price closes above the Point C level of ₹613.

At the time of this writing, the stock price was trading around ₹880 levels. If the price of ₹880 is taken into account to calculate the mark to market profit / loss account then trading higher top, higher bottom and lower top, lower bottom pattern formations would have resulted in a profit of 241 points.

~

Example 16: Sundaram Clayton

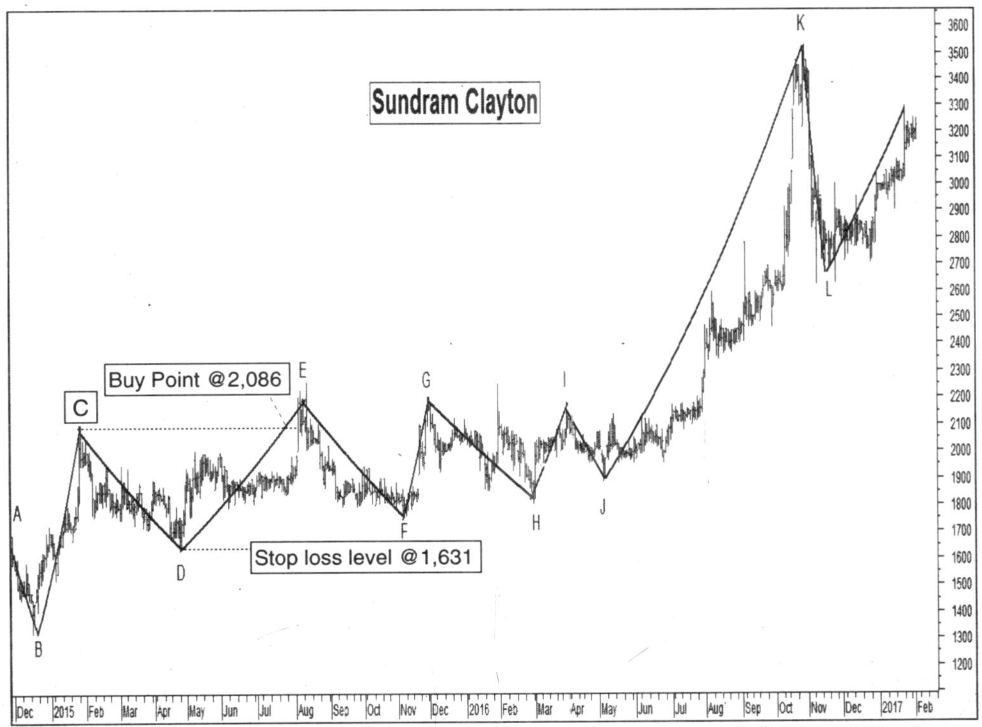

Figure 5.16: **Daily stock price chart of Sundaram Clayton with profitable Dow trades highlighted**

~

Higher top, higher bottom and lower top, lower bottom pattern formations in Figure 5.16 would suggest buying as and when the level made earlier by Point C at ₹2,086 is cracked in the subsequent up move from Point D to Point E. The stock price then enters a higher top, higher bottom pattern. At the time of buying, the stop loss can be placed at Point D, i.e. at about ₹1,631 levels.

After a consolidation phase, the stock price rallied upward strongly to the highs of Point K.

Trade Summary

1. Buying at ₹2,157 levels, i.e. buying after the price closes above the Point C levels of ₹2,086.

2. At the time of this writing, the stock price was trading around ₹3,200 levels. If the price of ₹3,200 is taken into account to calculate the mark to market profit / loss account, then trading higher top, higher bottom and lower top, lower bottom pattern formations would have resulted in a profit of 1,043 points in this example.

~

Example 17: Swan Energy

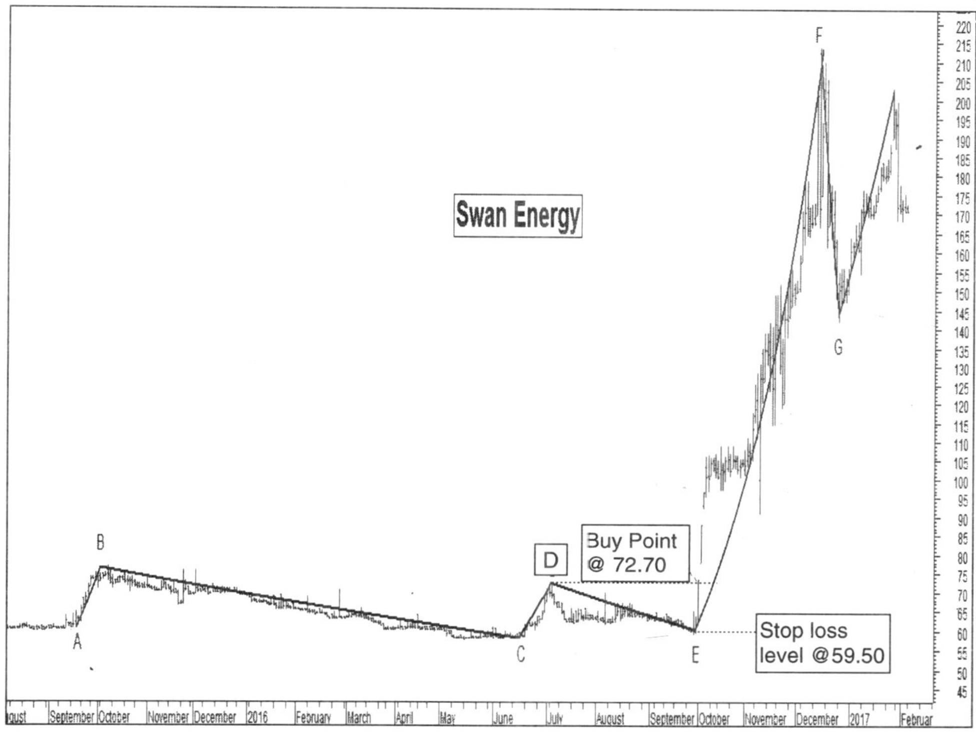

Figure 5.17: **Profitable Dow trades highlighted on the daily stock price chart of Swan Energy**

~

Higher top, higher bottom and lower top, lower bottom pattern formations in Figure 5.17 would suggest buying as and when the level made earlier by Point D at about ₹72.70 is cracked in the up move from Point E to Point F because the stock price then enters a higher top, higher bottom pattern regime. At the time of buying, the stop loss can be placed at Point E, i.e. at around ₹59.50 levels.

The price rallied upward strongly to the highs of around ₹220 levels, i.e. to around Point F, from where it slid down.

At the time of this writing, the stock price was trading around ₹170 on the upside.

Trade Summary

1. Buying at around ₹73.25, i.e. buying after the price closes above the Point D levels of ₹72.70.
2. At the time of this writing, the stock price was trading around ₹170 levels. If the price of ₹170 is taken into account to calculate the mark-to-market profit / loss account, then trading higher top, higher bottom and lower top, lower bottom pattern formations would have resulted in a profit of 96.75 points in this case.

~

Example 18: Symphony

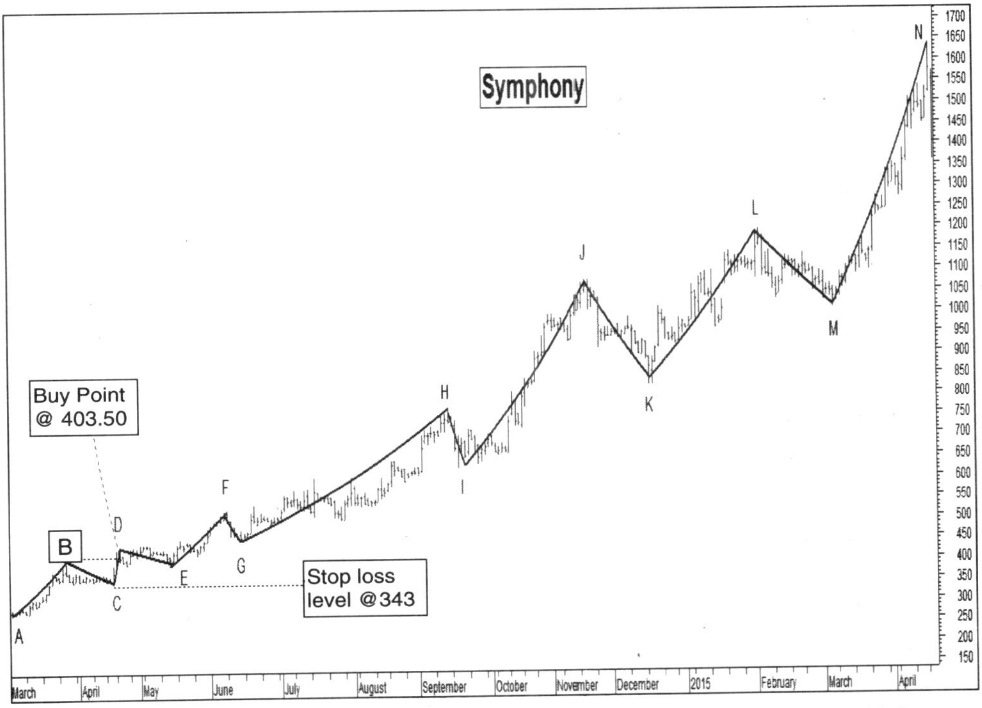

Figure 5.18: **Daily stock price chart of Symphony with profitable Dow trades highlighted**

~

Trading higher top, higher bottom and lower top, lower bottom pattern formations in the case of Symphony depicted in Figure 5.18 would suggest buying as and when the level made earlier by Point B at about ₹403.50 levels is cracked in the subsequent up move from Point C to Point D, because the stock price then enters a higher top, higher bottom pattern regime. At the time of buying, the stop loss can be placed at around the Point C level of ₹343.

Thereafter the stock price rallied upward and made successive higher tops at points F, H, J, L and M, and successive higher bottoms at points E, G, I, K and M.

The last traded price in Chart 5.18 is about ₹1,300.

Trade Summary

1. Buying at ₹404 levels, i.e. buying after the price closes above the Point B level of about ₹403.50.
2. If the last traded price of ₹1,300 is taken into account to calculate the mark-to-market profit / loss account, then trading higher top, higher bottom and lower top, lower bottom pattern formations in this case would have resulted in a profit of 896 points.

~

Example 19: Syngene

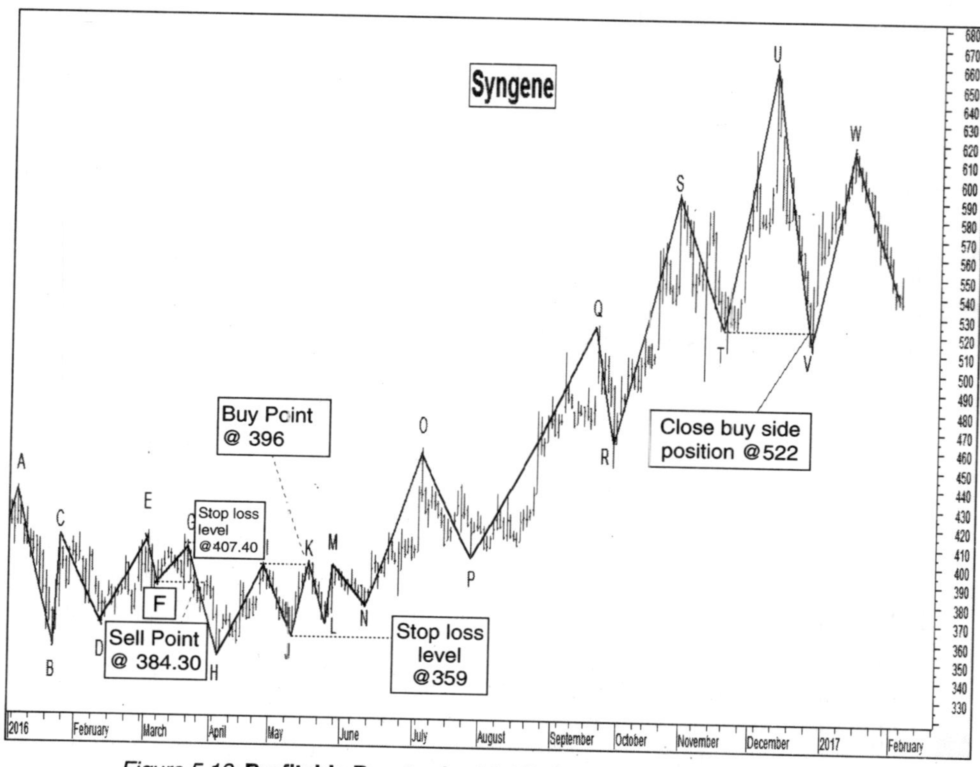

Figure 5.19: **Profitable Dow trades highlighted on the daily stock price chart of Syngene**

~

Higher top, higher bottom and lower top, lower bottom pattern formations in Figure 5.19 would suggest initiating a sell trade as and when the level made earlier by Point F at around ₹384.30 is cracked in the subsequent down move from Point G to Point H. This is because the stock price thereupon enters a lower top, lower bottom pattern regime. At the time of selling, the stop loss can be placed at around the Point G level of ₹407.40.

Thereafter the stock price declined to the lows of around ₹350 levels on the downside, i.e. to around Point H, from where it rallied strongly upward and cracked the level made earlier by Point I at around ₹396 in the up move from Point J to Point K. One should close the sell position when this occurs and instead initiate a fresh buy position because the stock price then enters a higher top, higher bottom pattern regime. At the time of buying, the stop loss can be placed at Point J, i.e. at about ₹359 levels.

Thereafter the stock price made successive higher tops at points O, P, S and U, and successive higher bottoms at points E, L, N, P, R and T.

Then from the highs of around ₹657, i.e. from Point U, the stock price declined and cracked the level made earlier by Point T at ₹522 in its down move from Point U to Point V. One should close the buy position as and when the Point T level of ₹522 is cracked on the downside because the ongoing higher top, higher bottom pattern formation gets distorted when this happens.

Trade Summary

1. Selling at ₹382 levels, i.e. selling after the price closes below the Point F level of ₹384.30.
2. Initiating a buy trade at ₹397 levels, i.e. after the price closes above the Point I level of ₹396.
3. Closing the buy positions at ₹518 levels, i.e. exiting after the price closes below the Point T level of ₹522.
4. Trading higher top, higher bottom and lower top, lower bottom pattern formations in this example would have resulted in a profit of 106 points.

~

Example 20: Tata Motors

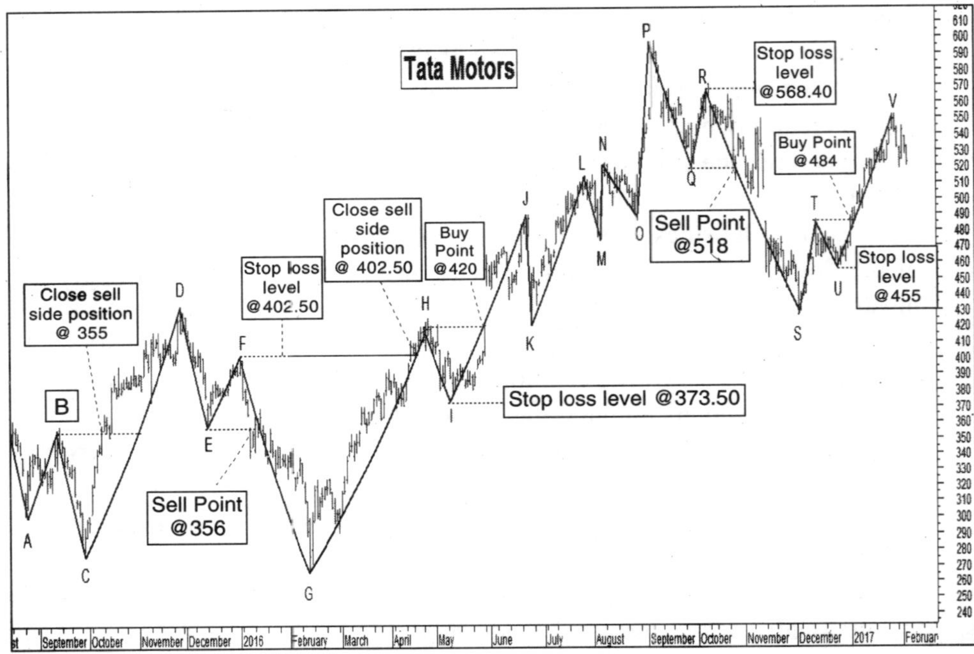

Figure 5.20: **Daily stock price chart of Tata Motors with profitable Dow trades highlighted**

~

Trading higher top, higher bottom and lower top, lower bottom pattern formations in Figure 5.20 would suggest closing the sell position as and when the level made earlier by Point B at around ₹355 is cracked in the up move from Point C to Point D because at that time the ongoing lower top, lower bottom pattern formation gets distorted.

Then from the highs of around ₹430 levels, i.e. from Point D, the stock price declined sharply and cracked the level made earlier by Point E during its down move from Point F to Point G. One should sell as and when the Point E level of ₹356 is cracked on the downside. The stock price then enters a lower top, lower bottom pattern regime. At the time of selling, the stop loss can be placed at the Point F level of ₹402.50.

Thereafter the stock price declined to the lows of around ₹273 on the downside, i.e. to Point G, from where it rallied strongly and cracked the level made earlier by Point F at about ₹402.50 in its up move from Point G to Point H. One should close all sell positions as and when the Point F level of ₹402.50 is cracked in this up move because the ongoing lower top, lower bottom pattern formation gets distorted at that time.

Thereafter the stock price rose further and cracked the level made earlier by Point H at around ₹420 in its up move from Point I to Point J. One should buy as and when this happens because the stock price thereupon enters a higher top, higher bottom pattern regime. At the time of buying, the stop loss can be placed at Point I, i.e. at ₹373.50 levels.

The stock price rose to the highs of around ₹590 levels in a higher top, higher bottom pattern regime and made successive higher tops at points J, L, N and P, — and successive higher bottoms at points I, K, M, O and Q.

The price then declined sharply from the highs of around ₹590 and cracked the level made earlier by Point Q at around ₹518 in its down move from Point R to Point S. One should close all buy positions — and instead initiate a fresh sell position as and when this happens because the stock price then enters a lower top, lower bottom pattern regime. At the time of selling, the stop loss can be placed at the Point R level of around ₹568.40.

Thereafter the stock price declined to around ₹430 levels on the downside, i.e. to around the level made earlier by Point S, from where it rallied back up strongly and cracked the level made earlier by Point T at around ₹484 in the up move from Point U to Point V. One should have closed the sell position — and instead initiated a fresh buy position — as and when the ₹484 levels was cracked on the upside as the stock price then entered a higher top, higher bottom pattern regime. At the time of buying, the stop loss could have been placed at the Point U level of ₹455.

At the time of this writing, the stock price was trading around ₹525 levels.

Trade Summary

1. Selling at ₹343 levels, i.e. exiting after the price closes below the Point E level of ₹356.
2. Exiting the sell positions at ₹409 levels, i.e. exiting after the price closes above the Point F level of ₹402.50.

3. Buying at ₹421 levels, i.e. after the price closes above the Point H level of ₹420.
4. Selling at ₹513 levels, i.e. exiting after the price closes below the Point Q level of ₹518.
5. Buying at ₹487 levels, i.e. buying after the price closes above the Point T level of ₹484.
6. At the time of this writing, the stock price was trading around ₹525 levels. If the price of ₹525 is taken into account to calculate the mark to market profit / loss account, then trading higher top, higher bottom and lower top, lower bottom pattern formations resulted in a profit of 90 points in this case.

~

Example 21: Tata Communication

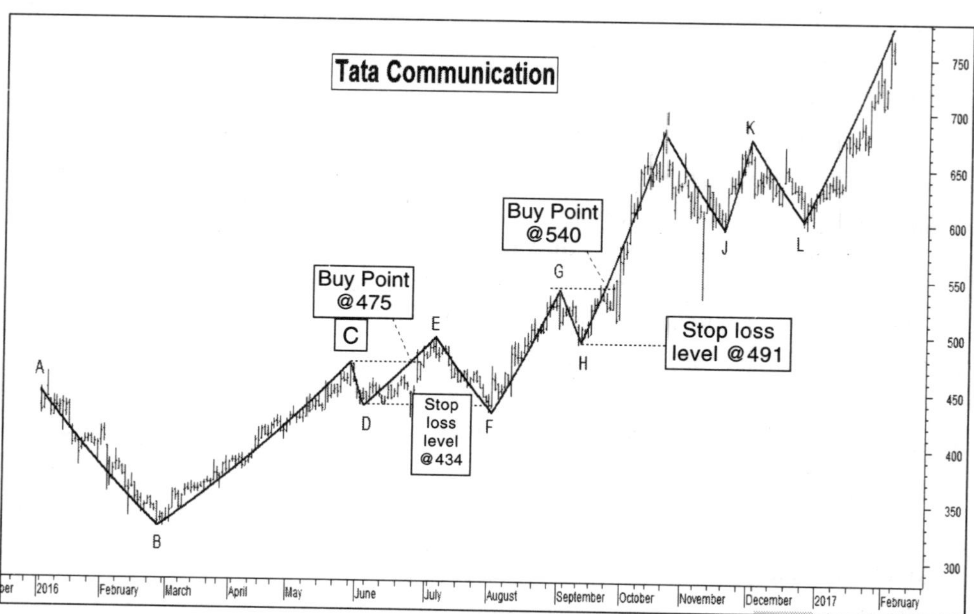

Figure 5.21: **Profitable Dow trades highlighted in the daily stock price chart of Tata Communication**

~

Higher top, higher bottom and lower top, lower bottom pattern formations in Figure 5.21 would suggest buying as and when the level made earlier by Point C at around ₹475 is cracked during the up move from Point D to Point E. The stock price then enters a higher top, higher bottom pattern regime. At the time of buying, the stop loss can be placed at Point D, i.e. at about ₹434 levels.

Thereafter the stock price declined sharply and cracked the level made earlier by Point D at around ₹434. One should close all the long positions as the stop loss gets triggered at this point.

From the lows of around ₹432, i.e. from Point F, the stock price rallied strongly upward and cracked the level made earlier by Point G at around ₹540 during the up move from Point H to Point I. One should buy as and when this happens as the stock price then enters a higher top, higher bottom pattern regime. At the time of buying, the stop loss can be placed at Point H, i.e. at ₹491 levels.

Thereafter the stock price rallied in a higher top, higher bottom pattern regime and made successive higher tops at points I and M, and higher bottoms at points H, J and L.

At the time of this writing, the stock price was trading around ₹755 levels.

Trade Summary

1. Initiate a buy trade at ₹480 levels, i.e. after the price closes above the Point C level of around ₹475.

2. Closing buy positions at ₹433.80 levels, i.e. exiting after the price closes below the Point D level of ₹434.

3. Buying at around ₹543 levels, i.e. after the price closes above the Point G level of ₹540.

4. At the time of this writing, the stock price was trading around ₹755 levels. If the price of ₹755 is considered to calculate mark to market profit / loss account, then trading higher top, higher bottom and lower top, lower bottom pattern formations would have resulted in a profit of 165.80 points in this case.

~

Example 22: Tata Elxsi

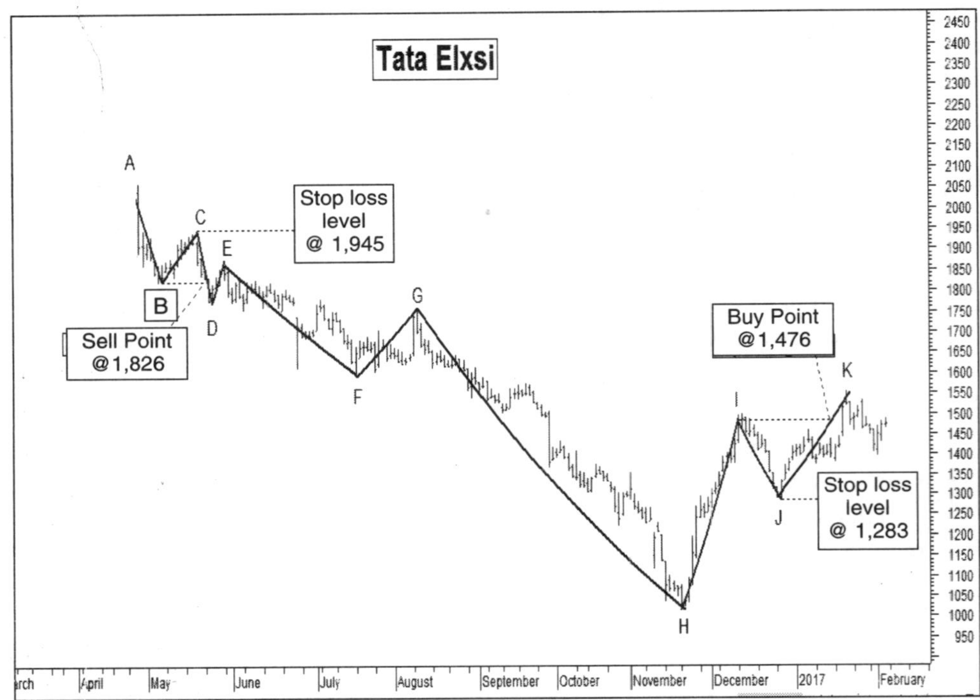

Figure 5.22: **Profitable Dow trades highlighted in the daily stock price chart of Tata Elxsi**

~

Higher top, higher bottom and lower top, lower bottom pattern formations in the chart of Tata Elxsi in Figure 5.22 suggest initially selling as and when the level made earlier by Point B at about ₹1,826 is cracked in the down move from Point C to Point D. The stock price then enters a lower top, lower bottom pattern regime. At the time of initiating the sell trade, the stop loss can be placed at Point C, i.e. at about ₹1,945 levels.

The stock price duly declined to the lows of around ₹1,030 levels, making a lower top at Point G and lower bottoms at points F and H.

From the lows of around ₹1,030 levels, i.e. from around Point H, the price rallied upward strongly and cracked the level made earlier by Point I at about ₹1,476 in the up move from Point J to Point K. One should close all sell side positions — and instead initiate a fresh buy position as and when the Point I level of ₹1,476 is cracked on the upside because the stock price then enters a higher top, higher bottom pattern. At the time of buying, the stop loss can be placed at Point J, i.e. at about ₹1,283 levels.

At the time of this writing, the stock price was trading around ₹1,468.

Trade Summary

1. Selling at ₹1,779 levels, i.e. after the price closes below the Point B level of ₹1,826.
2. Buying at ₹1,515 levels, i.e. after the price closes above the Point I level of ₹1,476.
3. At the time of this writing, the stock was trading around ₹1,468 price levels. If this price is used to calculate the mark to market profit / loss account, then trading higher top, higher bottom and lower top, lower bottom pattern formations would have resulted in a profit of 217 points in this example.

~

Example 23: Ambuja Cement

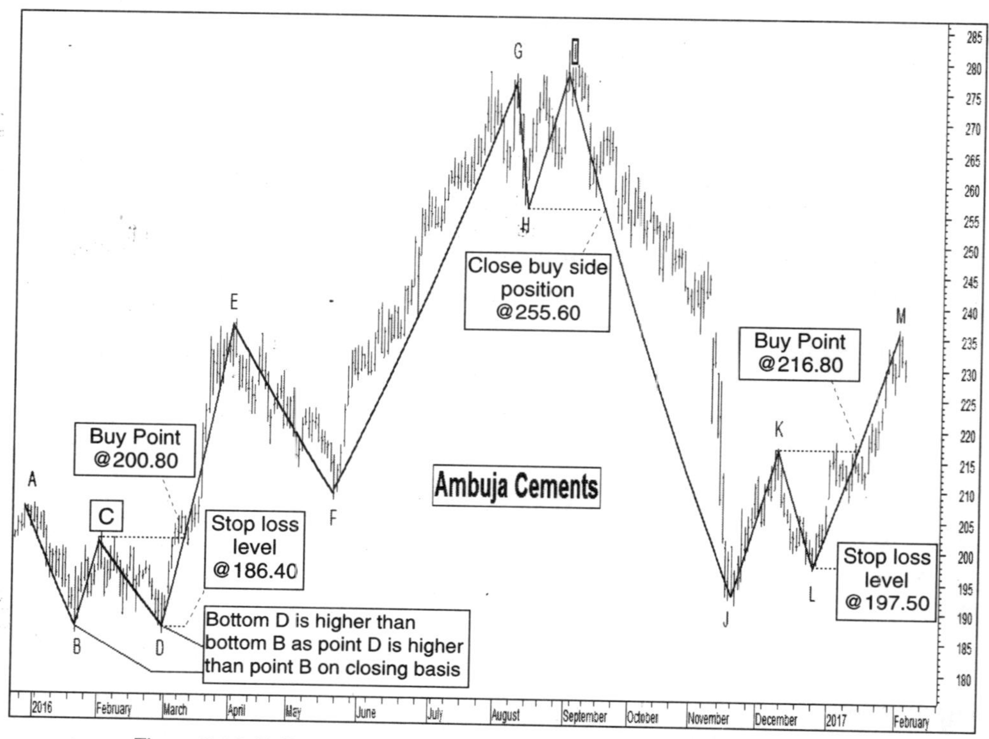

Figure 5.23: **Daily stock price chart of Ambuja Cement with profitable Dow trades highlighted**

~

Higher top, higher bottom and lower top, lower bottom pattern formations depicted in Figure 5.23 would suggest buying as and when the level made earlier by Point C at around ₹200.80 is cracked during the up move from Point D to Point E because the stock price then enters a higher top, higher bottom pattern regime. At the time of initiating the buy trade, the stop loss can be placed at Point D, i.e. at about ₹186.40 levels. In the chart in Figure 5.23 it appears that Point D is lower than Point B whereas in reality Point D did not close below Point B.

The stock price then rose in a higher top, higher bottom pattern regime and made successive higher tops at points E, G and I, and successive higher bottoms at points F and H.

From the highs of around ₹280 levels, i.e. from Point I, the stock price fell and cracked the level made earlier by Point H at around ₹255.60 in its down move from Point I to Point J. One should close the buy positions as and when the level of ₹255.60 is cracked on the downside because the ongoing higher top, higher bottom pattern formation then gets distorted.

Thereafter the stock price declined to the lows of around ₹194 levels, i.e. to Point J, in a pattern which does comply with the lower top, lower bottom pattern regime. As a result, Dow traders would not have been able to sell in this down move.

From the lows of around ₹194 levels, i.e. from Point J, the stock price rallied strongly upward and cracked the level made earlier by Point K at around ₹216.80 during its up move from Point L to Point M. One should buy as and when the Point K level of ₹216.70 is cracked on the upside as the stock price then enters a higher top, higher bottom pattern regime. At the time of buying, the stop loss can be placed at Point L, i.e. at about ₹197.50 levels.

At the time of this writing, the stock price was trading around ₹237 levels.

Trade Summary

1. Buying at ₹202.40 levels, i.e. after the price closes above the Point C level of ₹200.80.
2. Exiting buy side positions at ₹254 levels, i.e. after the price closes below the Point H level of ₹255.60.
3. Buying at ₹217.55 levels, i.e. after the price closes above the Point K level of ₹216.80.
4. At the time of this writing, the stock price was trading around ₹237 levels. If the price of ₹237 is reckoned to calculate the mark to market profit / loss account then trading higher top, higher bottom and lower top, lower bottom pattern formations would have resulted in profit of 71.05 points in this case.

~

Example 24: Ambika Cotton Mills

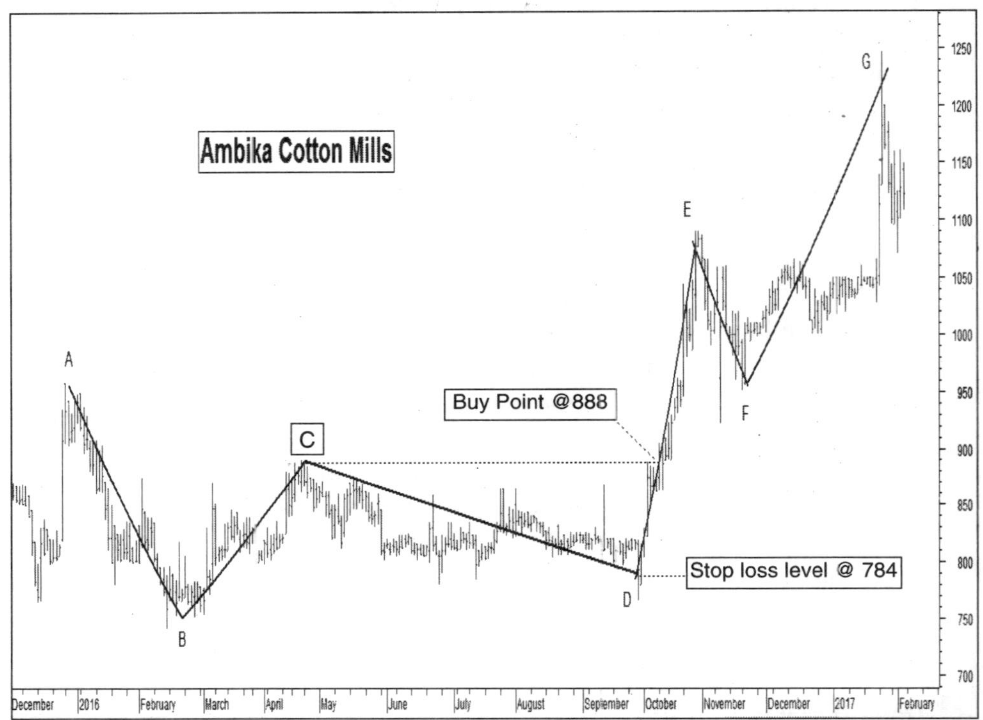

Figure 5.24: **Profitable Dow trades highlighted in the daily stock price chart of Ambika Cotton Mills**

~

Higher top, higher bottom and lower top, lower bottom pattern formations in Figure 5.24 would suggest buying as and when the level made earlier by Point C at around ₹888 is cracked in the up move from Point D to Point E. The stock price then enters a higher top, higher bottom pattern regime. At the time of buying, the stop loss can be placed at the Point D level of ₹784.

The stock price thereafter rallied in a higher top, higher bottom pattern formation and made successive higher tops at points E and G, and a higher bottom at Point F.

At the time of this writing, the stock price was trading around ₹1,150 levels.

Trade Summary

1. Initiating a buy trade at ₹897 levels, i.e. buying after the price closes above the Point C levels of ₹888.
2. At the time of this writing, the stock price was trading around ₹1,150 levels. If this price is used to calculate a mark to market profit / loss account, then trading higher top, higher bottom and lower top, lower bottom pattern formations would have resulted in a profit of 253 points in this case.

~

Example 25: Apollo Tubes

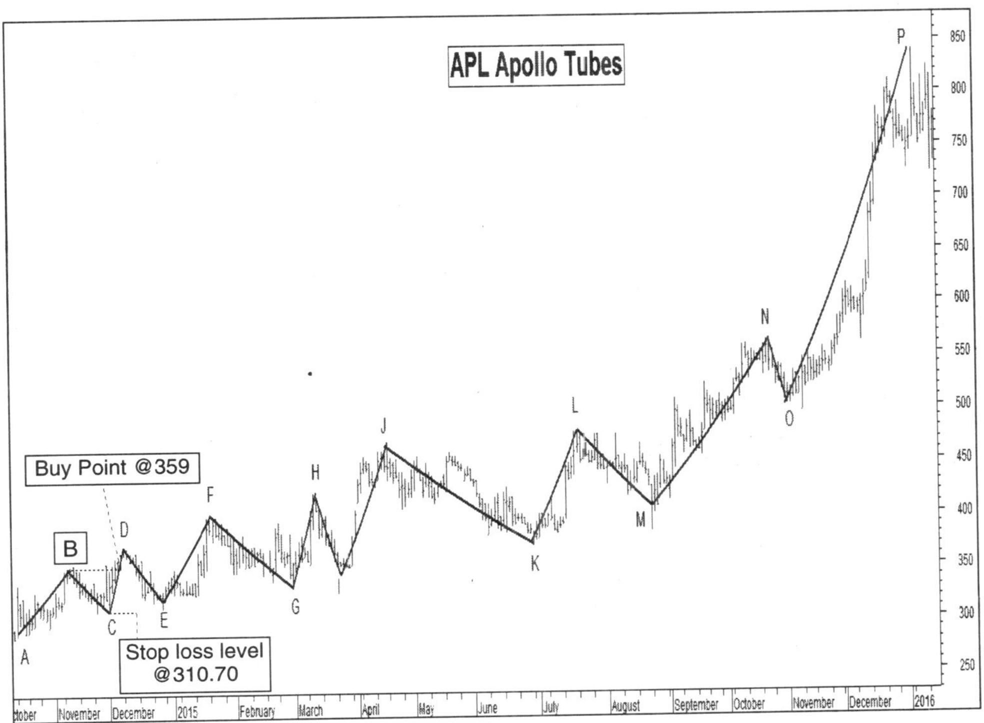

Figure 5.25: **Daily stock price chart of Apollo Tubes highlighting profitable Dow trades**

~

Higher top, higher bottom and lower top, lower bottom pattern formations in the chart of Apollo Tubes in Figure 5.25 suggest buying as and when the level made earlier by Point B at around ₹359 is cracked in the up move from Point C to Point D. At that time the stock price enters a higher top, higher bottom pattern regime. At the time of buying, the stop loss can be placed at Point C, i.e. at around ₹310.70 levels.

The stock price thereafter rallied upward making a higher top, higher bottom pattern regime and made successive higher tops at points F, H, J, L, N and P, and successive higher bottoms at points G, I, K, M and O.

At the time of this writing, the price of Apollo Tubes was trading around ₹745 levels.

Trade Summary

1. Initiating a buy trade at ₹369 levels, i.e. buying after the price closes above the Point B level of ₹359.
2. At the time of this writing, the stock price was trading around ₹745 levels. If the price of ₹745 is used to calculate the market profit / loss account, then trading higher top, higher bottom and lower top, lower bottom pattern formations would have resulted in a profit of 376 points in this example.

~

Example 26: Ashapura Intimates Fashion Ltd

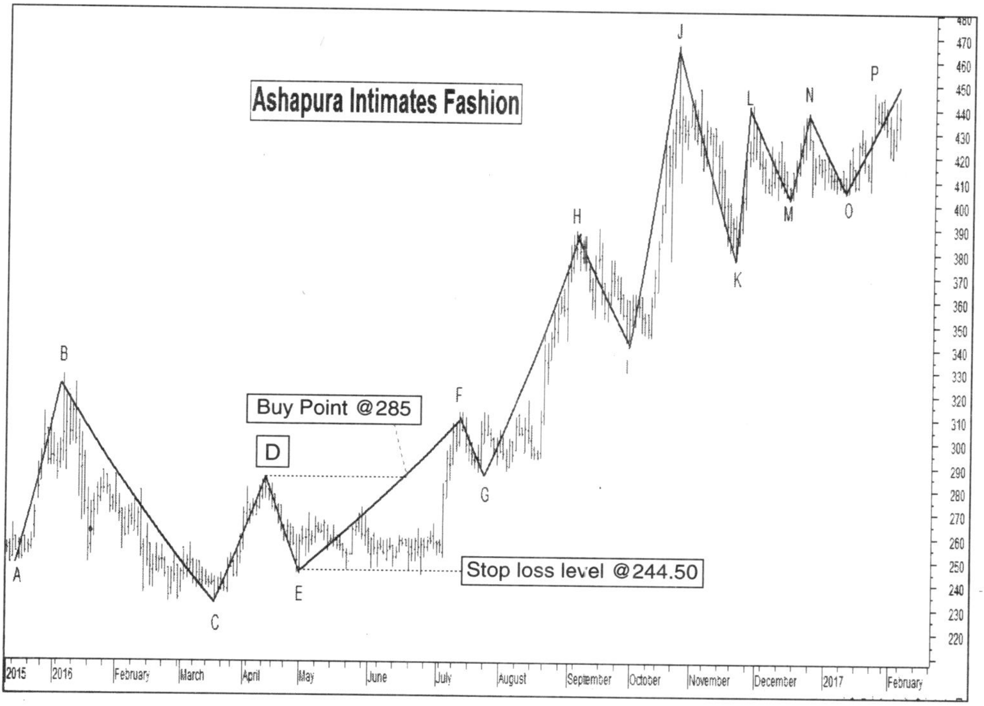

Figure 5.26: **Profitable Dow trades highlighted in the daily stock price chart of Ashapura Intimates Fashion**

~

Higher top, higher bottom and lower top, lower bottom pattern formations in Figure 5.26 would have suggested initiating a buy trade as and when the level made earlier by Point D at about ₹285 is cracked in the up move from Point E to Point F. The stock price then enters a higher top, higher bottom pattern regime. At the time of buying, the stop loss can be placed at the Point E level, i.e. around ₹244.50.

The stock price thereafter rallied in a higher top, higher bottom pattern regime and made successive higher tops at points F, H and J, and successive higher bottoms at points G, I, K, M and O.

At the time of this writing, the stock price was trading around ₹426 levels.

Trade Summary

1. Buying at ₹293 levels, i.e. after the price closes above the Point D level of ₹285.
2. At the time of this writing, the stock price was trading around ₹426 levels. If the price of ₹426 is used to calculate the mark to market profit / loss account, then trading higher top, higher bottom and lower top, lower bottom pattern formations in this case would have resulted in a profit of 133 points.

~

Example 27: ACC

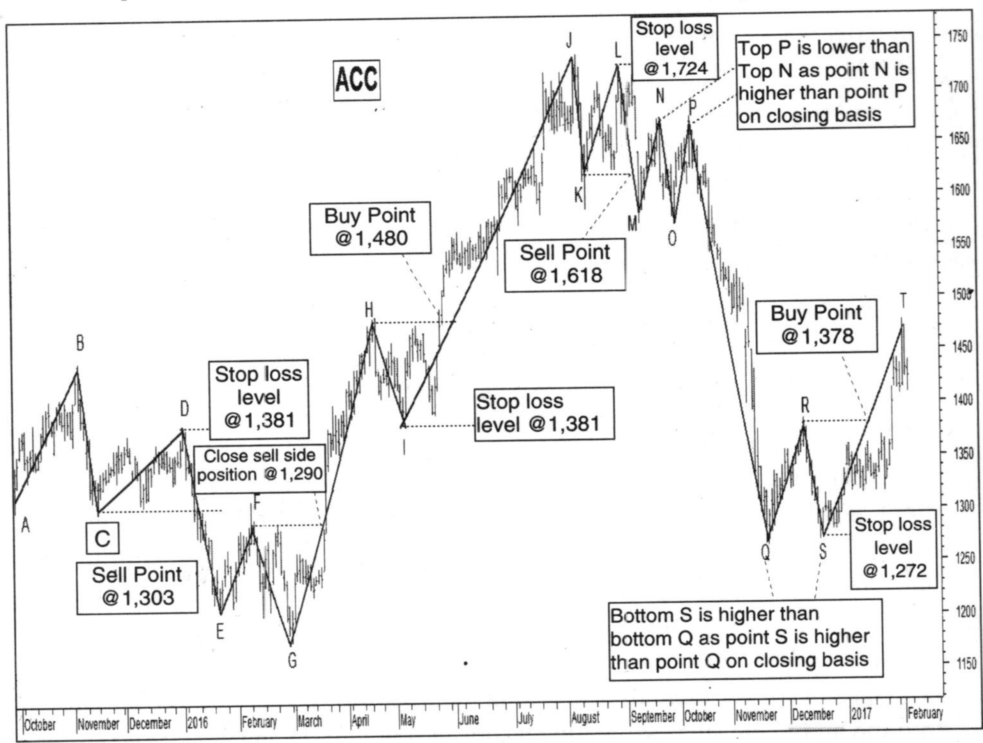

Figure 5.27: **Daily stock price chart of ACC with profitable Dow trades highlighted**

~

Higher top, higher bottom and lower top, lower bottom patterns in Figure 5.27 suggest selling ACC as and when the level made earlier by Point C at about ₹1,303 is cracked in the down move from Point D to Point E. The stock price then enters a lower top, lower bottom pattern regime. At the time of selling, the stop loss can be placed at the Point D level of ₹1,381.

The stock price thereafter declined in a lower top, lower bottom pattern regime and made a lower top at Point F and a lower bottom at Point G.

From the lows of around ₹1,180, i.e. from around Point G, the stock price rallied strongly and cracked the level made earlier by Point F at ₹1,290 in its up move from Point G to Point H. One should close the sell position as and when this happens as at that time the ongoing lower top, lower bottom pattern formation gets distorted.

The stock price rallied further and cracked the level made earlier by Point H at around ₹1,480 in its up move from Point I to Point J. One should buy as and when this break occurs as the stock price then enters a higher top, higher bottom pattern regime. At the time of buying, the stop loss can be placed at about the Point I level of ₹1,381.

The stock price thereafter rallied to the highs of around ₹1,733 levels on the upside, i.e. to around the level of Point J, from where it then declined and cracked the level made earlier by Point K at about ₹1,618 in its down move from Point L to Point M. One should close the buy trade — and instead initiate a fresh sell position — as and when this happens the stock price then enters a lower top, lower bottom pattern regime. At the time of selling, the stop loss can be placed at the Point L level of ₹1,724.

The stock price thereafter declined in a lower top, lower bottom pattern regime and made successive lower tops at points N, P and R, and successive lower bottoms at points M, O and Q. While it appears that Point P is seemingly higher than Point N, in reality Point P did not close above the level of Point N.

From the lows of around ₹1,276 levels, i.e. from around Point S, the stock price turned around and rallied strongly upward and cracked the

Point R level of ₹1,378 in its up move from Point S to Point T. One should close the sell position — and instead initiate fresh buy positions — when the Point R level of ₹1,378 is cracked on the upside because the stock price then enters a higher top, higher bottom pattern regime. At the time of buying, the stop loss can be placed at about the Point S level of ₹1,272.

The stock price rallied thereafter to the highs of around ₹1,495 levels.

At the time of this writing, the stock price was trading around ₹1,456 levels.

Trade Summary

1. Initiating a sell trade at ₹1,300 levels, i.e. after the price closes below the Point C level of ₹1,303.
2. Exiting short positions at ₹1,337 levels, i.e. after the price closes above the Point F level of ₹1,290.
3. Initiating a buy trade at ₹1,504 levels, i.e. after the price closes above the Point H level of ₹1,480.
4. Selling at ₹1,582 levels, i.e. after the price closes below the Point K level of ₹1,618.
5. Buying at ₹1,400 levels, i.e. buying after the price closes above the Point R level of around ₹1,378.
6. At the time of this writing, the stock price was trading around ₹1,456 levels. If ₹1,456 is used to calculate the mark to market profit / loss account, then trading higher top, higher bottom and lower top, lower bottom pattern formations would have resulted in a profit of 279 points in this case.

~

Example 28: Astec Lifesciences

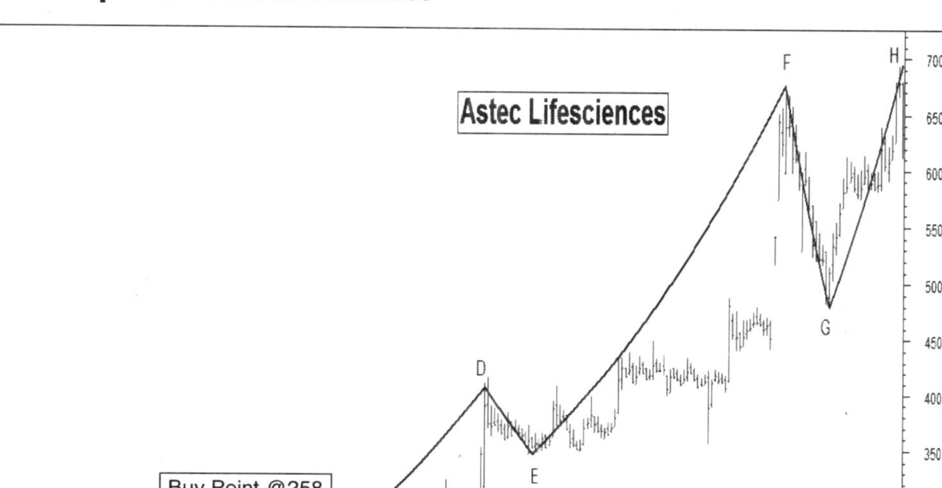

Figure 5.28: **Daily stock price chart of Astec Lifesciences highlighting profitable Dow trades**

~

Higher top, higher bottom and lower top, lower bottom pattern formations in Figure 5.28 would have suggested buying Astec Lifesciences as and when the level made earlier by Point B at around ₹258 is cracked in the up move from Point C to Point D. The stock price thereafter enters a higher top, higher bottom pattern regime. At the time of buying, the stop loss can be placed at Point C, i.e. at around ₹171.

Thereafter the stock price rallied making a higher top, higher bottom pattern and made successive higher tops at points D, F and H, and successive higher bottoms at points E and G.

At the time of writing, the stock price of Astec Lifesciences was trading around ₹592.

Trade Summary

1. Going long at ₹293 levels, i.e. after the price closes above the Point B levels of around ₹258.
2. At the time of this writing, the price was ₹592. If this price of ₹592 is taken into account to calculate the mark to market profit / loss account, then trading higher top, higher bottom and lower top, lower bottom pattern formations would have resulted in a profit of 299 points in this case.

~

Example 29: Atul Ltd

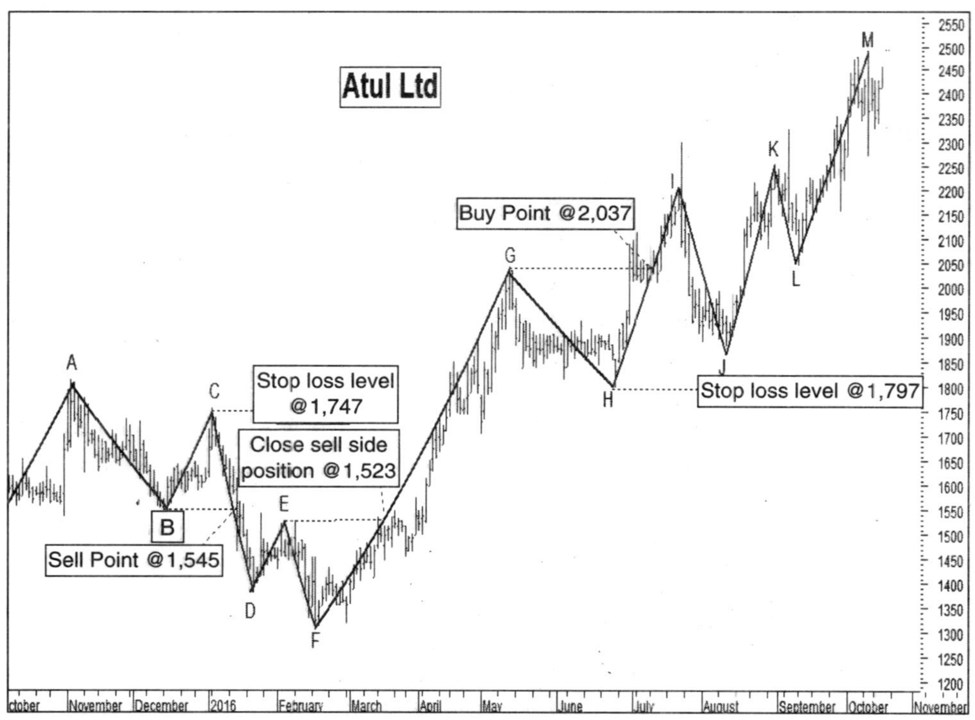

Figure 5.29: **Profitable Dow trades highlighted in the daily stock price chart of Atul Ltd**

~

Higher top, higher bottom and lower top, lower bottom pattern formations in the case of Figure 5.29 would have suggested selling as and when the level made earlier by Point B at around ₹1,545 is cracked in the down move from Point C to Point D because the stock price then enters a lower top, lower bottom pattern regime. At the time of going short, the stop loss can be placed at Point C, i.e. at around ₹1,747 levels.

Thereafter, the stock price made a lower top at E and lower bottoms at points D and F.

From the lows of around ₹1,313, however, i.e. from around Point F, the stock price rallied higher strongly and cracked the level made earlier by Point E at ₹1,523 in the up move from Point F to Point G. One should close the sell position when this happens because the ongoing lower top, lower bottom pattern formation then gets distorted.

Thereafter the stock price rallied further and cracked the level made earlier by Point G at around ₹2,037 in its up move from Point H to Point I. One should buy when this happens as the stock price then enters a higher top, higher bottom pattern regime. At the time of buying, the stop loss can be placed at Point H, i.e. around ₹1,797 levels.

The stock price thereafter rallied higher to around ₹2,475 levels, the last traded stock price in Chart 5.29.

Trade Summary

1. Going short at ₹1,534 levels, i.e. after the price closes below the Point B level of ₹1,545.
2. Exiting sell side positions at ₹1,535 levels, i.e. after the price closes above the Point E level of ₹1,523.
3. Buying at ₹2,050 levels, i.e. after the price closes above the Point G level of ₹2,037.
4. If the last traded price of ₹2,475 is taken into account to calculate the mark to market profit / loss account, then trading higher top, higher bottom and lower top, lower bottom pattern formations would have resulted in a profit of 424 points in this case.

~

Example 30: Tech Mahindra

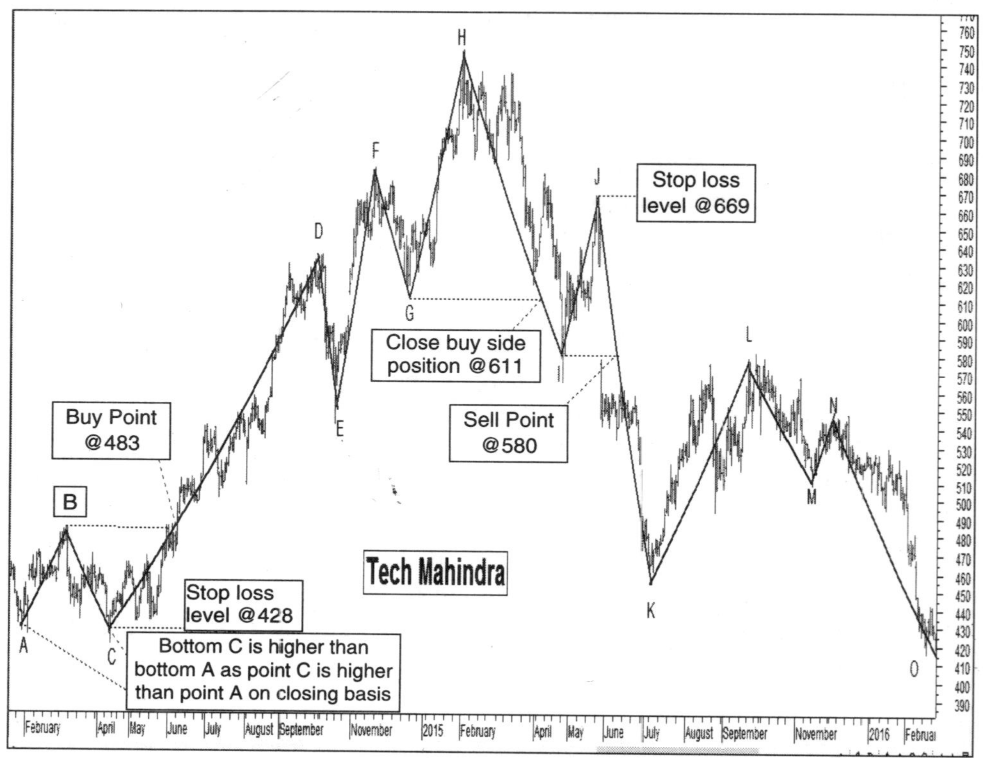

Figure 5.30: **Daily stock price chart of Tech Mahindra with profitable Dow trades highlighted**

~

Higher top, higher bottom and lower top, lower bottom patterns in the example of Figure 5.30 would suggest buying Tech Mahindra as and when the level made earlier by Point B at about ₹483 is cracked in the up move from Point C to Point D because the stock price then enters a higher top, higher bottom pattern regime. At the time of buying, the stop loss can be placed at Point C, i.e. at about ₹428 levels.

The stock price thereafter rallied upward to the highs of around ₹747 levels in a higher top, higher bottom pattern and made successive higher tops — at points D, F and H, and successive higher bottoms at points E, G.

From the highs of around ₹747 levels, the stock price began a decline and cracked the level made earlier by Point G at about ₹611 in its down move from Point H to Point I. One should close the long / buy position as and when this happens because the ongoing higher top, higher bottom pattern formation then gets distorted.

The stock price thereafter declined further and cracked Point I at ₹580 levels in the down move from Point J to Point K. One should sell at this point because the stock price then enters a lower top, lower bottom pattern regime. At the time of selling, the stop loss can be placed at the Point J level of around ₹669.

The stock price thereafter declined in a lower top, lower bottom pattern and made successive lower tops at points L and N, and successive lower bottoms at points K and O.

At the time of this writing, the stock price was trading around ₹415 levels.

Trade Summary

1. Initiating a buy trade at ₹489 levels, i.e. buying after the price closes above the Point B level of ₹483.
2. Exiting buy positions at ₹588 levels, i.e. after the price closes below the Point G level of ₹611.
3. Selling at ₹549 levels, i.e. selling after the price closes below the Point I level of ₹580.
4. At the time of this writing, the stock price was trading around ₹415 levels. If the price of ₹415 is used to calculate the mark to market profit / loss account, then trading higher top, higher bottom and lower top, lower bottom pattern formations would have resulted in a profit of 233 points in this instance.

~

Example 31: Suzlon

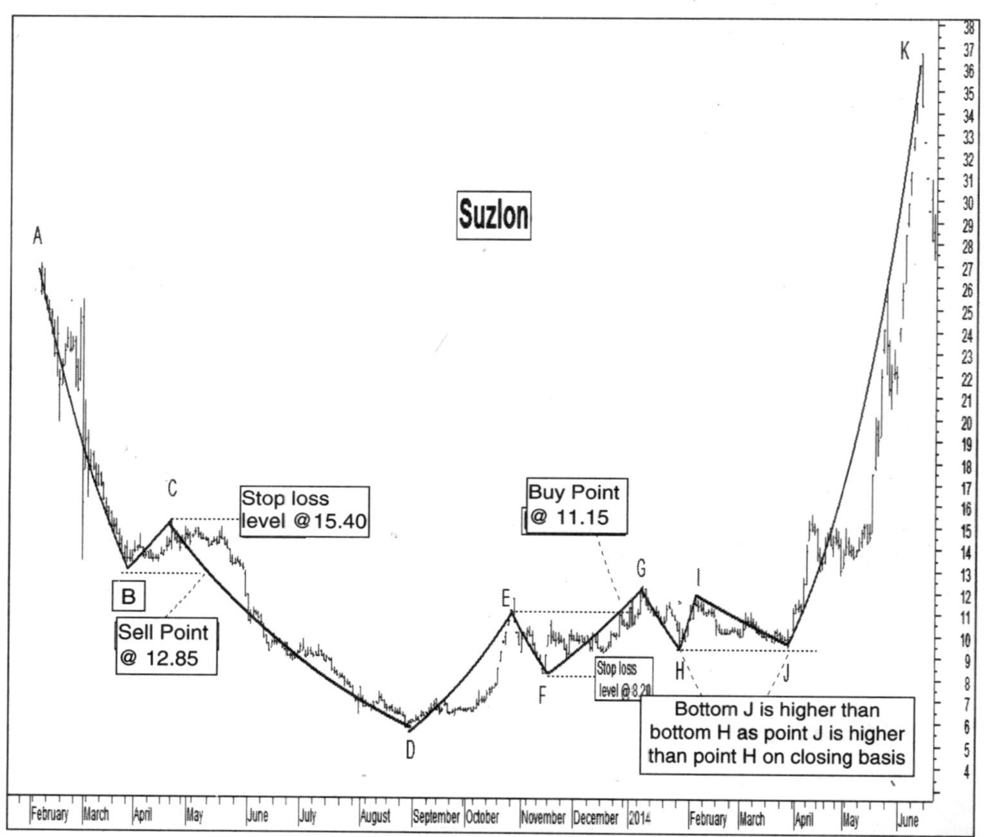

Figure 5.31: **Profitable Dow trades highlighted on the daily stock price chart of Suzlon**

~

Higher top, higher bottom and lower top, lower bottom pattern formations in the case of Figure 5.31 would have suggested selling or shorting, Suzlon as and when the level made earlier by Point B at around ₹12.85 is cracked in the down move from Point C to Point D. This is because the stock price then enters a lower top, lower bottom pattern regime. At the time of selling, the stop loss can be placed at Point C, i.e. at around ₹15.40 levels.

The stock price thereafter declined in a lower top, lower bottom pattern regime and made a lower top at Point E and a lower bottom at Point D.

Then from the lows of around ₹6, i.e. from Point D, the stock price rallied strongly upward and cracked the level made earlier by Point E at ₹11.15 in its up move from Point F to Point G. One should close the sell position — and instead initiate a fresh buy trade as and when the Point E level of ₹11.15 is cracked on the upside as the stock price then enters a higher top, higher bottom pattern. At the time of buying, the stop loss can be placed at Point F, i.e. at ₹8.20 levels.

The stock price thereafter rallied upward making a higher top, higher bottom pattern and made successive higher tops at points E, G, and K, and successive higher bottoms at points F, H and J. In the chart in Figure 5.31, it seemingly appears that bottom J is lower than bottom H, whereas in reality Point J did not close below Point H.

The last traded stock price in this chart is ₹35.

Trade Summary

1. Initiating a sell trade at ₹11.75 levels, i.e. selling after the price closes below the Point B level of ₹12.85.
2. Buying at ₹11.30 levels, i.e. buying after the price closes above the Point E level of ₹11.15.
3. If the last traded price of ₹35 is taken into account to calculate the mark to market profit / loss account, then trading higher top, higher bottom and lower top, lower bottom pattern formations would have resulted in a profit of 24.15 points in this case.

~

Example 32: Adani Port

Figure 5.32: **Daily stock price chart of Adani Port with profitable Dow trades highlighted**

~

Higher top, higher bottom and lower top, lower bottom pattern formations in Figure 5.32 would have suggested selling as and when the level made earlier by Point C at about ₹293 is cracked in the down move from Point D to Point E because the stock price then enters a lower top, lower bottom pattern regime. At the time of selling, the stop loss can be placed at Point D, i.e. at around ₹331 levels.

Thereafter the stock price declined and made successive lower tops at points F, H and J, and successive lower bottoms at points E, G and K.

Then, from the lows of around ₹170 levels, i.e. from Point K, the stock price rallied strongly upward and cracked the Point J level of ₹242.70 in its up move from Point K to Point L. One should close the sell position as and when this happens as the ongoing lower top, lower bottom pattern formation is then distorted.

The stock price thereafter rallied higher and cracked the level made earlier by Point L at around ₹279 levels in its move from Point M to Point N. One should buy as and when the ₹279 level is cracked on the upside since the stock price then enters a higher top, higher bottom pattern regime. At the time of buying, the stop loss can be placed at Point M at ₹250 levels.

The stock price thereafter rose further to the highs of around ₹315 levels.

Trade Summary

1. Selling short at ₹291 levels, i.e. after the price closes below the Point C level of ₹293.
2. Exiting the short positions at ₹259 levels, i.e. after the price closes above the Point J level of ₹242.70.
3. Initiating a buy trade at ₹286 levels, i.e. buying after the price closes above the Point L level of ₹279.
4. At the time of this writing, the stock price was trading around ₹315 levels. If ₹315 is taken into account to calculate the up to date mark to market profit / loss account, then trading higher top, higher bottom and lower top, lower bottom pattern formations resulted in a profit of 61 points in this example.

~

Example 33: Bajaj Auto

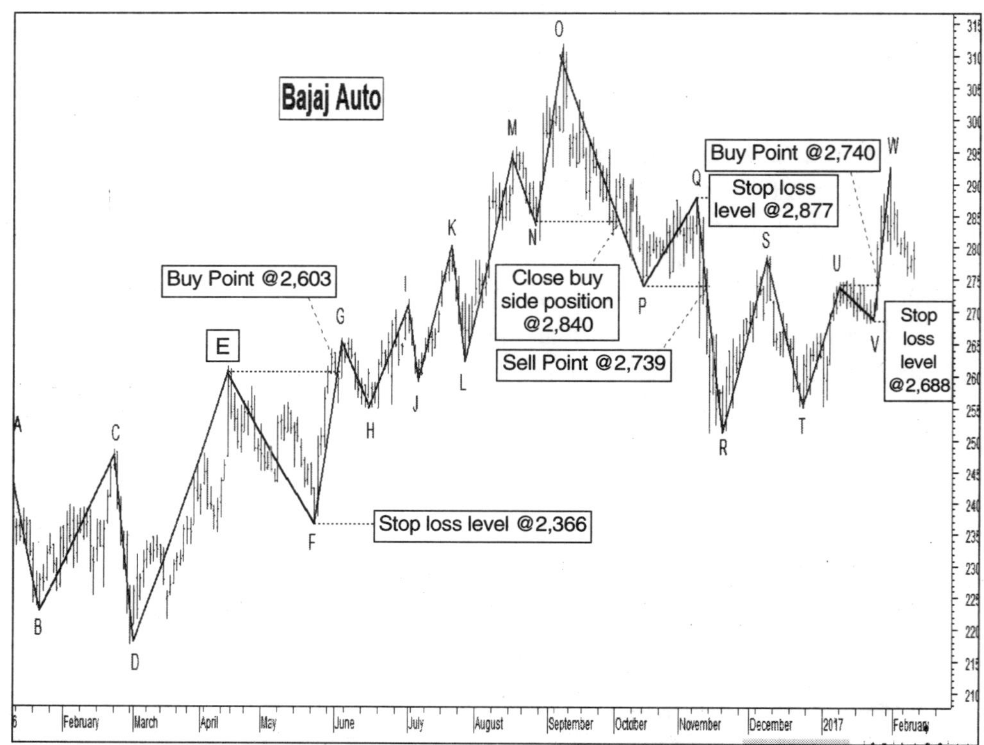

Figure 5.33: **Profitable Dow trades highlighted in the daily stock price chart of Bajaj Auto**

~

Higher top, higher bottom and lower top, lower bottom pattern formations in the case of the chart in Figure 5.33 suggests buying Bajaj Auto as and when the level made earlier at Point E around ₹2,603 is cracked during the up move from Point F to Point G. This is because the stock price then enters a higher top, higher bottom pattern. At the time of buying, the stop loss can be placed at Point F level of ₹2,366.

Thereafter the stock price made successive higher tops at points G, I, K, M and O, and successive higher bottoms at points H, J, L and N.

From the highs of around ₹3,100 levels, however, i.e. from around Point O, the stock price fell sharply and cracked Point N at around

₹2,840 levels in its down move from Point O to Point P. One should close the buy position when this happens as the ongoing higher top, higher bottom pattern formation then gets distorted.

Thereafter, the stock price declined further and cracked the level made earlier by Point P at around ₹2,739 in its down move from Point Q to Point R. One should sell when this happens because the stock price thereupon enters a lower top, lower bottom pattern regime. At the time of selling, the stop loss can be placed at the Point Q level of ₹2,877.

The stock price thereafter declined to the lows of around ₹2,530 levels on the downside and made a lower top at Point S and a lower bottom at Point R.

From around Point T, however, the stock price rallied upward strongly and cracked the level made earlier by Point U at around ₹2,740 during its up move from Point V to Point W. One should close the sell position — and instead initiate a fresh buy position — as and when the Point U level of ₹2,740 is cracked on the upside because the stock price then enters a higher top, higher bottom pattern. At the time of buying, the stop loss can be placed at Point V, i.e. at ₹2,688 levels.

The stock price thereafter rallied to a high of around ₹2,920 levels. At the time of this writing, the stock price was trading around ₹2,780 levels.

Trade Summary

1. Initiating a buy trade at ₹2,607 levels, i.e. buying after the price closes above the Point E level of ₹2,603.
2. Exiting buy side positions at ₹2,827 levels, i.e. after the price closes below the Point N level of ₹2,840.
3. Initiating a sell trade at ₹2,726 levels, i.e. selling short after the price closes below the Point P level of ₹2,739.
4. Buying afresh at ₹2,798 levels, i.e. after the price closes above the Point U level of ₹2,740.
5. At the time of this writing, the stock price was trading around ₹2,780 levels. If the price of ₹2,780 is taken into account to calculate the mark to market profit / loss account, then trading higher top, higher bottom and lower top, lower bottom pattern formations would have resulted in a profit of 130 points in this case.

Example 34: Bajaj Finance

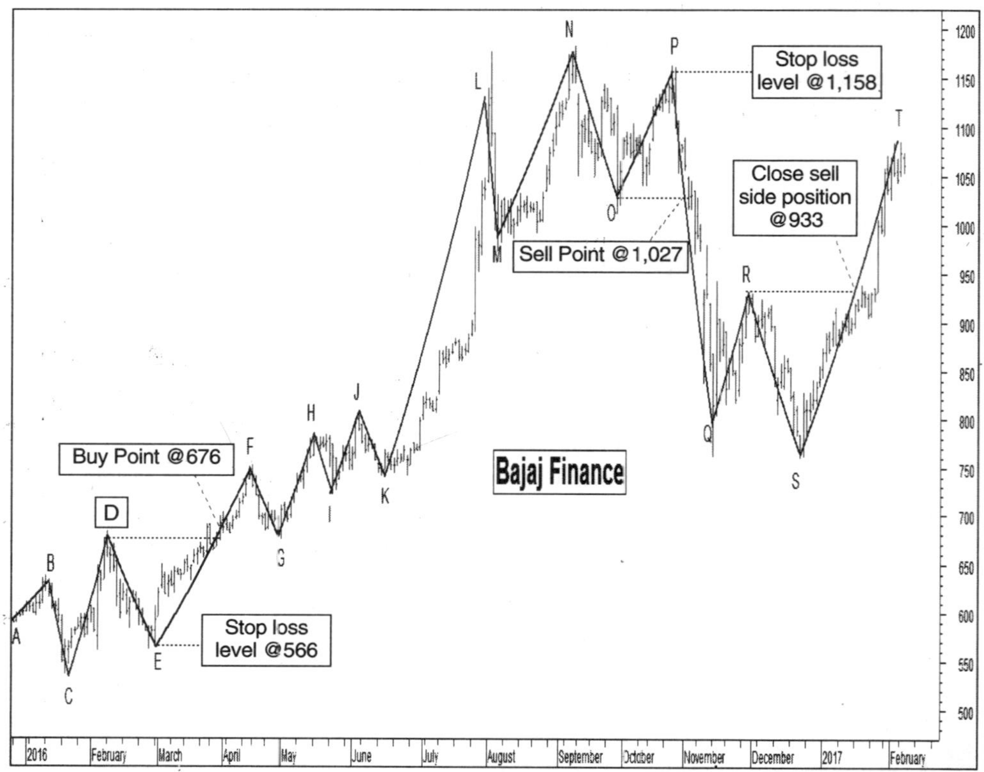

Figure 5.34: **Daily stock price chart of Bajaj Finance highlighting profitable Dow trades**

~

Higher top, higher bottom and lower top, lower bottom pattern formations in the chart in Figure 5.34 suggests buying Bajaj Finance as and when the level made earlier by Point D at around ₹676 is cracked in the up move from Point E to Point F. The stock price then enters a higher top, higher bottom pattern regime. At the time of buying, the stop loss could have been placed at Point E, i.e. at about ₹566 levels.

The stock price thereafter made a higher top, higher bottom pattern regime with successive higher tops at points F, H, J, L and N, and successive higher bottoms at points G, I, K, M and O.

From the highs of around ₹1,155 levels on the upside, i.e. from around Point P, the stock price then declined sharply and cracked the Point O level of ₹1,027 in its down move from Point P to Point Q. One should close the buy side position, and instead initiate a fresh sell side position as and when the Point O level at ₹1,027 is cracked on the downside as the stock price then enters a lower top, lower bottom pattern regime. At the time of selling, the stop loss can be placed at the Point P level of around ₹1,158.

The stock price thereafter declined to the lows of around ₹768 in a lower top, lower bottom pattern regime and made a lower top at Point R and lower bottoms at points Q and S.

From the lows of around ₹768, i.e. from around Point S, the stock price then rallied upward strongly and cracked the Point R level at around ₹933 in its up move from Point S to Point T. One should close the sell side position as and when this happens because at that particular time, the ongoing lower top, lower bottom pattern formation gets distorted.

The stock price then rallied upward to the highs of around ₹1,082 levels in a manner which does not comply with the higher top, higher bottom pattern regime. As a result, Dow Theory practitioners would not have been able to buy in this up move.

At the time of this writing, the stock price was trading around ₹1,040 levels.

Trade Summary

1. Initiating a buy trade at ₹687 levels, i.e. buying after the price closes above the Point D level of ₹676.
2. Selling at ₹1,019 levels, i.e. selling after the price closes below the Point O level of ₹1,027.
3. Exiting the sell positions at ₹999 levels, i.e. exiting after the price closes above the Point R level of ₹933.
4. In this case, trading higher top, higher bottom and lower top, lower bottom pattern formations would have resulted in a profit of 352 points.

~

Example 35: Bharat Electronics (BEL)

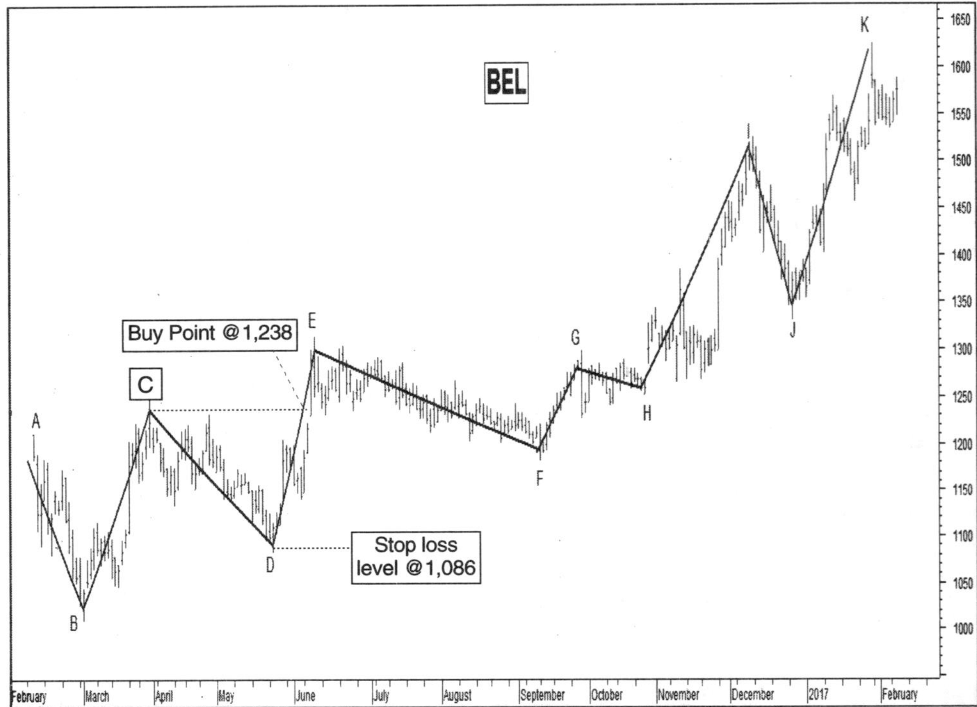

Figure 5.35: **Profitable Dow trades highlighted on the daily stock price chart of BEL**

~

Higher top, higher bottom and lower top, lower bottom pattern formations in the chart in Figure 5.35 suggests buying BEL as and when the level made earlier by Point C at about ₹1,238 levels is cracked in the up move from Point D to Point E. The stock price then enters a higher top, higher bottom pattern regime. At the time of buying, the stop loss can be placed at around the Point D levels of ₹1,086.

The stock price thereafter rallied higher to around ₹1,618 levels in a higher top, higher bottom pattern regime and made successive higher tops at points E, I and K, and successive higher bottoms at points F, H and J.

At the time of this writing, the stock price was trading around ₹1,564 levels.

Trade Summary

1. Initiating a buy trade at ₹1,290 levels, i.e. buying after the price closes above the Point C level of ₹1,238.
2. At the time of this writing, the stock price was trading around ₹1,564 levels. If the price of ₹1,564 is taken into account to calculate the mark to market profit / loss account, then trading higher top, higher bottom and lower top, lower bottom pattern formations in this case would have resulted in a profit of 274 points.

Example 36: Biocon

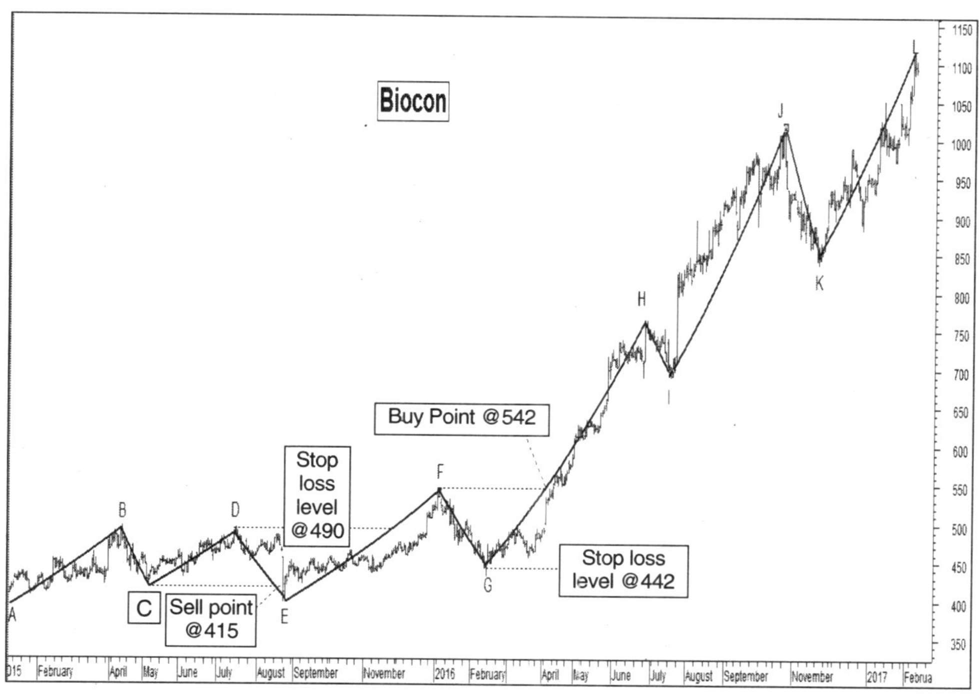

Figure 5.36: **Daily stock price chart of Biocon with profitable Dow trades highlighted**

~

Higher top, higher bottom and lower top, lower bottom pattern formations in the case of the chart in Figure 5.36 would have suggested selling short as and when the level made earlier by Point C at around ₹415 is cracked in the down move from Point D to Point E. This is because the stock price then enters a lower top, lower bottom pattern regime. At the time of selling, the stop loss can be placed at the Point D level of ₹490.

The stock price thereafter rallied strongly upward and cracked ₹490 levels on the upside, at which point the stop loss is triggered and the short trade aborted.

The stock price rose further and cracked the level made earlier by Point F at around ₹542 in its up move from Point G to Point H. One should initiate a buy trade as and when the Point F level of ₹542 is cracked on the upside as the stock price then enters a higher top, higher bottom pattern regime. At the time of buying, the stop loss can be placed at Point G, i.e. at ₹442 levels.

Thereafter the stock price rallied in a higher top, higher bottom pattern regime and made successive higher tops at points H, J and L, and successive higher bottoms at points I and K.

At the time of this writing, the stock price was trading around ₹1,090 levels.

Trade Summary

1. Initiating a sell trade at ₹409 levels, i.e. selling after the price closes below the Point C level of ₹415.
2. Exiting the sell positions at ₹508 levels, i.e. after the price closes above the Point D level of ₹490.
3. Buying at ₹546 levels, i.e. after the price closes above the Point F level of ₹542.
4. At the time of this writing, the stock price was trading around ₹1,090 levels. If the price of ₹1,090 is used to calculate the mark to market profit / loss account, then trading higher top, higher bottom and lower top, lower bottom pattern formations in this case would have resulted in a profit of 445 points.

~

Example 37: Bodal Chemical

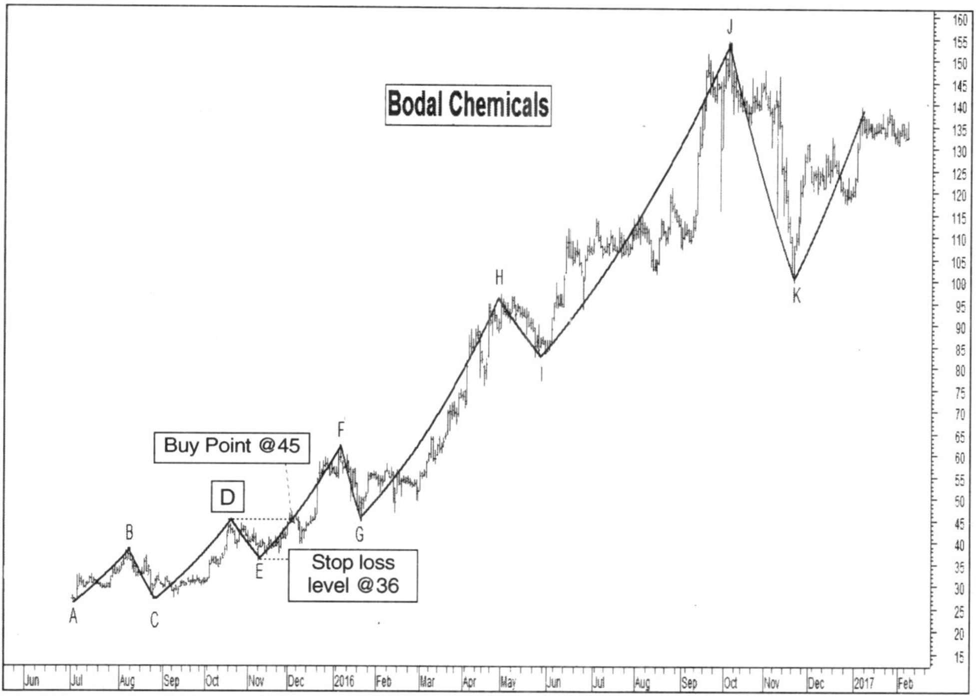

Figure 5.37: **Profitable Dow trades highlighted in the daily stock price chart of Bodal Chemical**

~

Higher top, higher bottom and lower top, lower bottom pattern formations in the Bodal Chemical chart in Figure 5.37 would suggest initiating a buy trade as and when the level made earlier by Point D at about ₹45 levels is cracked in the up move from Point E to Point F because the stock price thereafter enters a higher top, higher bottom pattern regime. At the time of buying, the stop loss can be placed at the Point E levels of ₹36.

The stock price then rallied higher to around ₹153 levels, making a higher top, higher bottom pattern with successive higher tops at points F, H and J, and successive higher bottoms at points G, I and K.

At the time of this writing, the stock price was trading around ₹132 levels.

Trade Summary

1. Initiating a buy trade at ₹54 levels, i.e. buying after the price closes above the Point D levels of ₹45.
2. At the time of this writing, the stock price was trading around ₹132 levels. If the price of ₹132 is used to calculate the mark to market profit / loss account, then trading higher top, higher bottom and lower top, lower bottom pattern formations in this case would have resulted in a profit of 78 points.

~

Example 38: BPL

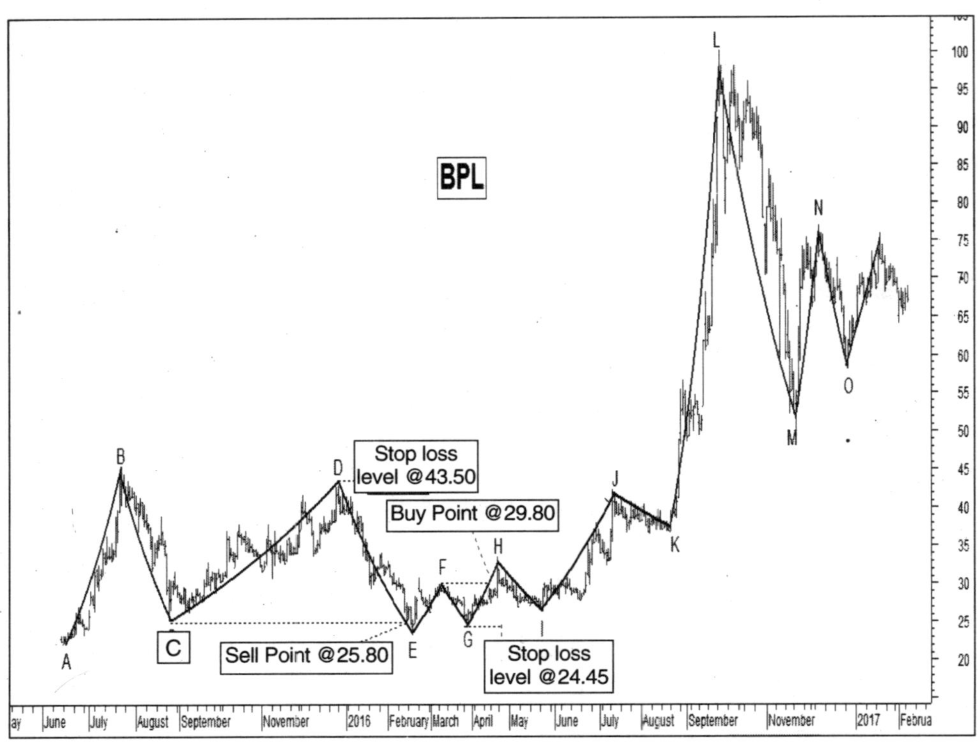

Figure 5.38: **Daily stock price chart of BPL with profitable Dow trades highlighted**

~

Higher top, higher bottom and lower top, lower bottom pattern formations in the case of chart in Figure 5.38 would have suggested selling BPL as and when the level made earlier by Point C at around ₹25.80 is cracked in the down move from Point D to Point E. The stock price then enters a lower top, lower bottom pattern regime. At the time of selling, the stop loss may be placed at Point D, i.e. at around ₹43.50 levels.

The stock price duly rallied upward strongly and cracked the level made earlier by Point F at ₹29.80 levels in its up move from Point G to Point H. One should close the sell position — and initiate instead a fresh buy position — as and when this level is cracked on the upside as the stock price then enters a higher top, higher bottom pattern. At the time of buying, the stop loss may be placed at Point G, i.e. at about ₹24.45 levels.

The stock price thereafter rallied upward to the highs of around ₹97 level in a higher top, higher bottom pattern regime and made successive higher tops at points H, J and L, and successive higher bottoms at points I, K, M and O.

At the time of this writing, the stock price was trading around ₹65 levels.

Trade Summary

1. Initiating a sell trade at ₹24.65 levels, i.e. after the price closes below the Point C level of ₹25.80.
2. Buying at ₹32 levels, i.e. buying after the price closes above the Point F level of ₹29.80.
3. At the time of this writing, the stock price was trading around ₹65 levels. If the price of ₹65 is used to calculate the mark to market profit / loss account, then trading higher top, higher bottom and lower top, lower bottom pattern formations would have resulted in a profit of 25.65 points in this case.

~

Example 39: Caplin Point Lab

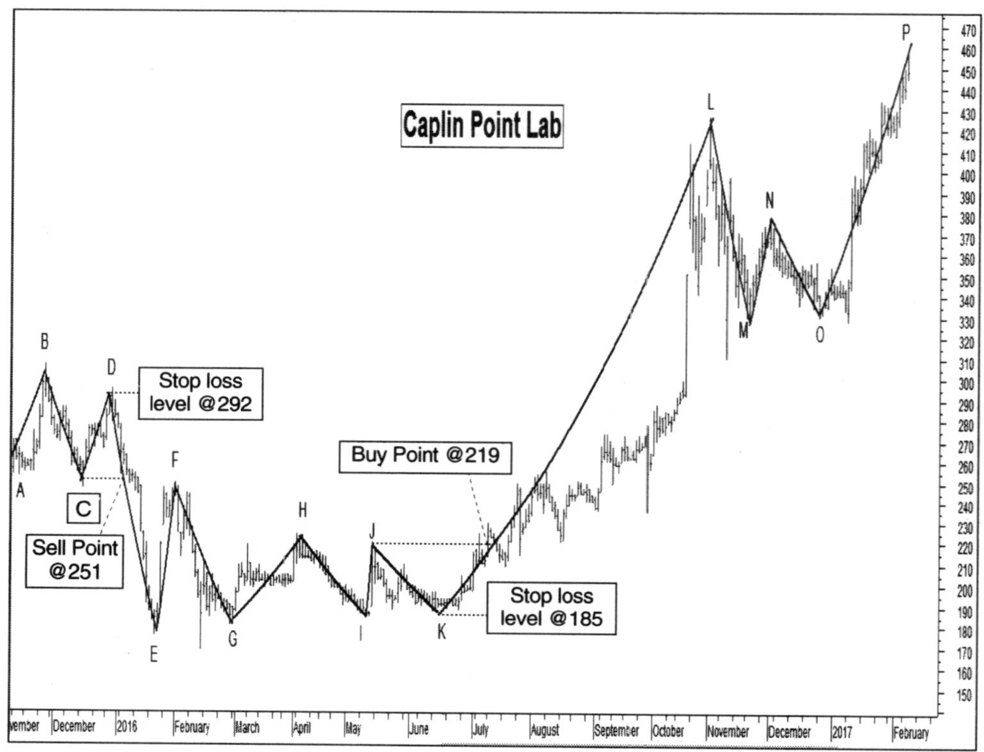

Figure 5.39: **Profitable Dow trades highlighted in the daily stock price chart of Caplin Point Lab**

~

Higher top, higher bottom and lower top, lower bottom pattern formations in the chart in Figure 5.39 would have suggested selling as and when the level made earlier by Point C at about ₹251 levels is cracked, in the down move from Point D to Point E. This is because the stock price then enters a lower top, lower bottom pattern regime. At the time of selling, the stop loss can be placed at Point D, i.e. at around ₹292 levels.

The stock price thereafter declined in a lower top, lower bottom regime and made successive lower tops at points F, H and J, and a lower bottom at Point E.

From the lows of around ₹187 levels, i.e. from Point K, the stock price rallied upward strongly and cracked the earlier Point J level of ₹219 in its up move from Point K to Point L. One should close the short sell position — and initiate instead a fresh buy position — as and when the earlier Point J level of ₹219 is cracked on the upside as the stock price enters a higher top, higher bottom pattern regime at that time. At the time of buying, the stop loss can be placed at Point K, i.e. at around ₹186 levels.

The stock price thereafter rallied upward to the highs of around ₹460 levels making a higher top, higher bottom pattern, with successive higher tops at points L and P, and successive higher bottoms at points K, M and O.

At the time of this writing, the stock price was trading around ₹429 levels.

Trade Summary

1. Going short at ₹246 levels, i.e. selling after the price closes below the Point C level of ₹251.
2. Buying at ₹224 levels, i.e. going long after the price closes above the Point J level of ₹219.
3. At the time of this writing, the stock price was trading around ₹429 levels. If the price of ₹429 is taken into account to calculate the mark to market profit / loss account, then trading higher top, higher bottom and lower top, lower bottom formations would have resulted in a profit of 227 points in this example.

~

Example 40: DCM Shriram Ltd

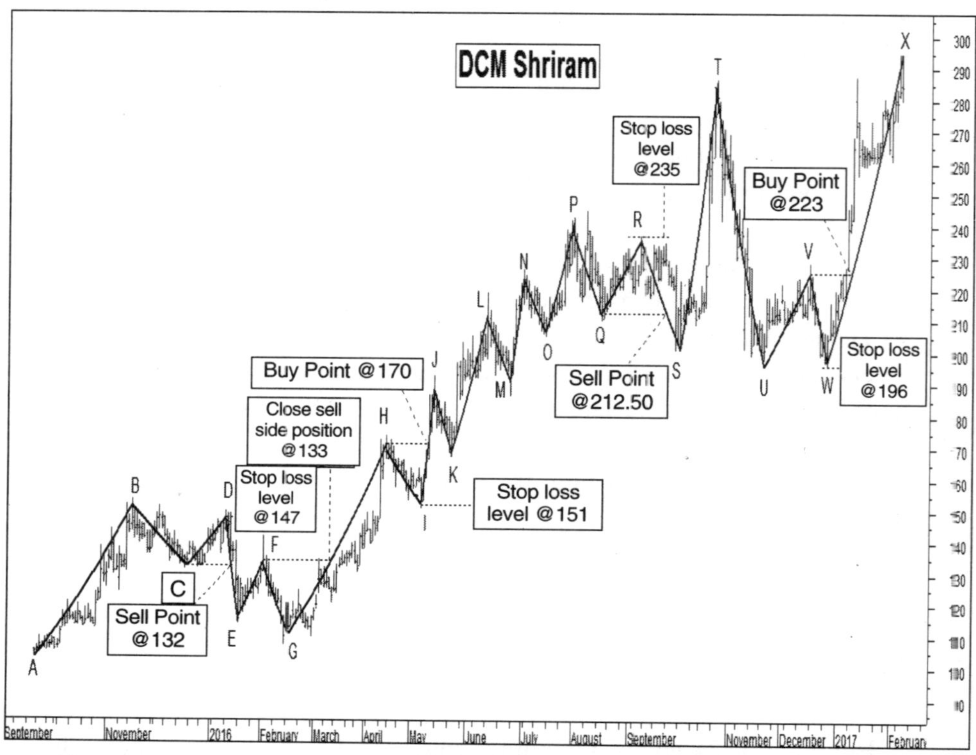

Figure 5.40: **Daily stock price chart of DCM Shriram Ltd with profitable Dow trades highlighted**

~

Higher top, higher bottom and lower top, lower bottom pattern formations in the chart in Figure 5.40 would suggest going short as and when the level made earlier by Point C at ₹132 levels is cracked in the down move from Point D to Point E. The stock price then enters a lower top, lower bottom pattern regime. At the time of selling, the stop loss can be placed at Point D, i.e. at about ₹147 levels.

The stock price thereafter declined making a lower top, lower bottom pattern and made a lower top at Point F and lower bottoms at points E and G.

From the lows of around ₹111 levels, i.e. from Point G, the stock price rallied upward strongly and cracked the level made earlier by Point F at about ₹133 in its up move from Point G to Point H. One should close the sell position as and when this happens as that distorts the ongoing lower top, lower bottom pattern.

Thereafter the stock price rallied higher and cracked the level made earlier by Point H at around ₹170 in the up move from Point I to Point J. One should go long and buy as and when the level of ₹170 is cracked on the upside because the stock price then enters a higher top, higher bottom regime. At the time of buying, the stop loss can be placed at Point I, i.e. at ₹151 levels.

The stock price then rose to the highs of around ₹240, making higher top, higher bottom patterns with successive higher tops at points H, J, L, N and P, and successive higher bottoms at points I, K, M, O and Q.

From around Point P at about ₹240, the stock price declined sharply and cracked the level made earlier by Point Q at ₹212.50 levels in the down move from Point R to Point S. One should close the buy position — and initiate instead a fresh sell position — as and when this happens because the stock price then enters a lower top, lower bottom pattern regime. At the time of selling, the stop loss can be placed around the Point R level of ₹235.

From the lows of around ₹203 levels, i.e. from Point S, the stock price then rallied strongly and cracked the level made earlier by Point R at about ₹235 levels in its up move from Point S to Point T. One should close the sell position when this happens as it triggers the stop loss.

The stock price thereafter rose almost upward to the highs of around ₹280 levels in a manner which did not comply with the higher top, higher bottom pattern. As a result, Dow Theory practitioners would not have been able to buy during this up move.

From the highs of around ₹280 levels, the stock price declined vertically to the lows of around ₹197 in a pattern which again did not comply with the lower top, lower bottom pattern. As a result, Dow Theory practitioners would not have been able to sell during this vertical decline.

From the lows of around Point W, the stock price rallied upward strongly and cracked the level made earlier by Point V at around ₹223 in its up move from Point W to Point X. One should buy as and when this occurs because the stock price then enters a higher top, higher bottom pattern regime. At the time of buying, the stop loss can be placed at Point W, i.e. at about ₹196 levels.

The stock price then rallied higher to around ₹291 levels.

At the time of this writing, the stock price was trading around ₹280 levels.

Trade Summary

1. Initiating a short trade at ₹127.50 levels, i.e. selling after the price closes below the Point C level of ₹132.
2. Exiting all short sell positions at ₹135 levels, i.e. after the price closes above the Point F level of ₹133.
3. Buying at ₹178 levels, i.e. going long after the price closes above the Point H level of ₹170.
4. Selling at ₹205 levels, i.e. after the price closes below the Point Q level of ₹212.50.
5. Closing short sell positions at ₹256 levels, i.e. exiting after the price closes above the Point R level of ₹235.
6. Buying at ₹225 levels, i.e. going long after the price closes above the Point V level of ₹223.
7. At the time of this writing, the stock price was trading around ₹280 levels. If this price of ₹280 is taken into account to calculate the mark to market profit / loss account, then trading higher top, higher bottom and lower top, lower bottom patterns would have resulted in a profit of 23.50 points in this example.

~

Example 41: IDFC

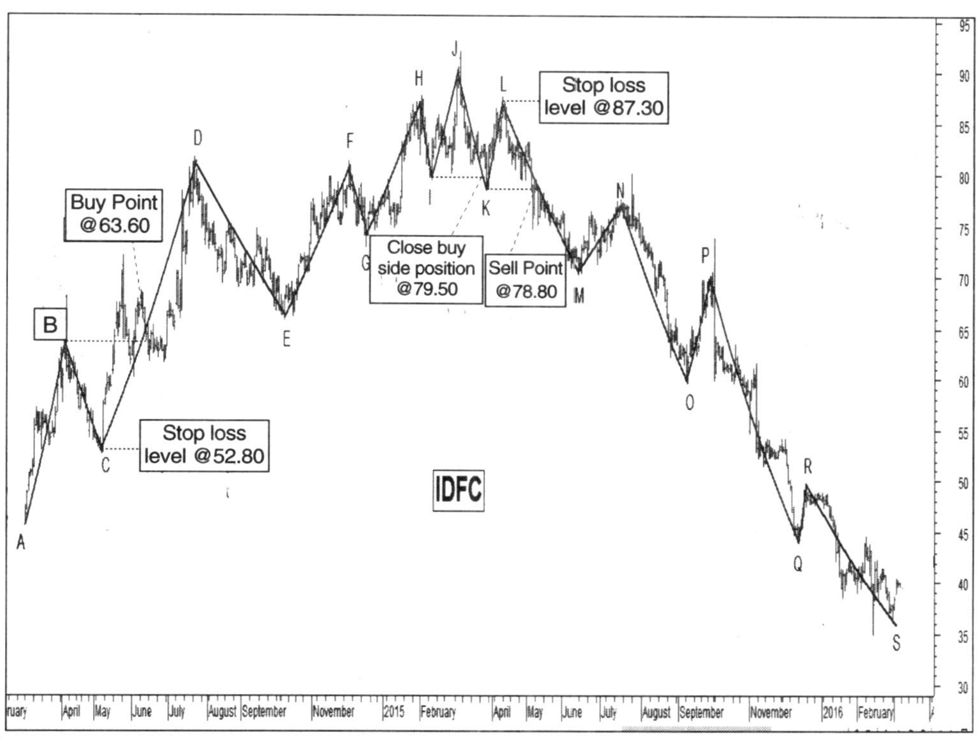

Figure 5.41: **Profitable Dow trades highlighted in the daily stock price chart of IDFC**

~

Higher top, higher bottom and lower top, lower bottom pattern formations in chart of IDFC in Figure 5.41 suggest buying as and when the level made earlier by Point B at about ₹63.60 levels is cracked in the up move from Point C to Point D because the stock price then enters a higher top, higher bottom pattern. At the time of buying, the stop loss can be placed at Point C, i.e. at about ₹52.80 levels.

The stock price thereafter rallied to the highs of around ₹89 levels making a higher top, higher bottom pattern with successive higher tops at points D, H and J, and successive higher bottoms at points E, G and I.

From the highs of around ₹89 levels, the stock price then declined sharply and cracked the level made earlier by Point I at around ₹79.60 in its down move from Point J to Point K. One should close the buy position when this crack occurs as this distorts the ongoing higher top, higher bottom pattern formation.

Thereafter the stock price declined further and cracked the level made earlier by Point K at about ₹78.80 in the down move from Point L to Point M. One should go short when this happens because the stock price then enters a lower top, lower bottom pattern regime. At the time of selling, the stop loss can be placed the Point L level of around ₹87.30.

The stock price thereafter declined making a lower top, lower bottom pattern with successive lower tops at points N, P and R, and successive lower bottoms, at points M, O, Q and S.

The last traded stock price on Chart 5.41 was ₹41.

Trade Summary

1. Buying at ₹64.20 levels, i.e. going long after the price closes above the Point B levels of ₹63.60.
2. Exiting buy side positions at ₹79.25 levels, i.e. after the price closes below the Point I level of ₹79.60.
3. Initiating a sell position at ₹75.85 level, i.e. going short after the price closes below the Point K level of ₹78.80.
4. The last traded price in Chart 5.41 is ₹41. If this price is taken into account to calculate the mark to market profit / loss account, then trading higher top, higher bottom and lower top, lower bottom pattern formations would have resulted in a profit in this case of ₹49.90 points.

~

Example 42: Edelweiss Financial Services

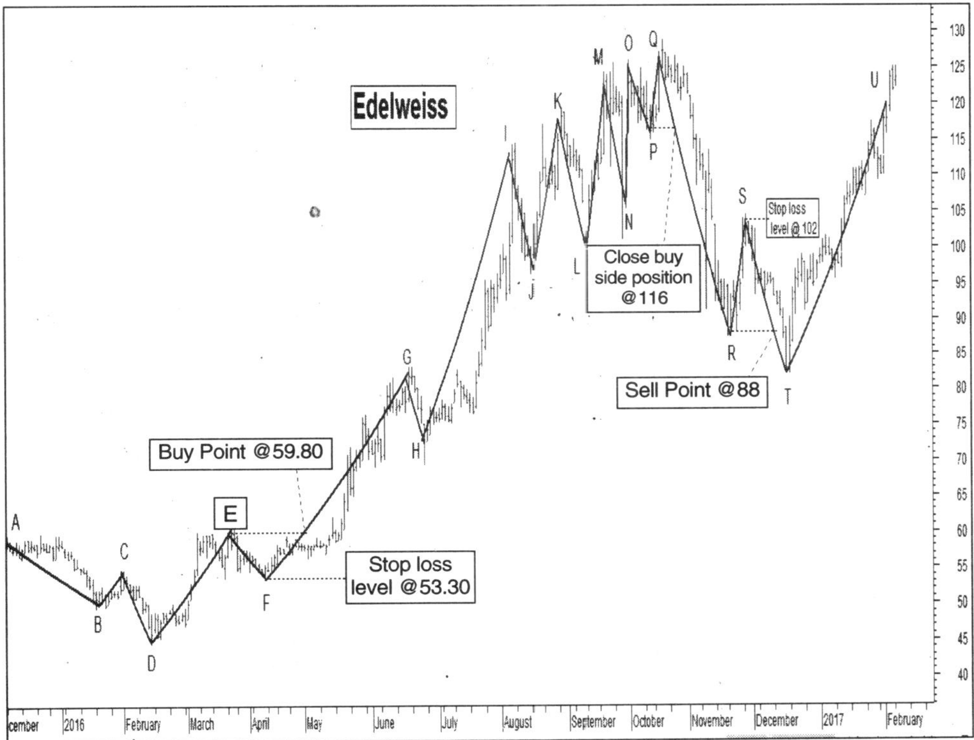

Figure 5.42: **Daily stock price chart of Edelweiss Financial Services with Dow trades highlighted**

~

Higher top, higher bottom and lower top, lower bottom patterns in the case of the Edelweiss chart in Figure 5.42 would suggest buying as and when the level made earlier by Point E at about ₹59.80 levels is cracked in the up move from Point F to Point G. This is because the stock price then enters a higher top, higher bottom pattern regime. At the time of buying, the stop loss can be placed at Point F, i.e. at about ₹53.30 levels.

The stock price thereafter rose to the highs of around ₹125 levels, making successive higher tops at points G, I, K, M, O and Q, and successive higher bottoms at points F, H, J, L, N and P.

From the highs of around ₹125 levels, i.e. from around Point Q, the stock price then declined sharply and cracked the level made earlier by Point P at ₹116 levels in its down move from Point Q to Point R. One should close the buy positions as and when the Point P level of ₹116 is cracked since the ongoing higher top, higher bottom pattern formation is then distorted.

Thereafter the stock price fell further and cracked the level made earlier by Point R at around ₹88 levels in its down move from Point S to Point T. One should sell as and when this level is cracked on the downside because the stock price then enters a lower top, lower bottom pattern regime. At the time of selling, the stop loss can be placed at Point S, i.e. around ₹102 levels.

From the lows of around ₹83 levels, i.e. from Point T, the stock price rallied strongly upward and cracked the level made earlier by Point S at around ₹102 levels in the up move from Point T to Point U. One should close the short sell positions when this level of ₹102 is cracked because the stop loss then gets triggered.

The stock price thereafter rallied to the highs of around ₹120 levels in a pattern which does not comply with the higher top, higher bottom formation. As a result, the Dow Theory practitioners would not have been able to buy in this up move.

Trade Summary

1. Buying at ₹59.85 levels, i.e. going long after the price closes above the Point E level of ₹59.80.
2. Closing long positions at ₹114.85 levels, i.e. exiting after the price closes below the Point P level of ₹116.
3. Selling short at ₹87.85 levels, i.e. after the price closes below the Point R level of ₹88.
4. Exiting sell side positions at ₹105.75 levels, i.e. exiting after the price closes above the Point S level of ₹102.
5. Trading higher top, higher bottom and lower top, lower bottom patterns in this study would have resulted in a profit of 37.10 points.

~

Example 43: Dewan Housing Finance Ltd (DHFL)

Figure 5.43: **Profitable Dow trades highlighted in the daily stock price chart of Dewan Housing Finance Ltd (DHFL)**

~

Higher top, higher bottom and lower top, lower bottom pattern formations in the chart in Figure 5.43 would suggest going short as and when the level made earlier by Point E at about ₹208 levels is cracked in the down move from Point F to Point G. This is because the stock price thereupon enters a lower top, lower bottom pattern regime. At the time of selling, the stop loss can be placed at Point F, i.e. at about ₹238 levels.

The stock price thereafter declined to the lows of around ₹148 and made a lower top at Point H as well as lower bottoms at points G and I.

From the lows of around ₹148 levels, i.e. from Point I, the stock price rallied strongly upward and cracked the level made earlier by Point H at ₹195 levels in its up move from Point I to Point J. One should close the sell position as and when this occurs as the ongoing lower top, lower bottom pattern formation then stands distorted.

The stock price then rallied higher and cracked the level made earlier by Point J at about ₹211 in its up move from Point K to Point L. One should buy as and when this level is cracked on the upside as the stock price then enters a higher top, higher bottom pattern regime. At the time of buying, the stop loss can be placed at Point K, i.e. at about ₹183.50 levels.

The stock price thereafter rallied to the highs of around ₹335 levels in a higher top, higher bottom pattern regime, making higher tops at points L, N and P, and higher bottoms at points K, M and O.

From the highs of around ₹335 levels, i.e. from around Point P, the stock price then declined sharply and cracked the earlier Point O level of ₹270 in its down move from Point P to Point Q. One should close the long position as and when this happens because the ongoing higher top, higher bottom pattern formation is then distorted.

The stock price thereafter declined to the lows of around ₹220 levels i.e. to around Point Q in a pattern which did not comply with the lower top, lower bottom pattern regime. As a result, the Dow Theory practitioners would not have been able to sell in this down move.

From the ₹228 lows, i.e. from around Point S, the stock price then rallied strongly upward and cracked the Point R level of ₹256 in the up move from Point S to Point T. One should buy when this level is cracked as at that time, the stock price enters a higher top, higher bottom pattern. At the time of buying, the stop loss can be placed at Point S, i.e. at about ₹227 levels.

The stock price then rallied higher in a higher top, higher bottom pattern and made successive higher tops at points T and U, and successive higher bottoms at points S and U.

At the time of this writing, the stock price was trading around ₹300 levels.

Trade Summary

1. Selling at ₹202 levels, i.e. going short after the price closes below the Point E level of ₹208.
2. Exiting short positions at ₹196 levels, i.e. closing after the price closes above the Point H level of ₹195.
3. Buying at ₹212 levels, i.e. buying after the price closes above the Point J levels of ₹211.
4. Exiting long positions at ₹251 levels, i.e. closing after the price closes below the Point O level of ₹270.
5. Buying at ₹265 levels, i.e. buying after the price closes above the Point R levels of ₹256.
6. At the time of this writing, the stock price was trading around ₹300 levels. If the price of ₹300 is taken into account to calculate the mark to market profit / loss account, then trading higher top, higher bottom and lower top, lower bottom pattern formations in this study would have resulted in a profit of 80 points.

~

Example 44: Federal Bank

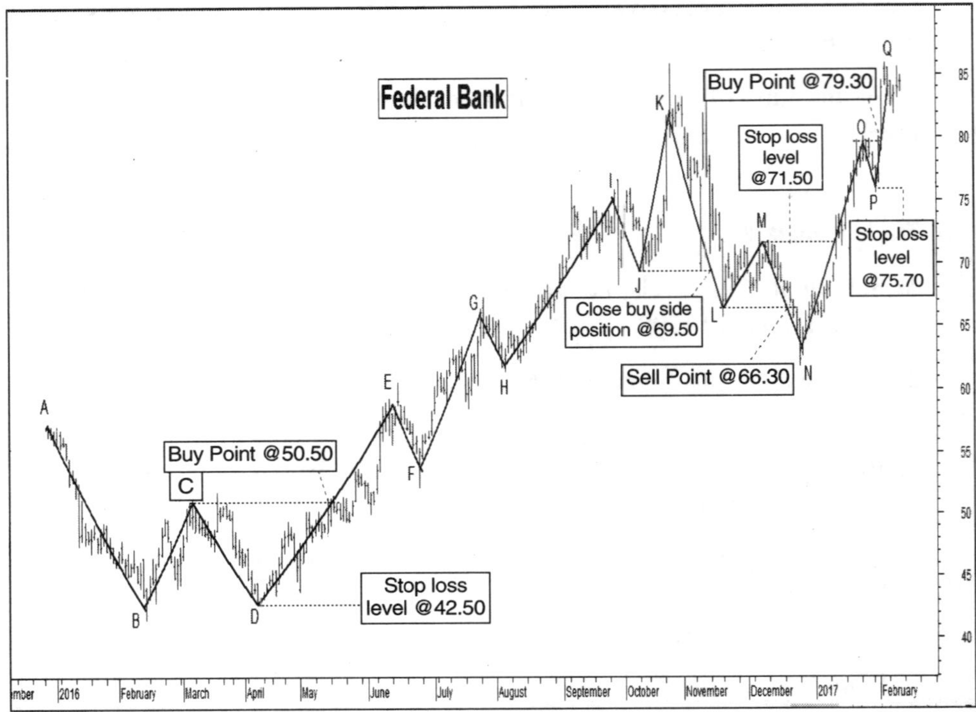

Figure 5.44: **Daily stock price chart of Federal Bank with profitable Dow trades highlighted**

~

Higher top, higher bottom of lower top, lower bottom pattern formations in the chart in Figure 5.44 suggest going long as and when the level made earlier by Point C at around ₹50.50 is cracked in the up move from Point D to Point E, because at that time, the stock price enters a higher top, higher bottom pattern regime. At the time of buying, the stop loss can be placed at Point D, i.e. at around ₹42.50 levels.

The stock price thereafter rose to around ₹83 levels in a higher top, higher bottom pattern regime and made successive higher tops at points E, G, I and K, and successive higher bottoms at points F, H and J.

From the highs of around ₹83 levels i.e. from around Point K, the stock price declined sharply and cracked the level made earlier by Point J at ₹69.50 levels in the down move from Point K to Point L. One should close the buy position as and when the Point J level of ₹69.50 is cracked on the downside because the ongoing higher top, higher bottom pattern formation is then distorted.

Thereafter the stock price fell further and cracked the level made earlier by Point L at ₹66.30 levels in the down move from Point M to Point N. One should go short as and when the Point L level is cracked on the downside because the stock price then enters a lower top, lower bottom pattern regime. At the time of selling, the stop loss can be placed at Point M, i.e. at about ₹71.60 levels.

Then, from the lows of around ₹66 levels, i.e. from around Point N, the stock price rallied upward strongly and cracked the level made earlier by Point M at about ₹71.60 in the up move from Point N to Point O. One should exit the sell position when this happens because the stop loss is then triggered.

Thereafter the stock price rallied higher and cracked the level made earlier by Point O at about ₹79.30 in the up move from Point P to Point Q. One should buy as and when this level is cracked on the upside because the stock price then enters a higher top, higher bottom pattern regime. At the time of buying, the stop loss can be placed at Point P, i.e. at ₹75.70 levels.

At the time of this writing, the stock price was trading around ₹84.50 levels, i.e. around Point Q.

Trade Summary

1. Buying at ₹50.85 levels, i.e. going long after the price closes above the Point C level of ₹50.50.
2. Exiting buy positions at ₹67 levels, i.e. exiting after the price closes below the Point J level of ₹69.50.
3. Going short at ₹65.50 levels, i.e. selling after the price closes below the Point L level of ₹66.30.
4. Exiting sell positions at ₹72.50 levels, i.e. after the price closes above the Point M level of ₹71.60.

5. Going long at ₹79.35 levels, i.e. buying after the price closes above Point O levels of ₹79.30.

6. At the time of this writing, the stock price was trading around ₹84.50 levels. If the price of ₹84.50 is used to calculate the mark to market profit / loss account, then trading higher top, higher bottom and lower top, lower bottom pattern formations in this study would have resulted in a profit of 14.30 points.

~

Example 45: Divis Lab

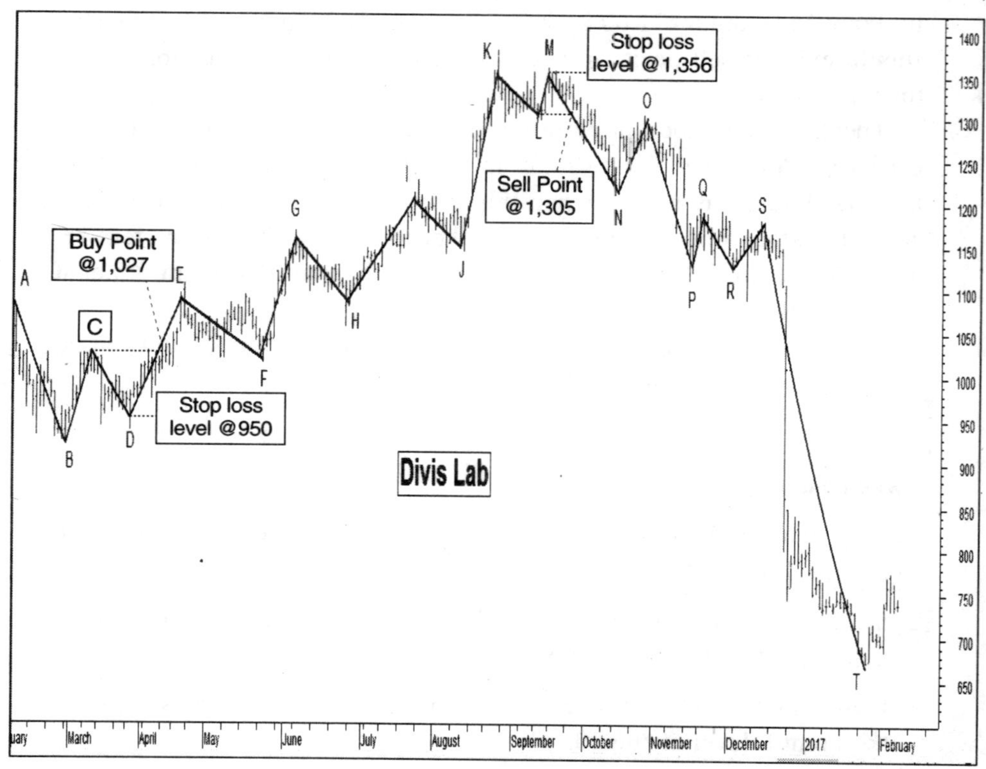

Figure 5.45: **Profitable Dow trades highlighted in the daily stock price chart of Divis Lab**

~

Trading higher top, higher bottom and lower top, lower bottoms in the case of Divis Lab's chart in Figure 5.45 would suggest buying as and when the level earlier made by Point C at around ₹1,027 levels is cracked in the up move from Point D to Point E because the stock price then enters a higher top, higher bottom pattern regime. At the time of buying, the stop loss can be placed at Point D, i.e. at around ₹950 levels.

The stock price thereafter rose up to around ₹1,335 levels and made successive higher tops at points E, G, K and M; and successive higher bottoms at points F, H, J and L.

From the highs of around ₹1,335 levels the stock price then declined sharply and cracked the level made earlier by Point L at about ₹1,305 levels in its down move from Point M to Point N. One should exit the buy position — and instead initiate a fresh sell position — as and when this occurs as the stock price then enters a lower top, lower bottom pattern regime. At the time of going short, the stop loss can be placed at Point M, i.e. at about ₹1,356 levels.

Thereafter the stock price declined in a lower top, lower bottom pattern regime, and made successive lower tops at points O, Q and S, and successive lower bottoms at points N, P and T.

At the time of this writing, the stock price was trading around ₹755 levels.

Trade Summary

1. Buying at ₹1,039 levels, i.e. going long after the price closes above the Point C level of ₹1,027.
2. Selling at ₹1,295 levels, i.e. after the price closes below the Point L level of ₹1,305.
3. At the time of this writing, the stock price was trading around ₹755 levels. If the price of ₹755 is taken into account to calculate the mark to market profit / loss account, then trading higher top, higher bottom and lower top, lower bottom pattern formations in this example would have resulted in a profit of 796 points.

~

Example 46: Ajanta Pharma

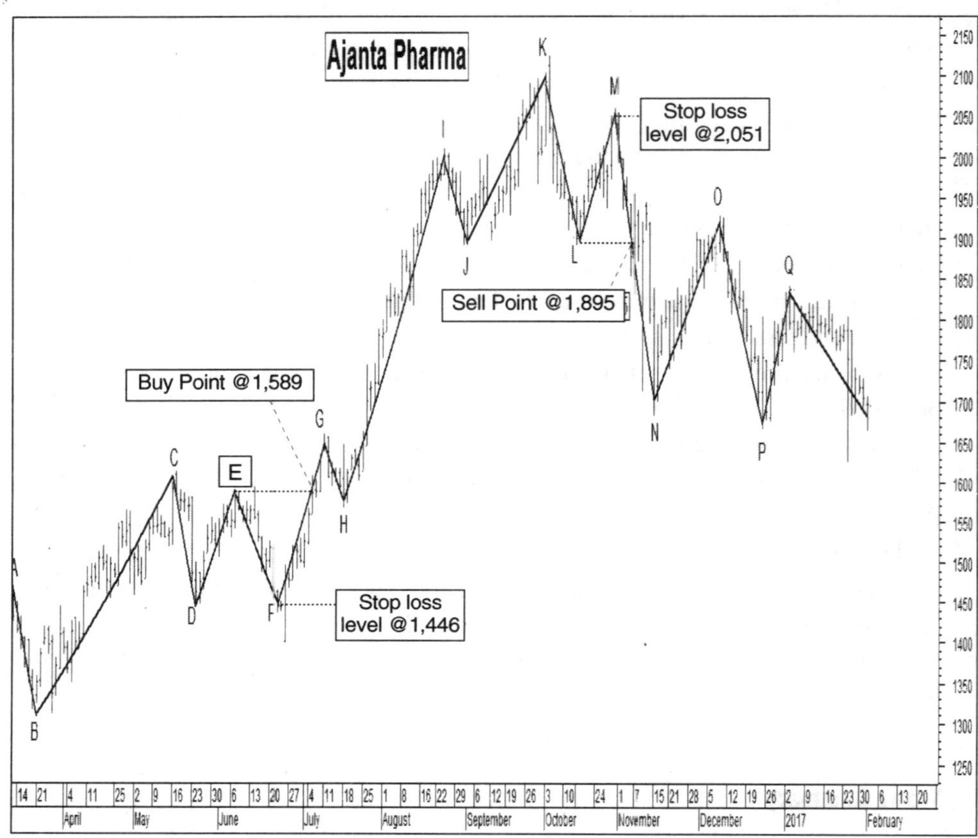

Figure 5.46: **Daily stock price chart of Ajanta Pharma with profitable Dow trades highlighted**

~

Higher top, higher bottom and lower top, lower bottom pattern formations in the chart in Figure 5.46 would suggest buying as and when the level made earlier by Point E at about ₹1,589 levels is cracked in the up move from Point F to Point G. This is because the stock price then enters a higher top, higher bottom pattern regime. At the time of buying, the stop loss can be placed at around Point F levels, i.e. at about ₹1,446.

The stock price thereafter rose to the highs of around ₹2,100 levels, making successive higher tops at points G, I and K, and successive higher bottoms at points H and J.

From the highs of around ₹2,100 level the stock price declined sharply and cracked the level made earlier by Point L at around ₹1,895 in its down move from Point M to Point N. One should exit the buy position — and instead initiate fresh sell position —when the Point L level at ₹1,895 is cracked on the downside as the stock price then enters a lower top, lower bottom pattern regime. At the time of going short, the stop loss can be placed at Point M, i.e. at about ₹2,051 levels.

The stock price thereafter declined in a lower top, lower bottom pattern regime and made successive lower tops at points O and Q, and successive lower bottoms at points N and P.

At the time of this writing, the stock price was trading around ₹1,700 levels.

Trade Summary

1. Initiating a buy trade at ₹1,630 levels, i.e. buying after the price closes above the Point E level of ₹1,589.
2. Going short at ₹1,876 levels, i.e. after the price closes below the Point L level of ₹1,895.
3. At the time of this writing, the stock price was trading around ₹1,700 levels. If the price of ₹1,700 is taken into account to calculate the mark to market profit / loss account, then trading higher top, higher bottom and lower top, lower bottom pattern formations in this study would have resulted in a profit of 422 points.

~

Example 47: Granules India Ltd

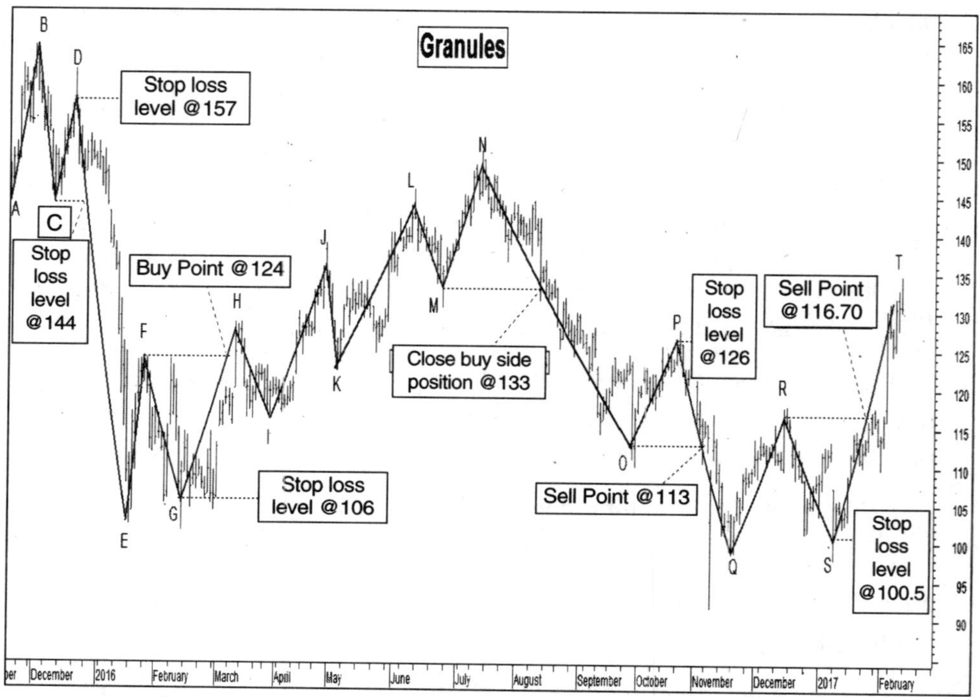

Figure 5.47: **Profitable Dow trades highlighted in the daily stock price chart of Granules India Ltd**

~

Higher top, higher bottom and lower top, lower bottom patterns in the chart in Figure 5.47 would suggest selling as and when the level made earlier by Point C at ₹144 levels is cracked in the down move from Point D to Point E. This is because the stock price then enters a lower top, lower bottom pattern regime. At the time of selling, the stop loss can be placed at Point D, i.e. at about ₹157 levels.

The stock price thereafter declined vertically to the lows of around ₹103 levels, i.e. to Point E.

From the lows of around ₹103 levels, the stock price rallied upward strongly and cracked the level made earlier by Point F at ₹124 levels in the up move from Point G to Point H. One should exit the sell position

— and also initiate a fresh buy position — as and when the Point F level at ₹124 is cracked on the upside because the stock price then enters a higher top, higher bottom pattern regime. At the time of buying, the stop loss can be placed at the Point G level of ₹106.

Thereafter the stock price rallied to the highs of around ₹148 levels in a higher top, higher bottom pattern regime and made successive higher tops at points H, J, L and N, and successive higher bottoms at points I, K and M.

From the highs of around ₹148 levels, i.e. from Point N, the stock price declined sharply and cracked the level made earlier by Point M at ₹133 levels in a down move from Point N to Point O. One should exit the buy position as and when the Point M level of ₹133 is cracked on the downside as the ongoing higher top, higher bottom pattern formation then gets distorted.

Thereafter the stock price declined further and cracked the level made earlier by Point O at about ₹113 in its down move from Point P to Point Q. One should initiate a sell trade as and when this occurs as the stock price then enters a lower top, lower bottom pattern regime. At the time of selling, the stop loss can be placed at Point P, i.e. at around ₹126 levels.

The stock price thereafter declined vertically to the lows of around ₹100 levels, i.e. to around Point Q.

From the lows of around ₹100 levels, the stock price then rallied upward strongly and cracked the level made earlier by Point R at ₹116.70 levels in its up move from Point S to Point T. One should exit the sell position when this occurs, and also initiate a fresh buy position, as the stock price then enters a higher top, higher bottom pattern regime. At the time of buying, the stop loss can be placed at Point S, i.e. at about ₹100.50 levels.

At the time of this writing, the stock price was trading around ₹130 levels, i.e. around Point T.

Trade Summary

1. Going short at ₹139 levels, i.e. initiating a sell trade after the price closes below the Point C level of ₹144.
2. Buying at ₹124.75 levels, i.e. going long after the price closes above the Point F level of ₹124.

3. Closing buy / long positions at ₹132.25 levels, i.e. exiting after the price closes below the Point M level of ₹133.
4. Initiating a sell trade at ₹111.90 levels, i.e. after the price closes below the Point O level of ₹113.
5. Buying at ₹128 levels, i.e. going long after the price closes above the Point R level of ₹116.70.
6. At the time of this writing, the stock price was trading around ₹130 levels. If the price of ₹130 is used to calculate the mark to market profit / loss account, then trading higher top, higher bottom and lower top, lower bottom pattern formations in this study would have resulted in a profit of 7.65 points.

~

Example 48: ITC

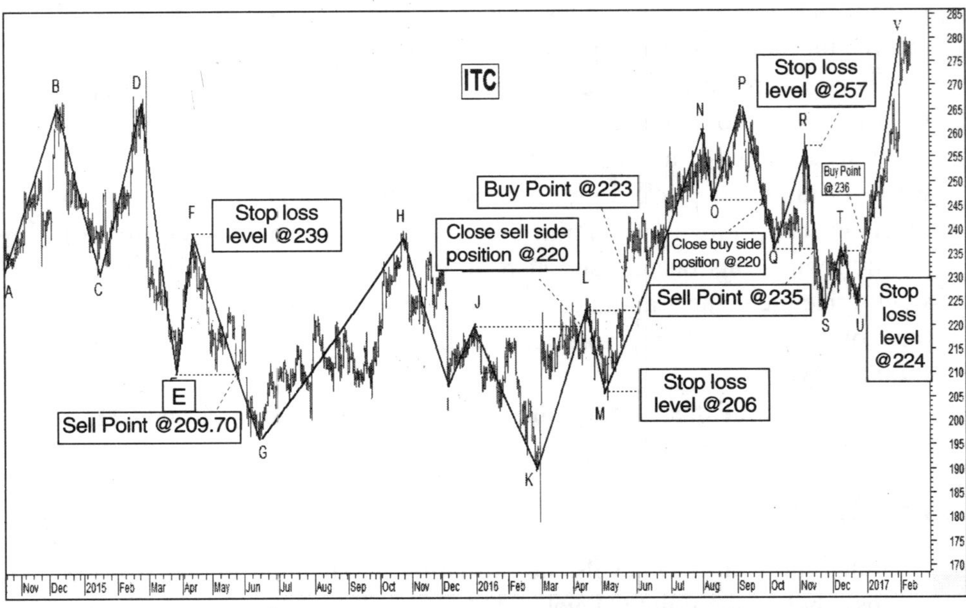

Figure 5.48: **Daily stock price chart of ITC with profitable Dow trades highlighted**

~

Higher top, higher bottom and lower top, lower bottom pattern formations in the chart of ITC in Figure 5.48 suggests initiating a sell trade as and when the level made earlier by Point E at ₹209.70 levels is cracked in the down move from Point F to Point G. This is because the stock price thereupon enters a lower top, lower bottom pattern regime. At the time of selling, the stop loss can be placed at Point F, i.e. at about ₹239 levels.

Thereafter the stock price declined to the lows of around ₹190 levels, i.e. to around Point K, from where it rallied strongly and cracked the level made earlier by Point J at around ₹220 levels in its up move from Point K to Point L. One should exit the sell positions as and when the earlier Point J level of ₹220 is cracked on the upside as at that time the ongoing lower top, lower bottom pattern formation is distorted.

The stock price thereafter rallied higher and cracked the level made earlier by Point L at ₹223 levels in its up move from Point M to Point N. One should initiate a buy trade at this point as the stock price thereupon enters a higher top, higher bottom pattern regime. At the time of buying, the stop loss can be placed at Point M, i.e. at about ₹206 levels.

The stock price then rallied upward to the highs of around ₹265 levels in a higher top, higher bottom pattern regime, making higher tops at points N and P, and a higher bottom at Point O.

From the highs of around ₹265 levels, i.e. from Point P, the stock price declined sharply and cracked the level made earlier by Point O at ₹246 in a down move from Point P to Point Q. One should close the buy trade position as and when the crack occurs because the ongoing higher top, higher bottom pattern formation is then distorted.

Thereafter the stock price declined even further and cracked the level made earlier by Point Q at ₹235 levels in its down move from Point R to Point S. One should initiate a sell trade when the Point Q level at ₹235 is cracked on the downside because the stock price then enters a lower top, lower bottom pattern regime. At the time of selling, the stop loss can be placed at Point R, i.e. at about ₹257 levels.

The stock price thereafter declined to the lows of around ₹225 in a lower top, lower bottom pattern, making a lower top at Point T and a lower bottom at Point S.

Then from the lows of around ₹225 levels, i.e. from around Point U, the stock price rallied higher strongly and cracked the level made earlier by Point T at ₹236 in its up move from Point U to Point V. One should close the sell position — and instead initiate a fresh buy position — as and when this crack occurs because the stock price then enters a higher top, higher bottom pattern regime. At the time of buying, the stop loss can be placed at Point U, i.e. at ₹224 levels.

The stock price thereafter rallied vertically upward to around ₹275 levels, where it was trading at the time of this writing.

Trade Summary

1. Going short at ₹203 levels, i.e. selling after the price closes below the Point E level of ₹209.70.
2. Exiting sell side positions at ₹221 levels, i.e. after the price closes above the Point J level of ₹220.
3. Buying at ₹231 levels, i.e. initiating a buy trade after the price closes above the Point L level of ₹223.
4. Exiting buy side positions at ₹245.70 levels, i.e. after the price closes below the Point O level of ₹246.
5. Selling at ₹231 levels, i.e. after the price closes below the Point Q level of ₹235.
6. Buying at ₹241 levels, i.e. after the price closes above the Point T levels of ₹236.
7. At the time of this writing, the stock price was trading around ₹275 levels. If the price of ₹275 is taken into account to calculate a mark to market profit / loss account, then trading higher top, higher bottom and lower top, lower bottom pattern formations in this example would have resulted in a profit of 20.70 points.

~

Example 49: Sun Pharma

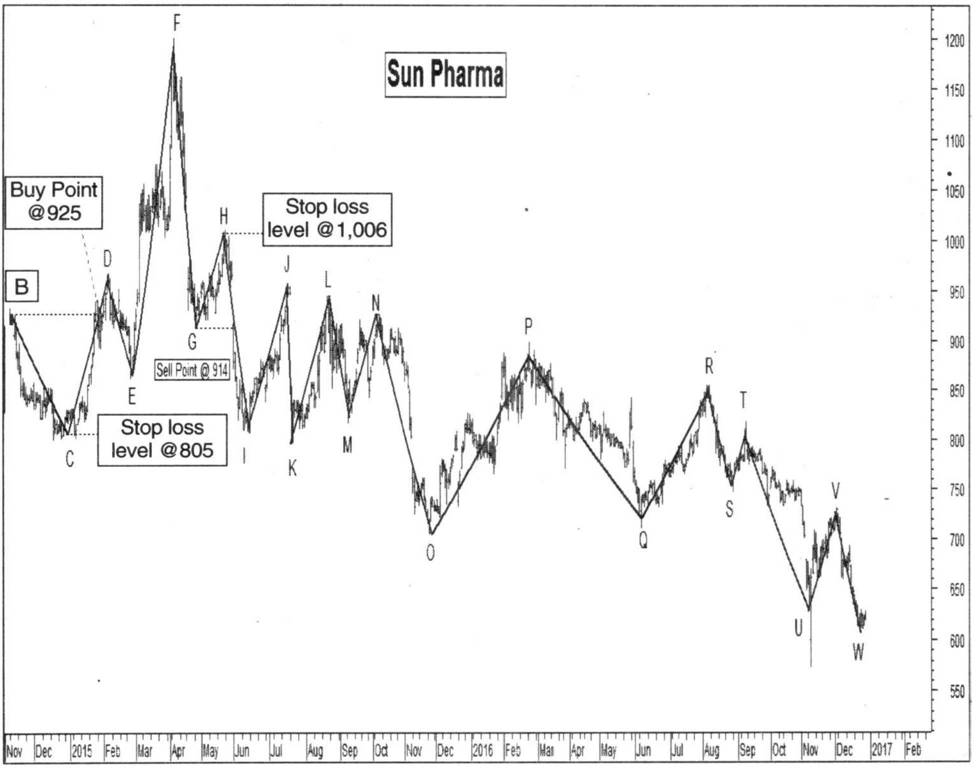

Figure 5.49: **Profitable Dow trades highlighted in the daily stock price chart of Sun Pharma**

~

Higher top, higher bottom and lower top, lower bottom pattern formations in the chart of Sun Pharma in Figure 5.49 would suggest buying as and when the level made earlier by Point B at about ₹925 is cracked in the up move from Point C to Point D. This is because the stock price thereupon enters a higher top, higher bottom pattern regime. At the time of buying, the stop loss may be placed at Point C, i.e. at about ₹805 levels.

The stock price thereafter rallied upward to the highs of around ₹1,180 levels in a higher top, higher bottom pattern and made a higher top at Point F and a higher bottom at Point E.

From around ₹1,180 levels the stock price declined sharply and cracked the level made earlier by Point G at ₹914 levels in its down move from Point H to Point I. One should close the buy trade position — and instead initiate a fresh sell trade — as and when the level made earlier by Point G at ₹914 levels is cracked on the downside because the stock price enters a lower top, lower bottom pattern regime at that time. At the time of selling, the stop loss can be placed at the Point H level of ₹1,006.

Thereafter the stock price declined making a lower top, lower bottom pattern and made successive lower tops at J, L, N, P, R, T and V, and lower bottoms at I, K, O, Q, U and W.

The last traded stock price in the chart in Figure 5.49 is ₹620.

Trade Summary

1. Buying at ₹927 levels, i.e. initiating a buy trade after the price closes above the Point B level of ₹925.
2. Initiating a sell trade at ₹877 levels, i.e. selling after the price closes below the Point G level of ₹914.
3. The last traded price in Chart 5.49 is ₹620. If the price of ₹620 is used to calculate the mark to market profit / loss account, then trading higher top, higher bottom and lower top, lower bottom patterns in this study would have resulted in a profit of 207 points.

~

Example 50: Jubilant Foodworks Ltd

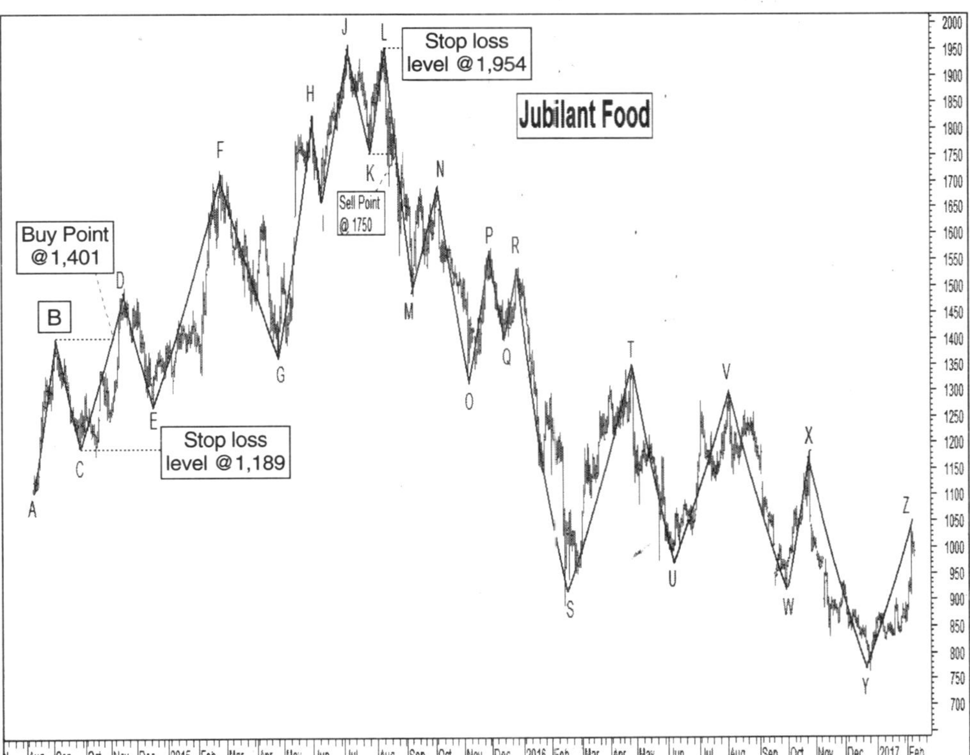

Figure 5.50: **Daily stock price chart of Jubilant Foodworks Ltd with profitable Dow trades highlighted**

~

Higher top, higher bottom and lower top, lower bottom pattern formations in the chart of Jubilant Foodworks in Figure 5.50 would suggest initiating a buy trade as and when the level made earlier by Point B at about ₹1,401 is broken in the up move from Point C to Point D. This is because at that time the stock price enters a higher top, higher bottom pattern regime. At the time of buying, the stop loss can be placed at Point C, i.e. at about ₹1,189 levels.

Thereafter the stock price rose to the highs of around ₹1,945 levels in a higher top, higher bottom pattern regime and made successive higher tops at points F, G, H and J — and successive higher bottoms at points E, G, I and K.

From the highs of around ₹1,955 levels, the stock price then declined sharply and cracked the level made earlier by Point K at ₹1,750 levels in its down move from Point L to Point M. One should close the long position — and instead initiate a fresh sell position — as and when the ₹1,750 level made earlier by Point K is cracked on the downside. The stock price then enters a lower top, lower bottom pattern. At the time of selling, the stop loss can be placed at Point L; i.e. at about ₹1,954 levels.

The stock price duly declined in a lower top, lower bottom pattern and made successive lower tops at points N, P, R, T, V, X and Z — and successive lower bottoms at points M, O, S and Y.

At the time of this writing, the stock price was trading around ₹994 levels.

Trade Summary

1. Buying at ₹1,417 levels, i.e. entering a buy trade after the price closes above the Point B level of ₹1,401.
2. Initiating a sell trade at ₹1,729 levels, i.e. selling after the price closes below the Point K level of ₹1,750.
3. At the time of this writing, the stock price was trading around ₹994 levels. If the price of ₹994 is taken into account to calculate the mark to market profit / loss account, then trading higher top, higher bottom and lower top, lower bottom pattern formations in this example would have resulted in a profit of 1,047 points.

~

Chapter 6

~

50 Profitable Dow Trades After Demonetisation

INDIAN PRIME MINISTER NARENDRA MODI made an announcement on the evening of 8 November 2016 that currency notes of ₹500 and ₹1,000 then in circulation would cease to be legal tender from midnight of 9 November 2016. As a result, the stock market turned volatile and most market participants incurred losses.

Dow Theory practitioners, however, actually ended up making handsome profits during same period.

What follow are 50 real examples from the Indian stock market of profitable Dow trading using hourly, i.e. 60-minute time frame, charts during the volatile demonetisation phase.

Example 1: Nifty

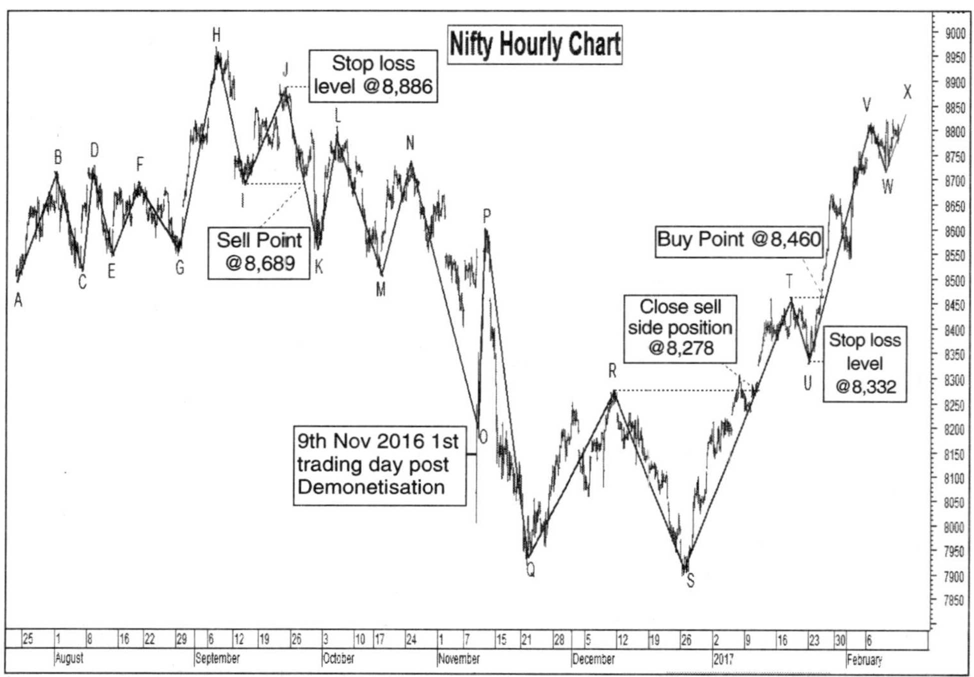

Figure 6.1 **Profitable Dow trades highlighted on the hourly, i.e. 60-minute, time frame price chart of Nifty**

~

Higher top, higher bottom and lower top, lower bottom pattern formations in Nifty's chart in Figure 6.1 shows Nifty initially rallying in a higher top, higher bottom pattern regime and making successive higher tops at points B, D and H, and successive higher bottoms at points A, C, E, G and I.

In this up move, Nifty made a high of around 8,947, i.e. at Point H.

From the highs of around 8,947 levels, Nifty fell and cracked the level it had made earlier at Point I at 8,689 levels in the down move from Point J to Point K. When this happens, one should close all buy positions and instead initiate fresh sell positions because at that time Nifty enters a lower top, lower bottom pattern regime. At the time of selling, the stop loss can be placed at Point J, i.e. at around 8,886 levels.

Thereafter, Nifty declined in a lower top, lower bottom pattern and made successive lower tops at points L and N, and successive lower bottoms at points K and M.

Demonetisation was announced on the night of 8 November 2016. At that time, Nifty was trading around Point M. The next day, i.e. on 9 November 2016, Nifty opened with a downside gap but closed above the highs of the previous day. Thereafter Nifty declined to the lows of around 7,930 levels on the downside, i.e. to Point Q.

Post demonetisation, Nifty rallied strongly from the lows of around 7,920 levels, i.e. from around Point S, and cracked the level made earlier by Point R at 8,278 levels in its up move from Point S to Point T. One should close the sell / short positions as and when this happens as the ongoing lower top, lower bottom pattern formation gets distorted at that particular time.

Nifty then rallied further and cracked the level it had made earlier at Point T at 8,460 levels in the up move from Point U to Point V. One should initiate a buy trade when this happens as Nifty then enters a higher top, higher bottom pattern. At the time of buying, the stop loss can be placed at about the Point U level of 8,322.

At the time of this writing, Nifty was trading around 8,794 levels, i.e. around Point X.

Trade Summary

1. Going short at 8,653 levels, i.e. selling after Nifty closes below the Point I level of 8,689.
2. Exiting sell positions at 8,300 levels, i.e. exiting after Nifty closes above the Point R level of 8,278.
3. Initiating a buy trade at 8,465 levels, i.e. buying after Nifty closes above the Point T level of 8,460.
4. At the time of this writing, Nifty was trading around 8,794 levels. If the level of 8,794 is used to calculate the mark to market profit / loss account, then trading higher top, higher bottom and lower top, lower bottom pattern formations in this study would have resulted in a profit of 682 points in the short span of around four months.

~

Example 2: ACC

Figure 6.2: **Hourly, i.e. 60-minute, time frame price chart of ACC with profitable Dow trades highlighted**

~

In Figure 6.2, the stock price initially rallied from Point A to Point B at ₹1,738 levels on the upside from mid-May to mid-August.

From the highs of around ₹1,738 levels, the stock price then declined sharply and cracked the Point C level made earlier at ₹1,586 levels in the down move from Point D to Point E. One should close all buy positions — and also initiate a fresh sell position — when this happens because at that time the stock price enters a lower top, lower bottom pattern regime. At the time of selling, the stop loss can be placed at the Point D level of ₹1,723.

Thereafter the stock price declined in a lower top, lower bottom pattern regime and made successive lower tops at points F, H and J, and successive lower bottoms at points E and I.

Demonetisation was announced after market hours on 8 November 2016. At that time, the ACC stock price was trading substantially below Point G. The next day, i.e. on 9 November 2016, the stock price opened with a downside gap but closed around the day's high. Thereafter the stock price declined to the lows of Point I at around ₹1,270 levels.

Post demonetisation, the stock price rallied strongly from the lows of around ₹1,276 levels, i.e. from around Point K, and cracked the level made earlier by Point J at ₹1,384 levels in the up move from Point K to Point L. One should close the sell position and, instead, initiate a fresh buy trade as and when this occurs because at that time the stock price enters a higher top, higher bottom pattern regime. At the time of buying, the stop loss can be placed at the Point K level of ₹1,271.

At the time of this writing, the stock price was trading around ₹1,485 levels, i.e. around Point L levels.

Trade Summary

1. Going short at ₹1,577 levels, i.e. selling after the price closes below the Point C level of ₹1,586.

2. Initiating a buy trade at ₹1,410 levels, i.e. buying after the price closes above the Point J level of ₹1,384.

3. At the time of this writing, the stock price was trading around ₹1,485 levels. If the price of ₹1,485 is taken into account to calculate the mark to market profit / loss account, then trading higher top, higher bottom and lower top, lower bottom pattern formation in this example would have resulted in a profit of 242 points in the short span of around five months.

~

Example 3: Adani Enterprises

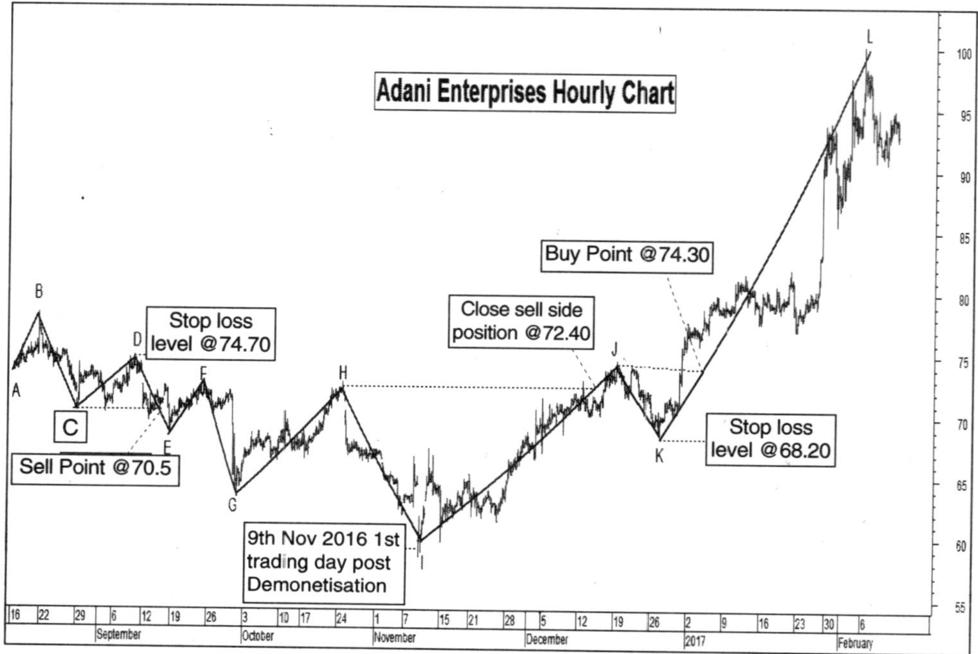

Figure 6.3: **Profitable Dow trades highlighted on the hourly, i.e. 60 minute, price chart of Adani Enterprises**

~

Trading higher top, higher bottom and lower top, lower bottom pattern formations in the case of Adani Enterprises in Figure 6.3 would suggest selling as and when the Point C level made earlier at ₹70.50 levels is cracked in the down move from Point D to Point E. At that time, the stock price enters a lower top, lower bottom pattern regime. At the time of initiating the sell trade, the stop loss can be placed at the Point D level of ₹74.70.

Thereafter the stock price declined in a lower top, lower bottom pattern regime and made successive lower tops at points B, D F and H and successive lower bottoms at points A, C, E, G and I.

Prior to demonetisation on the night of 8 November 2016, the stock price was trading below the level made earlier by Point G. The next day, i.e. on 9 November 2016, the stock price opened with a downside gap but closed above the highs of the previous day. Thereafter the stock price declined to the lows of around ₹59 levels on the downside, i.e. to around Point I.

Post demonetisation, the stock price rallied strongly from the lows of ₹59 levels, i.e. from around Point I, and cracked the earlier Point H levels of ₹72.40 in its up move from Point I to Point J. One should close the sell position when the Point H level is cracked on the upside as the ongoing lower top, lower bottom pattern formation gets distorted at that particular time.

Thereafter the stock price rallied upward further and cracked the earlier Point J level of ₹74.30 in its up move from Point K to Point L. One should initiate a buy trade as and when this happens as the stock price then enters a higher top, higher bottom pattern regime. At the time of buying, the stop loss can be placed at the Point K levels of about ₹68.20.

Thereafter the stock price rallied upward to around Point L.

At the time of this writing, the stock price was trading around ₹92 levels, i.e. around Point L.

Trade Summary

1. Selling at ₹70.10 levels, i.e. going short after the price closes below the Point C level of ₹70.50.
2. Exiting sell side positions at ₹73.25 levels, i.e. after the price closes above the Point H level of ₹72.40.
3. Initiating a buy trade at ₹75.15 levels, i.e. once the price closes above the Point J level of ₹74.30.
4. At the time of this writing, the stock price was trading around ₹92 levels. If the price of ₹92 is used to calculate the mark to market profit / loss account, then trading higher top, higher bottom and lower top, lower bottom formations resulted in a profit of 13.70 points in the short span of around five months.

~

Example 4: Aditya Birla Nuvo

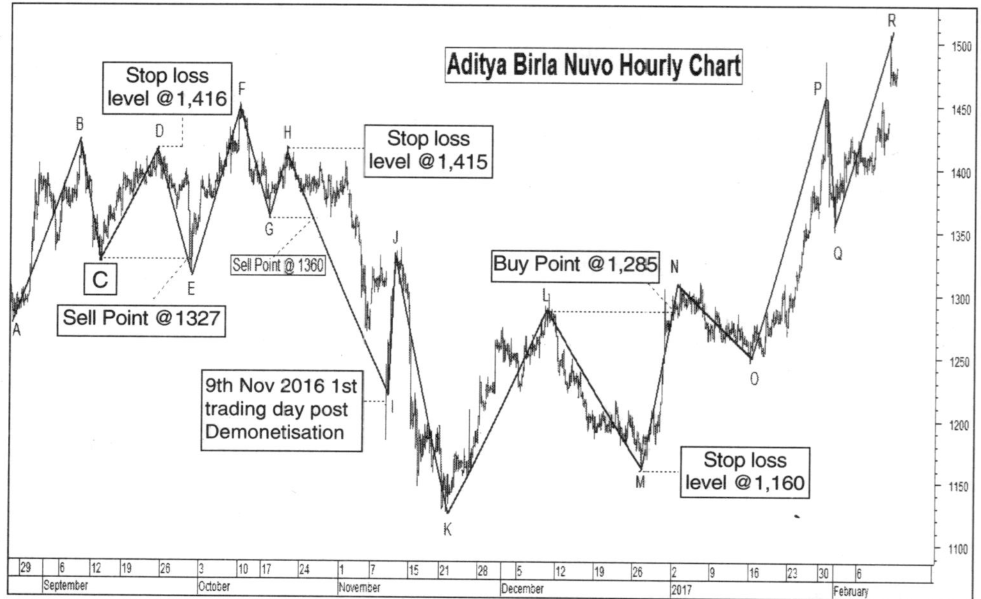

Figure 6.4: **Hourly, i.e. 60 minute, price chart of Aditya Birla Nuvo with profitable Dow trades highlighted**

~

Higher top, higher bottom and lower top, lower bottom pattern formations in the chart of Aditya Birla Nuvo in Figure 6.4 suggest selling as and when the level made earlier by Point C at about ₹1,327 is cracked in the down move from Point D to Point E. The stock price thereupon enters a lower top, lower bottom pattern regime. At the time of initiating the sell trade, the stop loss can be placed at Point D, i.e. at ₹1,416 levels.

After falling to Point E, the stock price moved up strongly from Point E and cracked the stop loss placed at the Point D level of ₹1,416, whereupon one should have closed the sell position.

Then, from the high level of Point F, the price first declined sharply and fell to the Point G levels of about ₹1,360 but then rose higher from Point G to Point H, from when it again began falling. In the down move from Point H to Point I, one should have initiated a sell trade on 2 November when the Point G level made earlier at ₹1,360 is cracked on the downside as thereafter the stock price enters a lower top, lower bottom pattern regime. At the time of selling, the stop loss can be placed at Point H, i.e. at about ₹1,415.

Thereafter the stock price declined in a lower top, lower bottom pattern regime and made a lower top at Point J and lower bottoms at points I and K.

When demonetisation was announced on the evening of 8 November 2016, the stock price was trading below the level made earlier by Point E. The next day, i.e. on 9 November 2016, the stock price opened with a downside gap but closed above the highs of the previous day. Thereafter the stock price declined to the lows of around ₹1,133 levels on the downside, i.e. to Point K level.

Post demonetisation, the stock price rallied strongly from the lows, i.e. from the Point K levels of ₹1,133 levels and it broke the Point L made earlier at ₹1,285 level in its up move from Point M to Point N. When this happens, one should close the sell position and instead initiate a fresh buy position since the price then enters a higher top, higher bottom pattern regime. At the time of buying, the stop loss can be placed at the levels earlier made by Point M at ₹1,160 levels.

At the time of this writing, the stock price was trading around ₹1,455 levels, i.e. around Point R.

Trade Summary

1. Selling at ₹1,326 levels, i.e. initiating a sell trade after the price closes below the Point C level of ₹1,327.
2. Exiting the sell positions at ₹1,416 levels, i.e. after the closes above the Point D level of ₹1,416.
3. Selling at ₹1,354 levels, i.e. initiating a sell trade after the price closes below the Point G level of ₹1,360.
4. Initiating a buy trade at ₹1,291 levels, i.e. after the price closes above the Point L level of ₹1,285.
5. At the time of this writing, the stock was trading around ₹1,455 levels. If the price of ₹1,455 is taken into account to calculate the mark to market profit / loss account, then trading higher top, higher bottom and lower top, lower bottom pattern formations in this example would have resulted in a profit of 137 points in the short span of around four months.

Example 5: Ambuja Cements

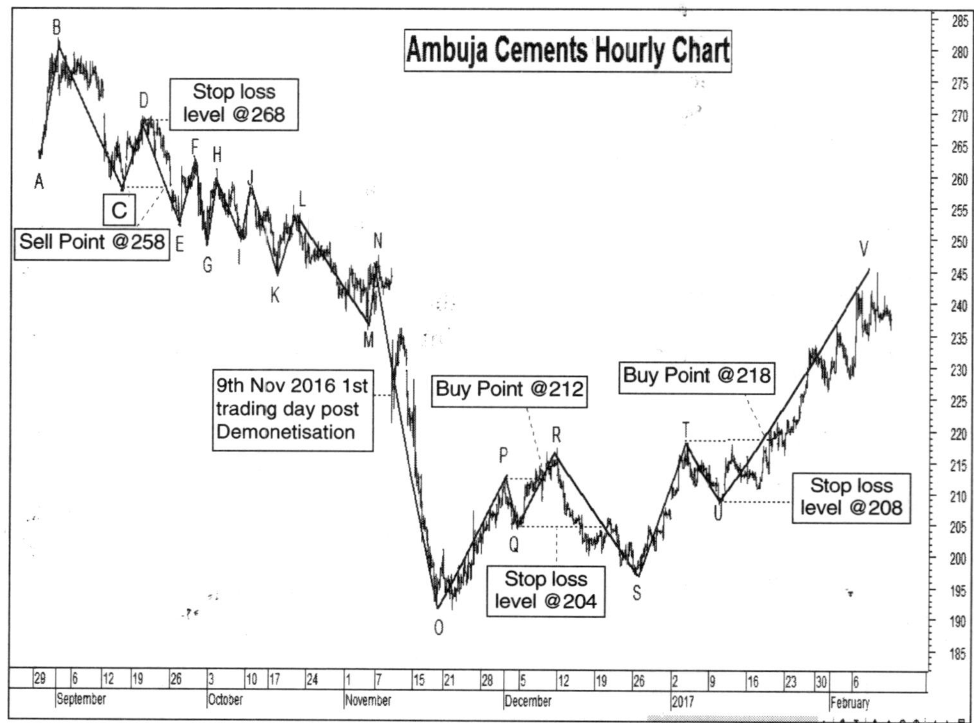

Figure 6.5: **Profitable Dow trades highlighted on the hourly, i.e. 60 minute, price chart of Ambuja Cements**

~

Higher top, higher bottom and lower top, lower bottom pattern formations in the chart of Ambuja Cements in Figure 6.5 suggest selling as and when the level made earlier by Point C at about ₹258 is cracked in the down move from Point D to Point E. This is because the stock price enters a lower top, lower bottom pattern regime at that time. At the time of initiating the sell trade, the stop loss can be placed at the Point D level of ₹268.

Thereafter the stock price declined and made successive lower tops, at points B, D F, H, J, L and N, and successive lower bottoms at points A, C, E, G, K and M.

Demonetisation was announced on the evening of 8 November 2016. At that time, the stock price was trading around Point M. The next day, i.e. on 9 November 2016, the price opened with a downside gap but closed around the day's high. Thereafter the stock price declined to the lows of around ₹193 levels, i.e. to around Point O.

Post demonetisation, the stock price rallied strongly from the lows around Point O, i.e. from around ₹193 levels, and cracked the level made earlier by Point P at ₹212 levels in its up move from Point Q to a higher top at Point R. One should close the sell position — and also initiate a fresh buy — as and when the Point P level of ₹212 levels is cracked on the upside as the stock price then enters a higher top, higher bottom pattern regime. At the time of buying, the stop loss can be placed at Point Q, i.e. at about ₹204 levels.

The stock price declined sharply thereafter and cracked the stop loss placed at Point Q on the downside. Hence one should close the buy position as and when the stop loss at Point Q level of ₹204 is cracked on the downside.

From the lows of around ₹197 levels on the downside, i.e. from around Point S, the stock price then rose up strongly and cracked the level made earlier by Point T at about ₹218 in its up move from Point U to Point V. One should initiate a buy trade as and when Point T level of ₹218 is cracked on the upside as the stock price then enters a higher top, higher bottom pattern regime. At the time of buying, the stop loss can be placed at the Point U level of ₹208.

At the time of this writing, the stock price was trading around ₹240 levels, i.e. around Point V.

Trade Summary

1. Initiating a sell trade at ₹254 levels, i.e. selling after the price closes below the Point C level of ₹258.
2. Buying at ₹213 levels, i.e. entering a buy trade after the price closes above the Point P level of ₹212.
3. Exiting the buy position at ₹202 levels, i.e. exiting after the price closes below the Point Q level of ₹204.

4. Buying at ₹219 levels, i.e. buying after the price closes above the Point T level of ₹218.

5. At the time of this writing, the Ambuja Cements stock price was trading around ₹240 levels. If this price is taken into account to calculate the mark to market profit / loss account, then trading higher top, higher bottom and lower top, lower bottom pattern formations would have resulted in a profit of 51 points in the short span of around five months.

~

Example 6: Balrampur Chini

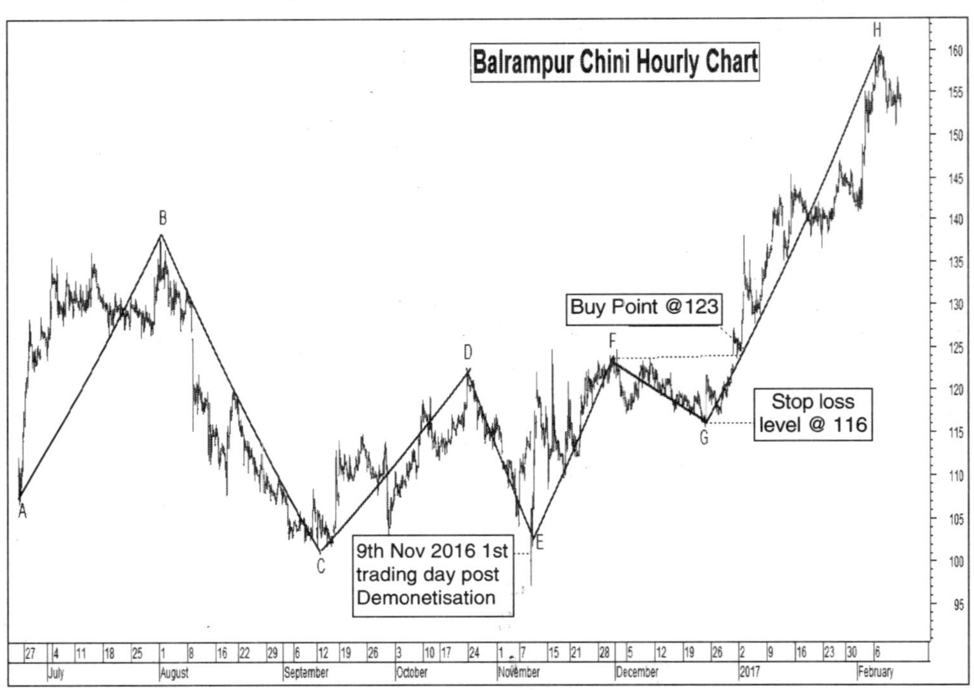

Figure 6.6: **Hourly, i.e. 60 minute, price chart of Balrampur Chini with profitable Dow trades highlighted**

~

In Figure 6.6, the stock price of Balrampur Chini initially declined in a lower top, lower bottom pattern regime, making successive lower tops at points B and D, and successive lower bottoms at points A and C.

Demonetisation was announced on the evening of 8 November 2016 when the stock price was trading around the level made earlier by Point E. The next day, i.e. on 9 November 2016, the stock price opened with a downside gap but closed around the day's high; and thereafter entered a consolidation phase.

The stock price broke out strongly from the lows of around ₹116 levels, i.e. from around the higher bottom at Point G and cracked the level made earlier by Point F at ₹123 levels in the up move from Point G to Point H. One should buy when this happens as the stock price then enters a higher top, higher bottom pattern regime. At the time of buying, the stop loss can be placed at Point G, i.e. at around ₹116 levels.

At the time of this writing, the stock price was trading around ₹155 levels, i.e. around Point H.

Trade Summary

1. Buying at ₹126 levels, i.e. buying after the price closes above the Point F level of ₹123.
2. At the time of this writing, the stock price was trading around ₹155 levels. If the price of ₹155 is taken into account to calculate the mark to market profit / loss account, then trading higher top, higher bottom and lower top, lower bottom pattern formations in this example would have resulted in a profit of 29 points in the short span of around two months.

~

Example 7: Bata

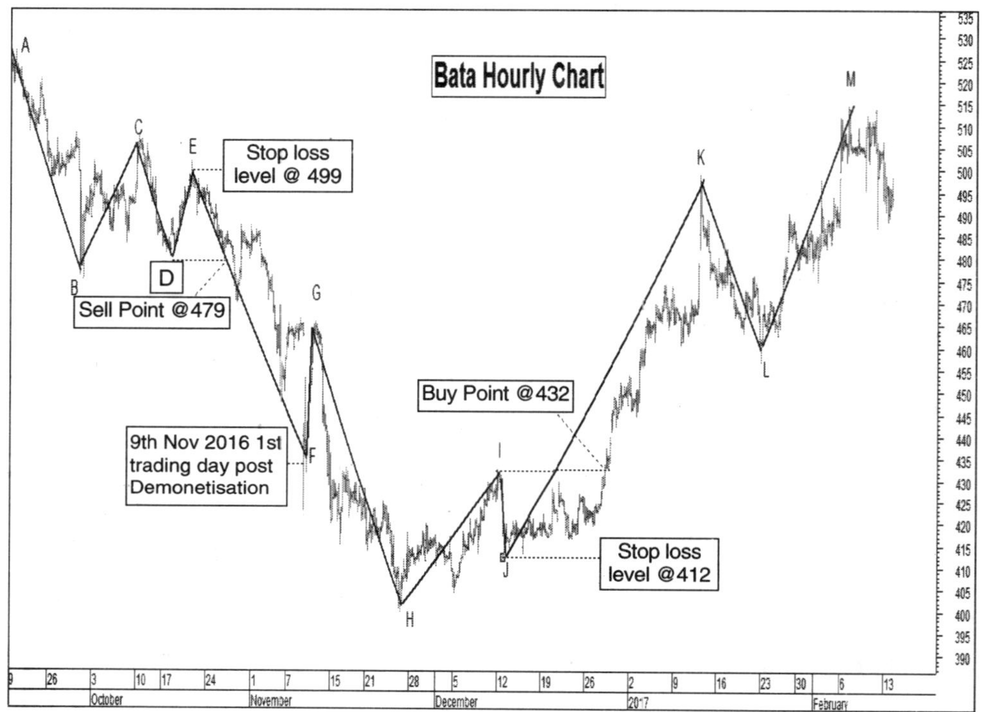

Figure 6.7: **Profitable Dow trades highlighted on the hourly, i.e. 60-minute, price chart of Bata**

~

Higher top, higher bottom and lower top, lower bottom pattern formations in the chart of Bata in Figure 6.7 would suggest initiating a sell trade as and when the level made earlier by Point D at about ₹479 is cracked in the down move from Point E to Point F because the stock price thereupon enters a lower top, lower bottom pattern regime. When initiating the sell trade, the stop loss can be placed at Point E levels of ₹499.

Thereafter the stock price made a lower top at Point G and successive lower bottoms at points F and H.

Demonetisation was announced on the evening of 8 November 2016 when the stock price was trading below Point C. The next day, i.e. on 9 November 2016, the stock price opened with a downside gap but closed around the day's high. The stock price thereafter declined to the lows of around ₹400 levels, i.e. to around Point H.

Post demonetisation, the stock price rallied strongly from the lows of around ₹400 levels, i.e. from around Point H. and cracked the level made earlier by Point I at ₹432 levels in its up move from Point J to Point K. One should close the sell position — and instead initiate a fresh buy trade — as and when the Point I level of ₹432 is cracked on the upside as the stock price then enters a higher top, higher bottom pattern regime. At the time of buying, the stop loss can be placed at Point J at ₹412 levels.

At the time of this writing, the stock price was trading around ₹495 levels, i.e. around Point M.

Trade Summary

1. Initiate a sell trade at ₹476 levels, i.e. selling after the price closes below the Point D level of ₹479.
2. Initiating a buy trade at ₹433 levels, i.e. buying after the price closes above the Point I level of ₹432.
3. At the time of this writing, the stock price was trading around ₹495 levels. If the market price of ₹495 is taken into account to calculate the market profit / loss accounts then trading higher top, higher bottom and lower top, lower bottom pattern formations in this example would have resulted in a profit of 105 points in the short span of around four months.

~

Example 8: Coromandel Fertilisers

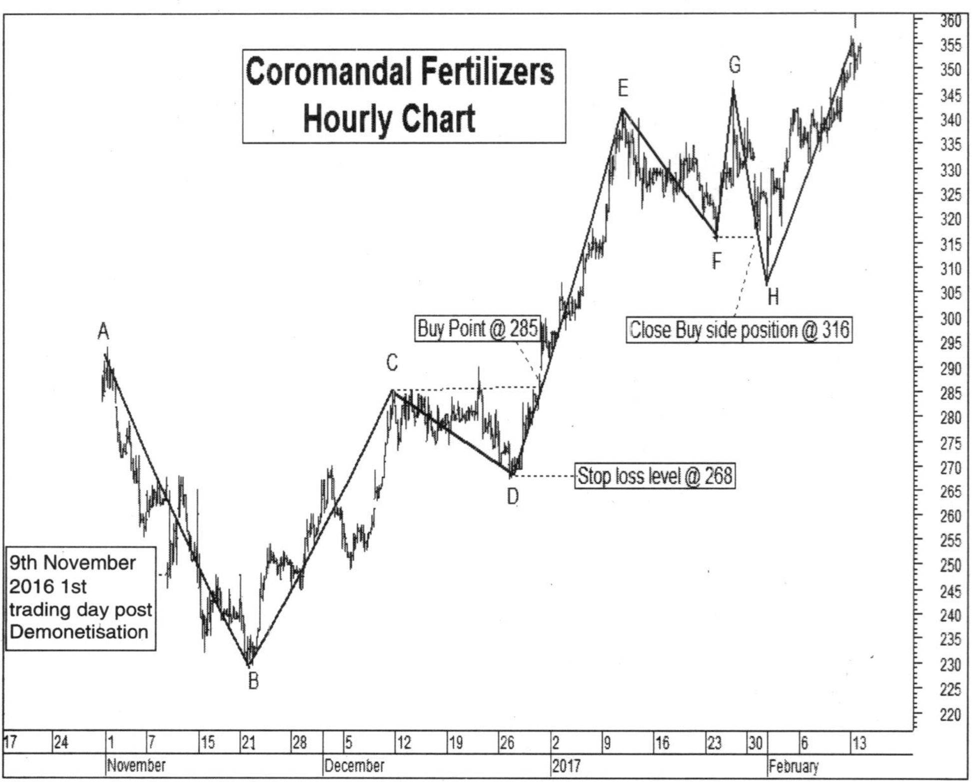

Figure 6.8: **Hourly, i.e. 60-minute, price chart of Coromandel Fertilisers with profitable Dow trades highlighted**

~

In Figure 6.8, the stock price of Coromandel Fertilisers initially declined in a straight line from Point A to Point B in a pattern which did not comply with the lower tops, lower highs pattern. As a result, the Dow Theory trader would not have been able to sell in this down move.

Demonetisation was announced on the evening of 8 November 2016. The stock price was then trading substantially below Point A. The next day, i.e. on 9 November 2016, while the stock price opened with a downside gap it closed around the day's high. Thereafter the stock price fell to the lows of around ₹230 levels, i.e. to Point B, from where it rallied upward strongly and cracked the level made earlier at the Point C levels of ₹285 in its up move from Point D to Point E. One should buy as and when the Point C level of ₹285 is cracked on the upside because the stock price then enters a higher top, higher bottom pattern regime. At the time of buying, the stop loss can be placed at Point D, i.e. at around ₹268 levels.

The stock price thereafter climbed up strongly to the highs of around Point G, from where it declined sharply and cracked the level made earlier by Point F at ₹316 levels in its down move from Point G to Point H. One should close the long positions as and when the Point F level of ₹316 is cracked on the downside as the ongoing higher top, higher bottom pattern formation gets distorted at that time.

Thereafter the stock price rallied sharply to a new life time high of around ₹354 levels on the upside, i.e. around the level made earlier by Point I, in a pattern which does not comply with the higher top, higher bottom regime. As a result, Dow Theory practitioners would not have been able to buy in this up move.

At the time of this writing book, the stock price was trading around ₹354 levels, i.e. around Point I.

Trade Summary

1. Initiating a buy trade at ₹287 levels, i.e. going long after the price closes above the Point C level of ₹285.
2. Exiting buy trade positions at ₹314 levels, i.e. exiting after the price closes below the Point F level of ₹316.
3. Here trading higher top, higher bottom and lower top, lower bottom patterns would have resulted in a profit of 27 points in the short span of around one month.

~

Example 9: Chennai Petroleum

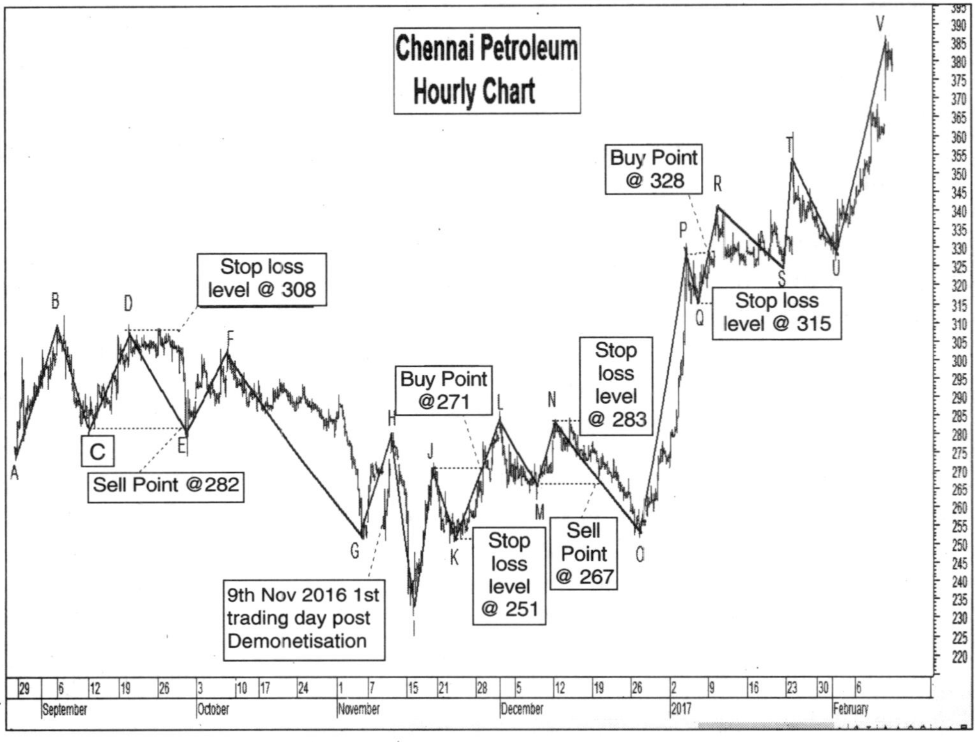

Figure 6.9: **Profitable Dow trades highlighted on the hourly, i.e. 60 minute, price chart of Chennai Petroleum**

~

Higher top, higher bottom and lower top, lower bottom pattern formations in the chart in Figure 6.9 suggest initiating a sell trade as and when the level made earlier by Point C at about ₹282 levels is cracked in the down move from Point D to Point E. The stock price then enters a lower top, lower bottom pattern regime. At the time of selling, the stop loss can be placed at Point D, i.e. at about ₹308 levels.

The stock price thereafter declined in a lower top, lower bottom pattern regime and made successive lower tops at points F and H, and successive lower bottoms at points E, G and I.

Demonetisation was announced on the evening of 8 November 2016 when the stock price of Chennai Petroleum was trading around Point H. Demonetisation resulted in massive price volatility. The next day, i.e. on 9 November 2016, the stock price opened with a downside gap but closed around the day's high. After that, the stock price declined to the lows of around ₹234 levels, i.e. to around Point I, from where it rallied upward strongly from the lows of around ₹234 levels and cracked the level made earlier by Point J at ₹271 levels in its up move from Point K to Point L. When this happens, one should close the sell position — and instead initiate a fresh buy position because the stock price then enters a higher top, higher bottom pattern regime. At the time of going long, the stop loss can be placed at around the Point K level of ₹251.

Thereafter the stock price rallied upward forming a higher top, higher bottom pattern and made a higher top at Point L and a higher bottom at Point M.

From the highs of around Point N, the stock price declined sharply and cracked the level made earlier by Point M at ₹267 levels in its down move from Point N to Point O. When this happens, one should close the buy position, and also instead initiate a fresh sell position as at that time, the stock price enters a lower top, lower bottom pattern regime. At the time of selling short, the stop loss can be placed at the Point N level of ₹283.

Then, from the lows of around ₹255 levels, i.e. from around Point O, the stock price rallied upward strongly and cracked the level made earlier by Point N at around ₹283 in the up move from Point O to Point P. One should close the sell position as and when the Point N level of ₹283 is cracked on the upside as the sell side stop loss placed at Point N then gets triggered.

Thereafter, the stock price rallied higher and cracked the level made earlier by Point P at around ₹328 in the up move from Point Q to Point R. One should buy as and when the Point P level of ₹328 is cracked on the upside as the stock price then enters a higher top, higher bottom pattern. At the time of buying, the stop loss can be placed at around Point Q, i.e. at about ₹315 levels.

Thereafter the stock price rallied in a higher top, higher bottom pattern regime and made successive higher tops at points P, R, T and V and successive higher bottoms at points Q, S and U.

At the time of this writing, the stock price was trading around ₹370 levels, i.e. around Point V.

Trade Summary

1. Initiate a sell trade at around ₹280 levels, i.e. after the price closes below the Point C level of ₹282.
2. Initiate a buy trade at ₹271 levels, i.e. buying after the price closes above the Point J level of ₹271.
3. Initiate a sell trade at around ₹265 levels, i.e. after the price closes below the Point M level of ₹267.
4. Exiting the sell trade at ₹284.50 levels, i.e. after the price closes above the Point N level of ₹283.
5. Initiating a buy trade at about ₹336 levels, i.e. buying after the price closes above the Point P level of ₹328,

At the time of this writing, the stock price was trading around ₹370 levels. If the price of ₹370 is taken into account to calculate mark to market profit / loss account, then trading higher top, higher bottom and lower top, lower bottom pattern formations resulted in a profit of 17.50 points in the short span of around five months.

~

Example 10: CESC

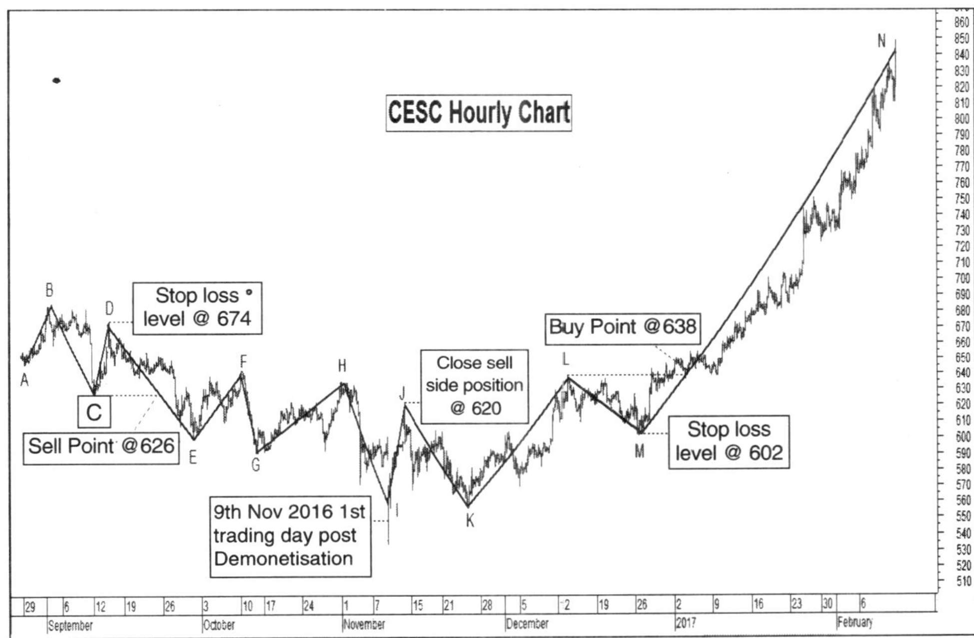

Figure 6.10: **Hourly, i.e. 60-minute, stock price chart of CESC with profitable Dow trades highlighted**

~

Higher top, higher bottom and lower top, lower bottom pattern formations in Figure 6.10 suggest initiating a sell trade as and when the level made earlier by Point C at about ₹626 levels is cracked in the down move from Point D to Point E. This is because the stock price then enters a lower top, lower bottom pattern regime. At the time of selling, the stop loss can be placed at Point D, i.e. at about ₹674 levels.

The stock price thereafter declined in a lower top, lower bottom pattern and made successive lower tops at points F, H, and J, and successive lower bottoms at points G, I and K.

Demonetisation was announced on the evening of 8 November 2016, when the stock price was trading below Point G. The very next day, i.e. on 9 November 2016, the stock price opened with a downside gap but closed around the day's high. Thereafter the stock price declined to the lows of around ₹558 levels, i.e. to Point K.

Post demonetisation, the stock price rallied strongly from the lows of around ₹558 levels, i.e. from around Point K, and cracked the level made earlier by Point J at ₹620 levels in the up move from Point K to Point L. One should close the sell position as and when the Point J level of ₹620 is cracked on the upside because the ongoing lower top, lower bottom pattern formation is then distorted.

Thereafter the stock price rallied further and cracked the level made earlier by Point L at around ₹638 levels in its up move from Point M to Point N. One should initiate a buy trade as and when this occurs because at that time the stock price enters a higher top, higher bottom pattern regime. At the time of buying, the stop loss may be placed at Point M, i.e. at about ₹602 levels.

Thereafter the stock price rallied upward to the highs of around Point N.

At the time of this writing, the stock price was trading around ₹867 levels, i.e. around Point N.

Trade Summary

1. Initiating a sell trade at ₹620 levels, i.e. after the price closes below the Point C level of ₹626.
2. Exiting short sell trade positions at about ₹627 levels, i.e. exiting after the price closes above the Point J level of ₹620.
3. Initiating a buy trade at about ₹643 levels, i.e. buying after the price closes above the Point L level of ₹638.

At the time of this writing, the stock price was trading around ₹867 levels. If the market price of ₹867 is taken into account to calculate mark to market profit / loss account, then trading higher top, higher bottom and lower top, lower bottom pattern formations would have resulted in a profit of 217 points in the short span of around five months in this case.

~

Example 11: Dhampur Sugar

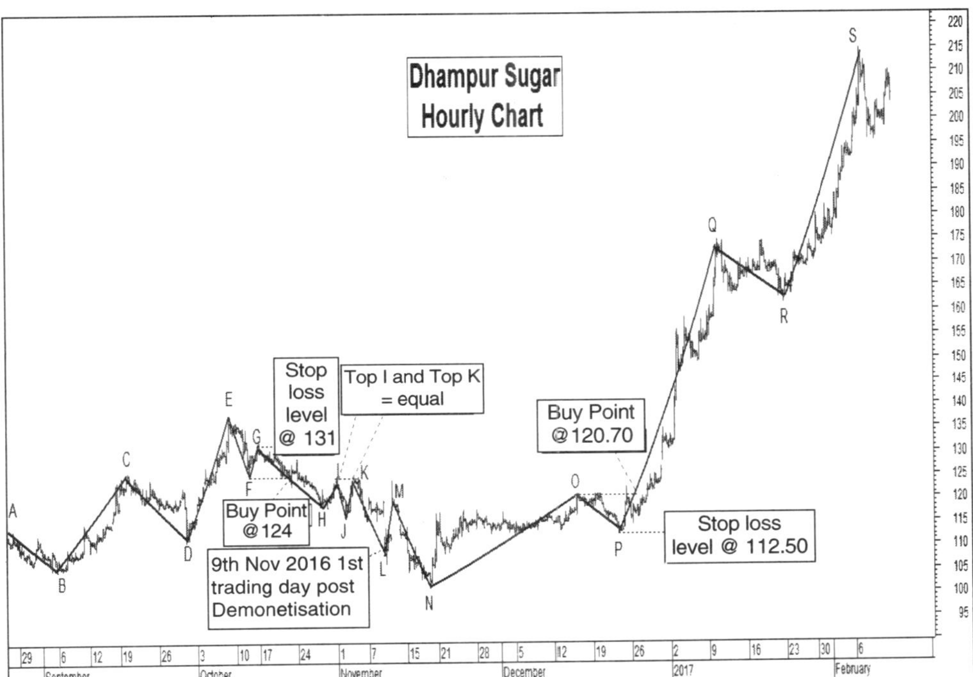

Figure 6.11: **Profitable Dow trades highlighted on the hourly, i.e. 60-minute, price chart of Dhampur Sugar**

~

Figure 6.11 shows the stock price of Dhampur Sugar initially rallying in a higher top, higher bottom pattern, making successive higher tops at points C and E, and successive higher bottoms at points B and D.

In this up move, the stock price made highs at around ₹137 levels, i.e. around Point E.

From the highs of around ₹137 levels, the stock price fell sharply and cracked the level made earlier by Point F at ₹124 levels in its down move from Point G to Point H. One should sell as and when this occurs because at that particular time, the stock price enters a lower top, lower bottom pattern. At the time of selling, the stop loss can be placed at the Point G level of ₹131.

Thereafter the stock price declined in a lower top, lower bottom pattern and made successive lower tops at points I and M, and successive lower bottoms at points H, J, L and M.

Demonetisation was announced on 8 November 2016 evening. At that time the stock price was trading below Point J. The very next day, i.e. on 9 November 2016, the price opened with a downside gap but closed around the day's high. Thereafter the stock price declined to the lows of around ₹103 levels, i.e. to Point N.

Post demonetisation, the stock price was volatile and rallied strongly from the lows of around ₹103 levels, i.e. from around Point N and cracked the level made earlier by Point O at ₹120.70 levels in its up move from Point P to Point Q. When this occurs, one should close the sell position — and instead initiate a fresh buy / long position — because the stock price then enters a higher top, higher bottom pattern regime. At the time of buying, the stop loss can be placed at Point P, i.e. at ₹112.50 levels.

At the time of this writing, the stock price was trading around ₹201 levels, i.e. around Point S.

Trade Summary

1. Initiate a sell trade at ₹123.50 levels, i.e. after the price closes below the Point F level of ₹124.
2. Initiate a buy trade at ₹122 levels, i.e. buying after the price closes above the Point O level of ₹120.70.

At the time of this writing, the stock price was trading around ₹201 levels. If the price of ₹201 is taken into account to calculate the market profit / loss account, then trading higher top, higher bottom and lower top, lower bottom pattern formations resulted in a profit of 80.50 points in the short span of around four months.

~

Example 12: Cummins India

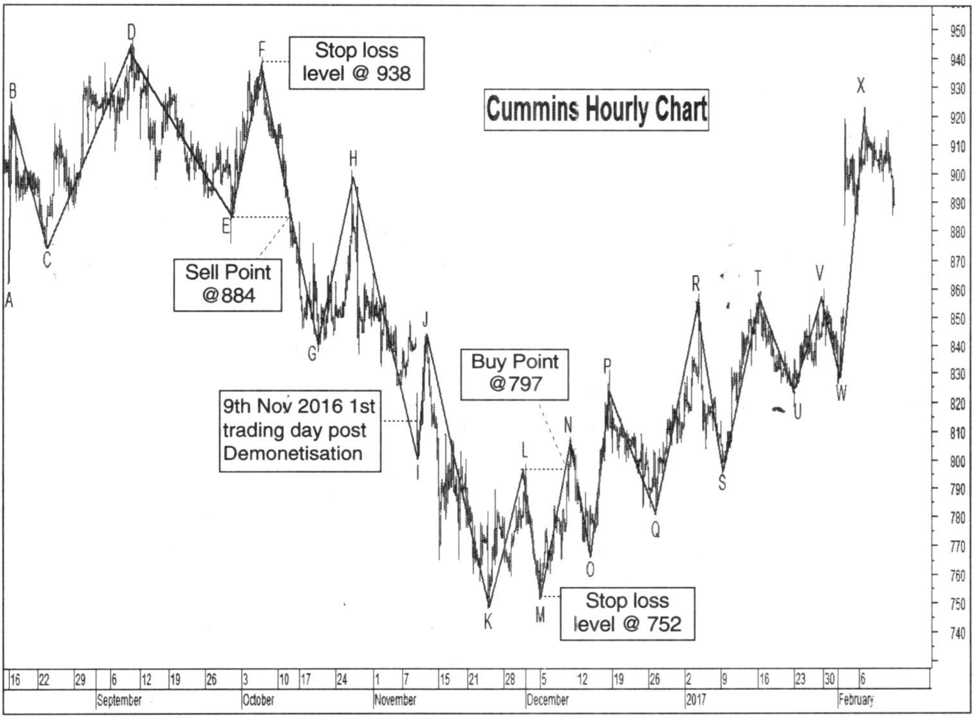

Figure 6.12: **Hourly, i.e. 60-minute, price chart of Cummins India with profitable Dow trades highlighted**

~

Figure 6.12 illustrates that the stock price of Cummins India initially rallied in a higher top, higher bottom pattern, making a higher top at Point D, and successive higher bottoms at points C and E.

During this up move, the stock price made a high of around ₹943 levels on the upside, i.e. around Point D, from where the stock price declined and cracked the level made earlier by Point E at ₹884 levels in the down move from Point F to Point G. One should close the buy position when this break occurs because at that time the stock price enters a lower top, lower bottom pattern. At the time of selling, the stop loss can be placed at Point F, at about ₹938 levels.

The stock price thereafter declined in a lower top, lower bottom pattern regime and made successive lower tops at points H and J and successive lower bottoms at points G, I and K.

Demonetisation was announced on 8 November 2016 night. At that time the stock price was trading below Point G. The very next day, i.e. on 9 November 2016, the stock price opened with a downside gap but closed around the day's high. Thereafter the stock price declined to the lows of around ₹750 levels on the downside, i.e. to around Point K.

Post demonetisation, the stock price rallied strongly from the lows of around ₹750 levels, i.e. from around Point K, and cracked the level made earlier by Point L at ₹797 levels in the up move from Point M to Point N.

One should close the sell position — and also initiate instead a fresh buy position — as and when the Point L levels of ₹797 is cracked on the upside since the stock price then enters a higher top, higher bottom pattern regime. At the time of buying, the stop loss can be placed at Point M, i.e. at about ₹752 levels.

Thereafter the stock price rallied in a higher top, higher bottom pattern regime and made successive higher tops at points N, P, R and X and successive higher bottoms at points M, O, Q, S, U and W.

At the time of this writing, the stock price was trading around ₹890 levels, i.e. around Point X.

Trade Summary

1. Selling at ₹880 levels, i.e. initiating a sell after the price closes below the Point E level of ₹884.
2. Buying at ₹798 levels, i.e. buying after the price closes above the Point L levels of ₹797.
3. At the time of this writing, the stock price was trading around ₹890 levels. If the price of ₹890 is taken into account to calculate the mark to market profit / loss account, then trading higher top, higher bottom and lower top, lower bottom pattern formations resulted in a profit of 174 points in the short span of around four months.

~

Example 13: Dwarikesh Sugar

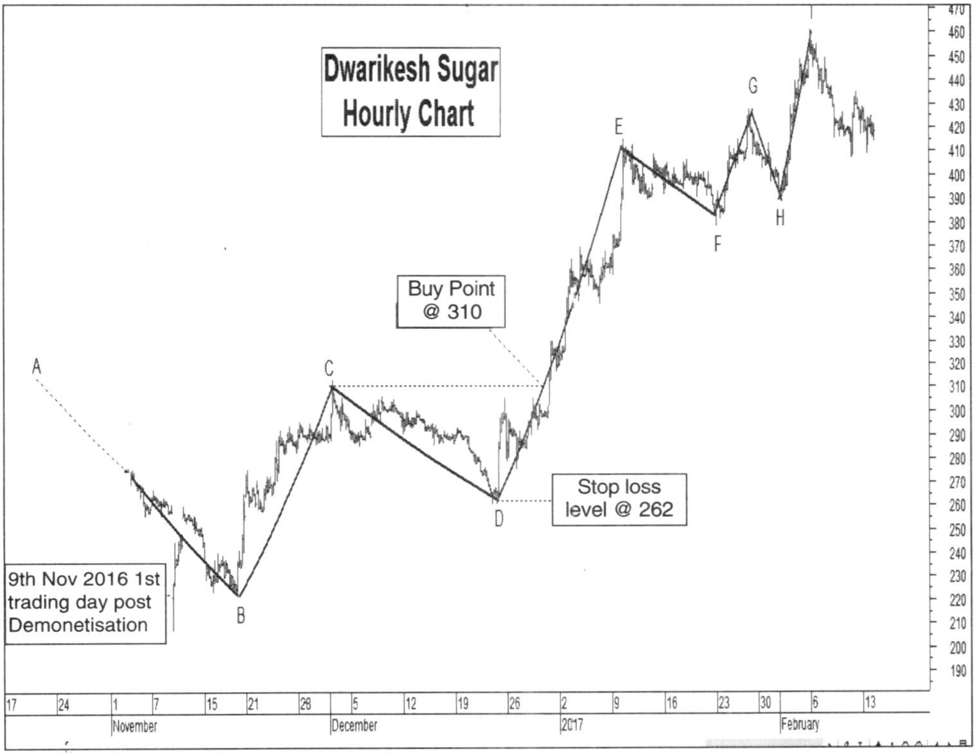

Figure 6.13: **Profitable Dow trades highlighted on the hourly, i.e. 60-minute, price chart of Dwarikesh Sugar**

~

In Figure 6.13, the stock price initially fell from Point A to Point B in a pattern which does not comply with a lower top, lower pattern regime. As a result, Dow Theory practitioners would not able to initiate a sell trade in this down move.

Demonetisation was announced on the night of 8 November 2016. At that time, the stock price was trading significantly below Point A. The next day, i.e. on 9 November 2016, while the stock price opened with a downside gap, it closed around the day's high. The stock price thereafter declined to the lows of around ₹224 levels, i.e. to around Point B.

The stock price then rallied strongly upward from the lows of around ₹230 levels, i.e. from Point B, and cracked the level made earlier by Point C at about ₹310 in the up move from Point D to Point E. One should buy as and when the Point C level of ₹310 is cracked on the upside. At that particular time, the stock price enters a higher top, higher bottom pattern regime. At the time of buying, the stop loss can be placed at about the Point D level of ₹262.

The stock price thereafter rallied in a higher top, higher bottom pattern regime and made successive higher tops at points E, G and I, and successive higher bottoms at points E and H.

At the time of this writing, the stock price was trading around ₹418 levels, i.e. around Point I.

Trade Summary

1. Initiating a buy trade at ₹313 levels, i.e. buying after the price closes above the Point C level of ₹310.
2. At the time of this writing, the stock price was trading around ₹418 levels. If the price of ₹418 is taken into account to calculate the mark to market profit / loss account, then trading higher top, higher bottom and lower top, lower bottom pattern formations resulted in a profit of 105 points in the short span of around two months.

~

Example 14: Escorts

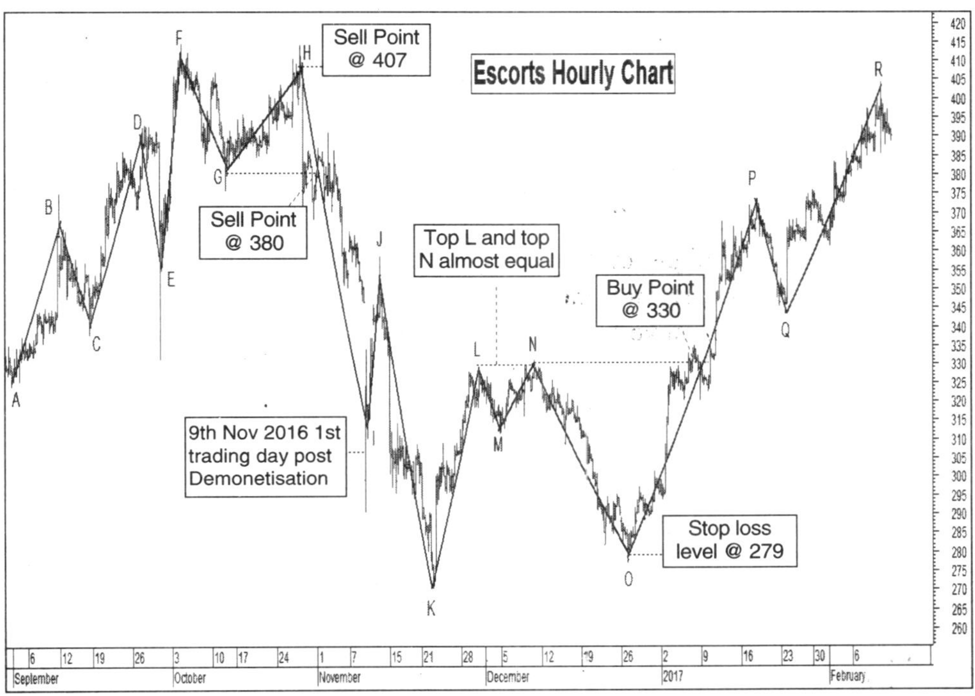

Figure 6.14: **Hourly, i.e. 60-minute, price chart of Escorts with profitable Dow trades highlighted**

~

Figure 6.14 shows that the stock price of Escorts initially rose in a higher top, higher bottom pattern regime, making successive higher tops at points D and F and successive higher bottoms at points C, E and G.

During this up move, the stock price made highs of around ₹411 levels, i.e. at Point F.

Then from the highs of around ₹411 levels, the stock price fell sharply and cracked the level made earlier by Point G at around ₹380 in a down move from Point H to Point I. One should close the buy trade — and instead initiate a fresh sell trade as and when the Point G level of ₹380 is cracked on the downside; at that particular time the stock price enters a lower top, lower bottom pattern regime. At the time of selling, the stop loss can be placed at around the Point H level of ₹407.

Thereafter the stock price declined in a lower top, lower bottom pattern regime and made a lower top at Point J and a lower bottom at Point I.

Demonetisation was announced on the evening of 8 November 2016. At that time the stock price of Escorts was trading below Point G. The very next day, i.e. on 9 November 2016, the stock price opened with a downside gap but closed around the day's high. The stock price thereafter declined to the lows of Point K at around ₹273 levels.

The stock price then rallied strongly upward from the lows of around ₹273, i.e. from around Point K; and cracked the level made earlier by Point N at about ₹330 levels in its up move from Point O to Point P. One should close the sell side position — and also initiate a fresh buy trade — as and when the Point N level of ₹330 is cracked on the upside. At that time, the stock price enters a higher top, higher bottom pattern regime. At the time of buying, the stop loss can be placed at Point O levels of ₹279.

The stock price thereafter rallied in a higher top, higher bottom pattern regime and made successive higher tops at Points P and R, and a successive higher bottom at Point Q.

At the time of this writing, the stock price was trading around ₹383 levels, i.e. around Point R.

Trade Summary

1. Initiating a sell trade at ₹375 levels, i.e. after the price closes below the Point G level of ₹380.
2. Initiating a buy trade at ₹331 levels, i.e. after the price closes above the Point N level of ₹330.
3. At the time of this writing, the stock price was trading around ₹383 levels. If the price of ₹383 is taken into account to calculate a mark to market profit / loss account, then trading higher top, higher bottom and lower top, lower bottom pattern formations resulted in a profit of 96 points in the short span of around four months.

~

Example 15: Gitanjali Gems

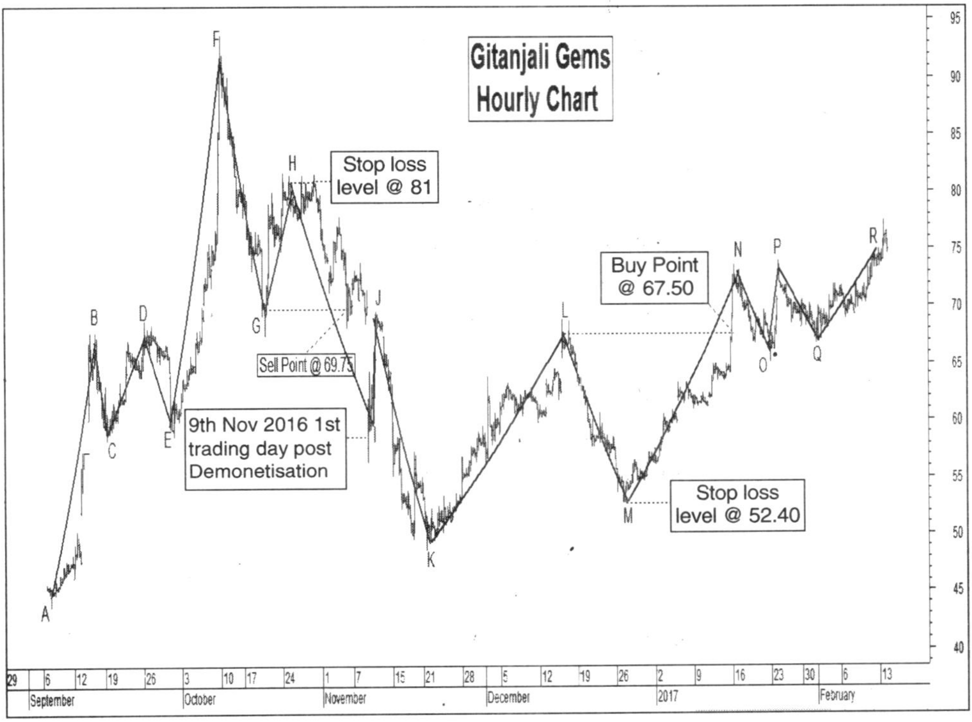

Figure 6.15: **Profitable Dow trades highlighted on the hourly, i.e. 60-minute, price chart of Gitanjali Gems**

~

Figure 6.15 demonstrates that the stock price of Gitanjali Gems initially rose in a higher top, higher bottom pattern regime, making successive higher tops at points D and F, and successive higher bottoms at points C and E. During this up move, the stock price made the high of around ₹91 levels at Point F. Thereafter, the price fell sharply and cracked the level made earlier by Point G at around ₹69.75 in its down move from Point H to Point I. One should close the buy position — and also initiate a fresh sell trade — as and when the Point G level of ₹69.75 is cracked on the downside as at that time, the stock price enters a lower top, lower bottom pattern regime. At the time of selling, the stop loss can be placed at Point H, i.e. at ₹81 levels.

The stock price thereafter declined in a lower top, lower bottom pattern regime and made a lower top at Point J and a lower bottom at Point I.

Demonetisation was announced on the evening of 8 November 2016 when the stock price was trading below Point G. The next day, i.e. on 9 November 2016, the stock price opened with a downside gap but closed around the day's high. Thereafter, though, the stock price fell to the lows of around ₹50 levels, i.e. to around Point K., It then rallied strongly from the lows of around ₹50 levels, and cracked Point L at ₹67.50 levels, in the up move from Point M to Point N. One should close the sell position — and instead initiate a new buy trade — as and when this break occurs. At that time, the stock price enters a higher top, higher bottom pattern regime. At the time of buying, the stop loss can be placed at the Point M level of ₹52.40.

The stock price thereafter rallied in a higher top, higher bottom pattern regime and made successive higher tops at points N, P and R and successive higher bottoms at points O and Q.

At the time of this writing, the stock price was trading around ₹75 levels, i.e. around Point R.

Trade Summary

1. Initiating a sell trade at ₹68.75 levels, i.e. after the price closes below the Point G level of ₹69.75
2. Going long at ₹71.75 levels, i.e. after the price closes above the Point L level of ₹67.50
3. At the time of this writing, the stock price was trading around ₹75 levels. If the price of ₹75 is taken into account to calculate the mark to market profit / loss account, then trading higher top, higher bottom and lower top, lower bottom pattern formations would have resulted in a profit of only 0.25 points.

~

Example 16: Future Enterprises

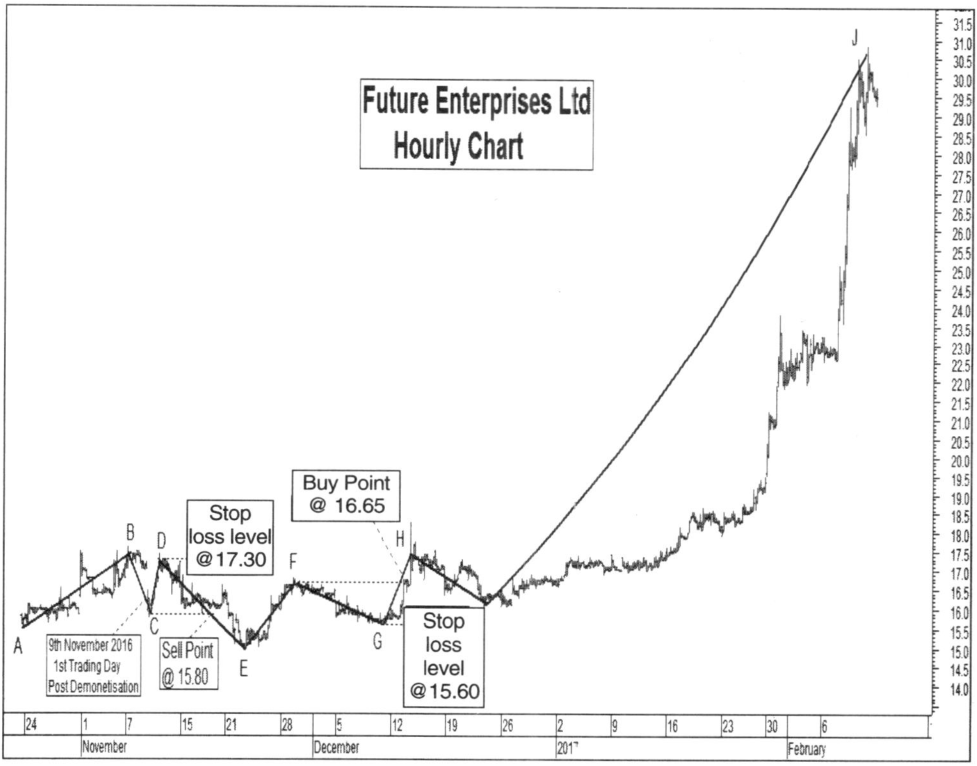

Figure 6.16: **Hourly, i.e. 60-minute, price chart of Future Enterprises with profitable Dow trades highlighted**

~

As Figure 6.16 illustrates, the Future Enterprises stock price initially rallied from Point A to Point B.

Demonetisation was announced on the evening of 8 November 2016 when the stock price was trading around Point B. The next day, i.e. on 9 November 2016, the stock price opened with a downside gap and closed around the day's low. On 10 November, however, the stock price opened with an upside gap and rallied higher to around Point D at about ₹17.20 levels. Thereafter, it declined sharply and cracked the level made earlier by Point C at around ₹15.80 in a down move from Point D to Point E.

One should close the buy position — and also initiate a fresh sell position instead — as when the Point C level of ₹15.80 is cracked on the downside at that time, the stock price enters a lower top, lower bottom pattern regime. At the time of selling, the stop loss can be placed at the Point D level of 17.30.

The stock price thereafter declined to the lows of around ₹15 levels, i.e. to Point E.

From around Point E, however, the stock price rallied upward strongly and cracked the level made earlier by Point F at about ₹16.65 in its up move from Point G to Point H. One should close the sell side position — and instead initiate a fresh buy trade — as and when the Point F level of ₹16.65 is cracked on the upside as the stock price then enters a higher top, higher bottom pattern regime at that time. At the time of buying, the stop loss can be placed at the Point G level of ₹15.60.

Thereafter the stock price rallied up to around ₹26.6 levels, i.e. to Point J, where it stood at the time of this writing.

Trade Summary

1. Initiating a sell trade at ₹15.40 levels, i.e. after the price closes below the Point C level of ₹15.80.
2. Going long at ₹16.80 levels, i.e. after the price closes above the Point H level of ₹16.65.
3. At the time of this writing, the stock price was trading around ₹26.60 levels. If the price of ₹26.60 is taken into account to calculate the mark to market profit / loss account, then trading higher top, higher bottom and lower top, lower bottom pattern formations in this example would have resulted in a profit of 8.40 points in the short span of around three months.

~

Example 17: Gateway Distriparks

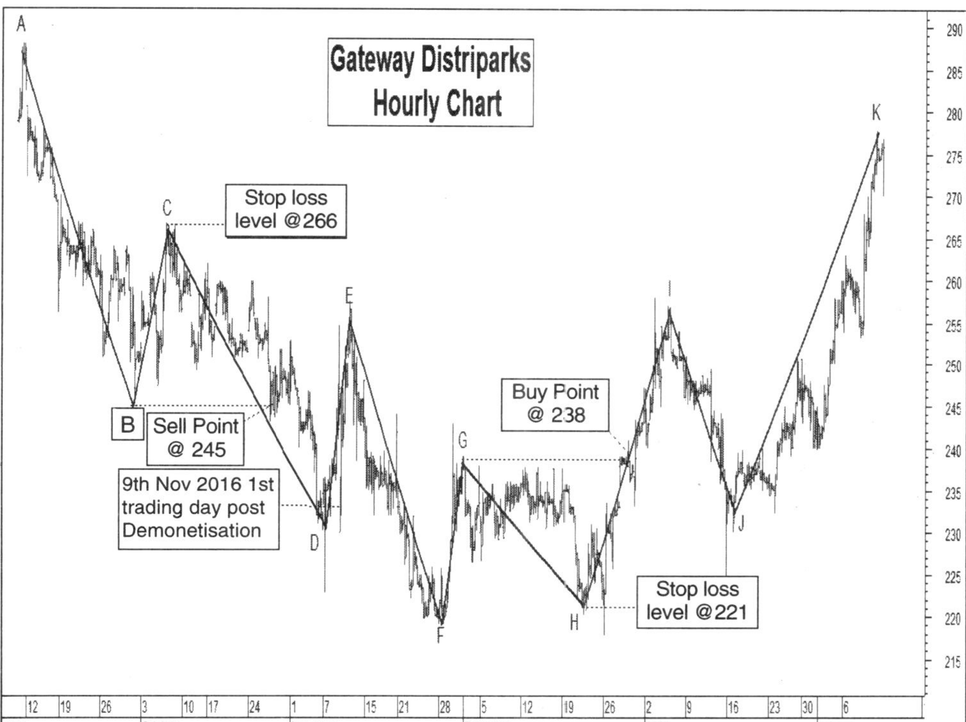

Figure 6.17: **Profitable Dow trades highlighted on the hourly, i.e. 60-minute, stock price chart of Gateway Distriparks**

~

Trading higher top, higher bottom and lower top, lower bottom pattern formations in the case of Figure 6.17 would suggest selling as and when the level made earlier by Point B at around ₹245 levels is cracked in the down move from Point C to Point D. This is because the stock price then enters a lower top, lower bottom pattern regime. At the time of selling, the stop loss can be placed at Point C, i.e. at about ₹266 levels.

The stock price thereafter declined in a lower top, lower bottom pattern regime and made a lower top at Point E, and successive lower bottoms at points D and F.

When demonetisation was announced on the evening of 8 November 2016 night, the stock price was trading below Point B. The next day, i.e. on 9 November 2016, the price opened with a downside gap but closed around the day's high. Thereafter the stock price fell to the lows of around ₹220 levels, i.e. to Point F, from where it rallied strongly and cracked the level made earlier by Point G at ₹238 levels in an up move from Point H to Point I.

One should have closed the sell side position — and also initiated a fresh buy trade— as and when the Point G level of ₹238 was cracked on the upside. This is because the stock price then enters a higher top, higher bottom pattern regime. At the time of buying, the stop loss can be placed at Point H level at ₹221.

Thereafter the stock price rallied in a higher top, higher bottom pattern regime and made a higher top at Point I and a higher bottom J. At the time of this writing, the stock price was trading around ₹270 levels, i.e. around Point N.

Trade Summary

1. Initiating a sell trade at ₹244 levels, i.e. after the price closes below Point B at ₹245 level.
2. Buying at ₹239 levels, i.e. after the price closes above Point G at ₹238 levels,
3. At the time of this writing, the stock price was trading around ₹270 levels. If the price of ₹270 is taken into account to calculate the mark to market profit / loss account, then trading higher top, higher bottom and lower top, lower bottom pattern formations in this example would have resulted in a profit of 36 points in the short span of around four months.

~

Example 18: JP Associates

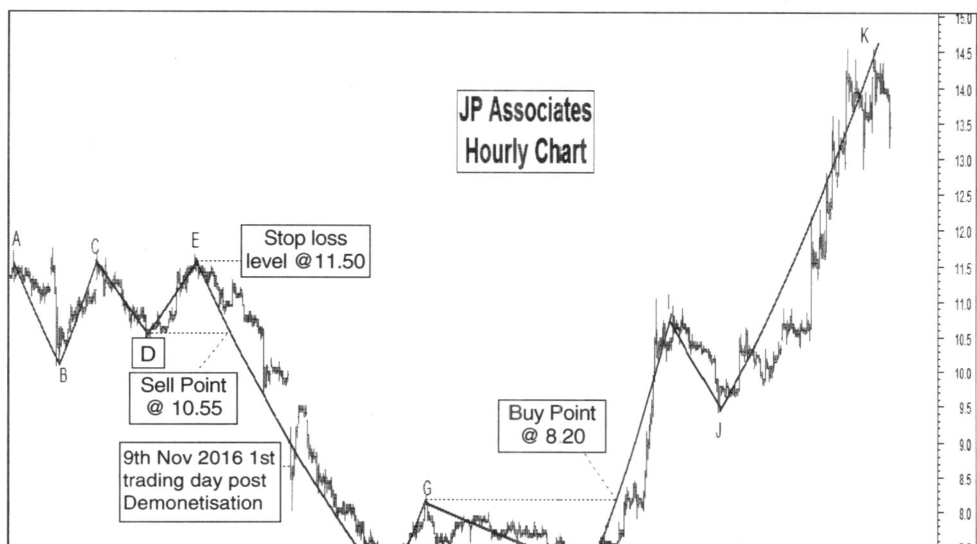

Figure 6.18: **Hourly, i.e. 60-minute, price chart of JP Associates with profitable Dow trades highlighted**

~

Trading higher top, higher bottom and lower top, lower bottom pattern formations in Figure 6.18 would suggest selling as and when the level made earlier by Point D at ₹10.55 is cracked on the downside in the down move from Point E to Point F. This is because the stock price then enters a lower top, lower bottom pattern regime. At the time of selling, the stop loss can be placed at Point E, i.e. at ₹11.50 levels.

The stock price thereafter declined to the lows of around ₹6.90 levels on the downside, i.e. to around Point F.

Demonetisation was announced on the evening of 8 November 2016. At that time the stock price of JP Associates was trading significantly below Point B. The very next day, i.e. on 9 November 2016, the stock price opened with a downside gap but closed around the day's high. Thereafter, however, the stock price fell to the lows of around ₹6.90 levels, i.e. to Point F, from where it rallied upward strongly and cracked the level made earlier by Point G at about ₹8.20 in the up move from Point H to Point I.

One should close the sell position, — and instead initiate a fresh buy trade — as and when the Point G level of ₹8.20 is cracked on the upside, because at that time the stock price enters a higher top, higher bottom pattern regime. At the time of buying, the stop loss can be placed at Point H, i.e. at around ₹7.15 levels.

The stock price thereafter rallied upward in a higher top, higher bottom pattern regime and made successive higher tops at points I and K and a higher bottom at Point J.

At the time of this writing, the stock price was trading around ₹13.70 levels, i.e. at around Point K.

Trade Summary

1. Initiating a sell trade at ₹9.65 levels, i.e. after the price closes below Point D at ₹10.55 level.
2. Going long at ₹8.25 levels, i.e. after the price closes above the Point G level of ₹8.20.
3. At the time of this writing, the stock price was trading around ₹13.70 levels. If the price of ₹13.70 is taken into account to calculate the mark to market profit / loss account, then trading higher top, higher bottom and lower top, lower bottom pattern formations in this example would have resulted in a profit of 6.85 points in the short span of around four months.

~

Example 19: India Cement

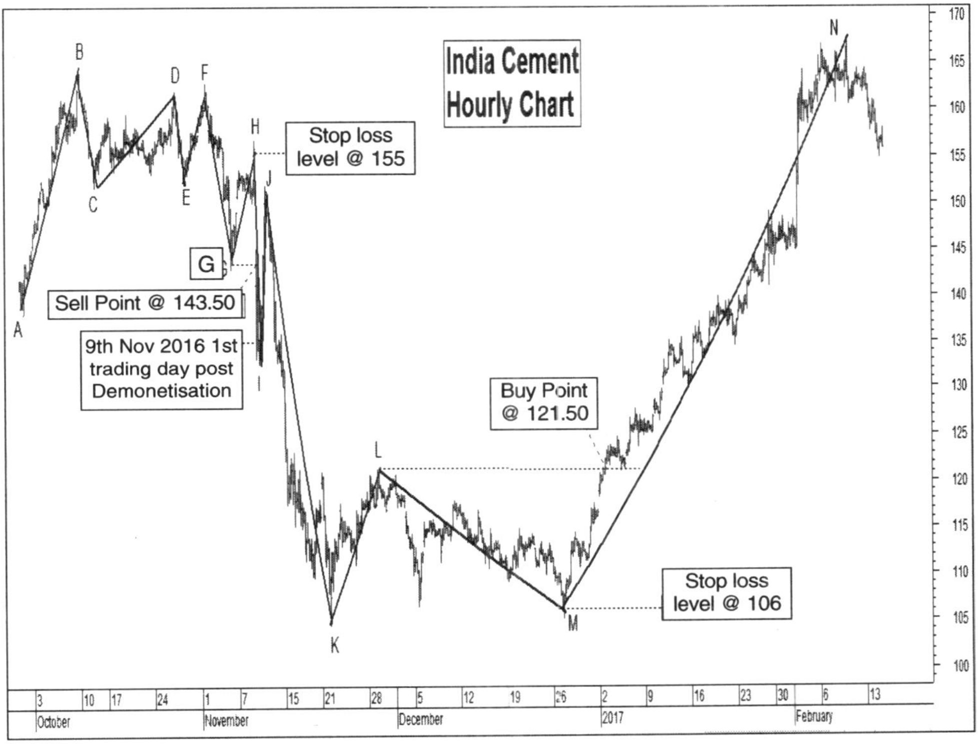

Figure 6.19: **Profitable Dow trades highlighted on the hourly, i.e. 60-minute, price chart of India Cement**

~

Trading higher top, higher bottom and lower top, lower bottom pattern formations in the case of Figure 6.19 would have suggested selling as and when the level made earlier by Point G at about ₹143.50 is cracked in the down move from Point H to Point I. This is because the stock price then enters a lower top, lower bottom pattern regime. At the time of selling, the stop loss can be placed at Point H, i.e. at around ₹155 levels.

Thereafter the stock price declined in a lower top, lower bottom pattern regime and made a lower top at Point J and a lower bottom at Point K.

Demonetisation was announced post market hours on 8 November 2016 when the stock price was trading a little above Point G. The next day, i.e. on 9 November 2016, the stock price opened with a downside gap but closed around the day's high. Thereafter the stock price declined to the lows of around ₹106 levels on the downside, i.e. to around Point K, from where it rallied strongly upward and cracked the level made earlier by Point L at about ₹121.50 in the up move from Point M to Point N. One should close the sell position, and instead initiate a fresh buy trade, as and when the Point L level of ₹121.50 is cracked on the upside as at that particular time the stock price enters a higher top, higher bottom pattern regime. At the time of buying, the stop loss can be placed at the Point M level of ₹106.

Thereafter the stock price rallied higher vertically to the highs of around Point N, where it stood at the time of this writing.

Trade Summary

1. Initiating a sell trade at ₹139.60 levels, i.e. after the price closes below the Point G level of ₹143.50.
2. Going long at ₹123 levels, i.e. after the price closes above Point L at ₹121.50 levels.
3. At the time of this writing, the stock price was trading around ₹162 levels. If the price of ₹162 is taken into account to calculate the mark to market profit / loss account, then trading higher top, higher bottom and lower top, lower bottom pattern formations in this example would have resulted in a profit of 55.60 points in the short span of around three months.

~

Example 20: Idea

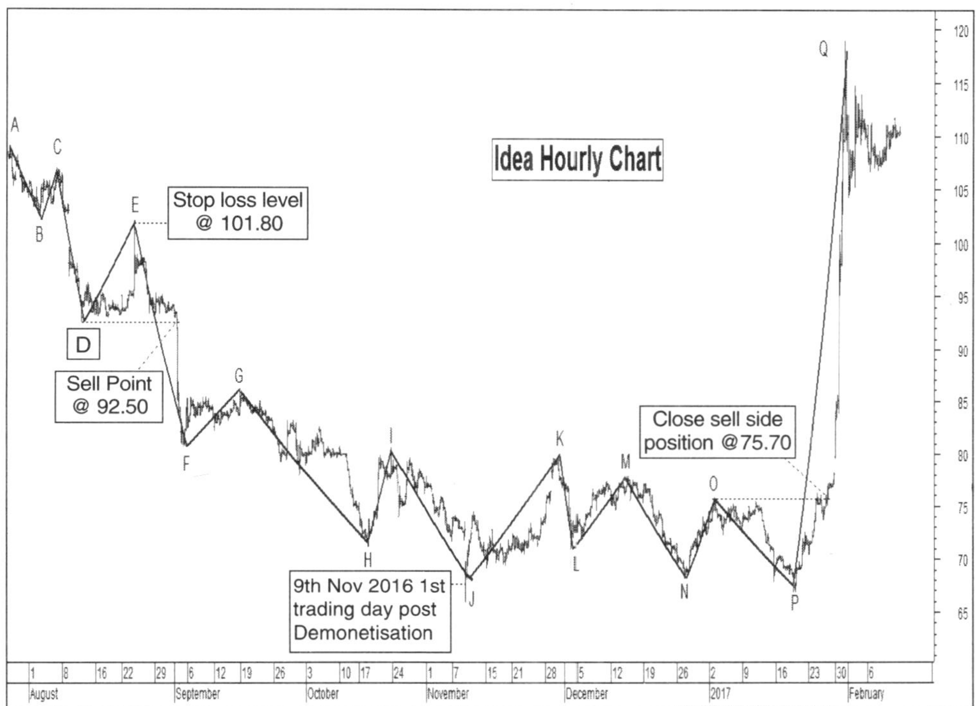

Figure 6.20: **Hourly, i.e. 60-minute, price chart of Idea with profitable Dow trades highlighted**

~

Trading higher top, higher bottom and lower top, lower bottom pattern formations in the case of Idea in Figure 6.20 would suggest selling as and when the level made earlier by Point D at around ₹92.50 is cracked in the down move from Point E to Point F. This is because at that time the stock price enters a lower top, lower bottom pattern regime. At the time of selling, the stop loss can be placed at Point E, i.e. at ₹101.80 levels.

Thereafter the stock price declined in a lower top, lower bottom pattern and made successive lower tops at points G, I, K, M and O and successive lower bottoms at points F, H, J and P.

Demonetisation was announced after market hours on 8 November 2016 when Idea's stock price was trading just below Point H. The next day, i.e. on 9 November 2016, the stock price opened with a downside gap but closed around the day's high. Thereafter the stock price declined to the lows of around ₹68 levels, i.e. to around Point P, from where it rallied strongly and cracked the level made earlier by Point O at about ₹75.70 in the up move from Point P to Point Q. One should close the sell trade position as and when this occurs as at that particular time the ongoing lower top, lower bottom pattern formation gets distorted.

Thereafter the stock price rallied vertically higher to around ₹115 levels, i.e. to around Point Q, in a pattern which does not comply with the higher top, higher bottom pattern regime. As a result, practitioners of Dow Theory would not have been able to buy during this up move.

Trade Summary

1. Initiating a sell trade at ₹91.95 levels, i.e. after the price closes below the Point D level of ₹92.50.
2. Exiting the sell positions at ₹76.20 levels, i.e. after the price closes above the Point O levels of ₹75.70.
3. Trading higher top, higher bottom and lower top, lower bottom pattern formations would have resulted in a profit of 15.75 points in the short span of around four months in this example.

~

Example 21: IOC

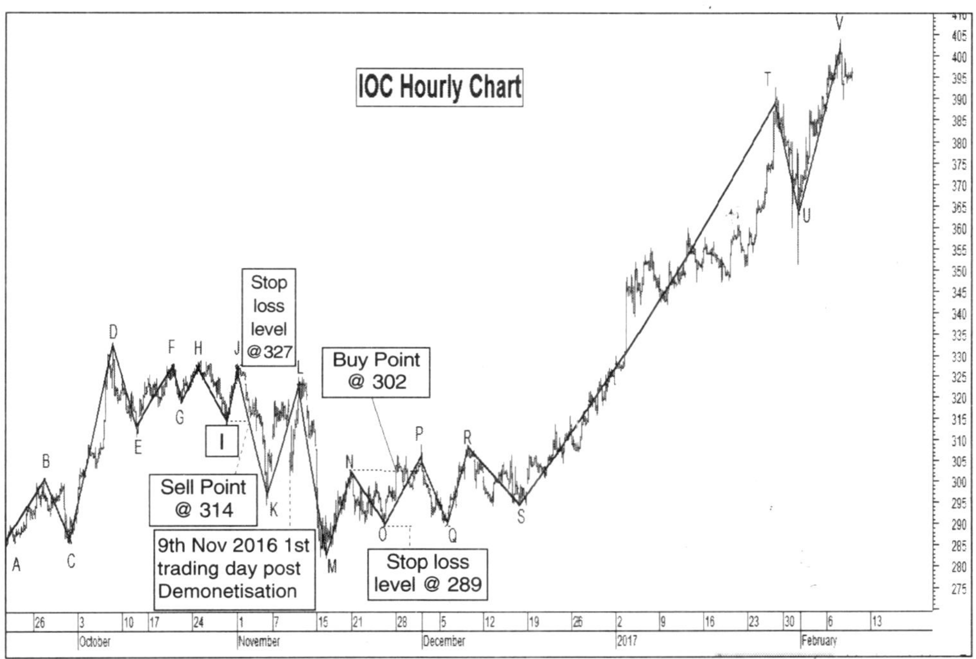

Figure 6.21: **Profitable Dow trades highlighted on the hourly, i.e. 60-minute, price chart of IOC**

~

Trading higher top, higher bottom and lower top, lower bottom pattern formations in the case of Figure 6.21 would suggest selling IOC as and when the level made earlier by Point I at about ₹314 is cracked in the down move from Point J to Point K. This is because at that time the stock price enters a lower top, lower bottom pattern regime. At the time of selling, the stop loss can be placed at Point J at ₹327 levels.

Thereafter the stock price declined in a lower top, lower bottom pattern regime and made a lower top at Point L and a lower bottom at Point M.

Demonetisation was announced after market hours on 8 November 2016 when IOC's price was trading a little above Point K. The next day, i.e. on 9 November 2016, the price opened with a downside gap but closed around the day's high. Thereafter the stock price declined to Point M, i.e. to around ₹284 levels, from where it rallied upward strongly and cracked the level made earlier by Point N at around ₹302 in the up move from Point O to Point P. One should close the sell position — and instead initiate a fresh buy trade position — as and when the crack occurs as at that particular time the stock price enters a higher top, higher bottom pattern regime. At the time of buying, the stop loss can be placed at Point O at about ₹289 levels.

Thereafter the stock price rallied higher in a higher top, higher bottom pattern regime and made successive higher tops at points P, R, T and V and successive higher bottoms at points O, Q, S and U.

At the time of this writing, the stock price was trading around ₹394 levels, i.e. around Point V.

Trade Summary

1. Selling at ₹309 levels, i.e. after the price closes below Point I at around ₹314 level.
2. Going long at ₹304 levels, i.e. after the price closes above Point N at around ₹302 levels.
3. At the time of this writing, the stock price was trading around ₹394 levels. If the market price of ₹394 is taken into account to calculate the mark to market profit / loss account, then trading higher top, higher bottom and lower top, lower bottom pattern formations would have resulted in a profit of 95 points in the short span of around four months in this case.

~

Example 22: Indian Hotels

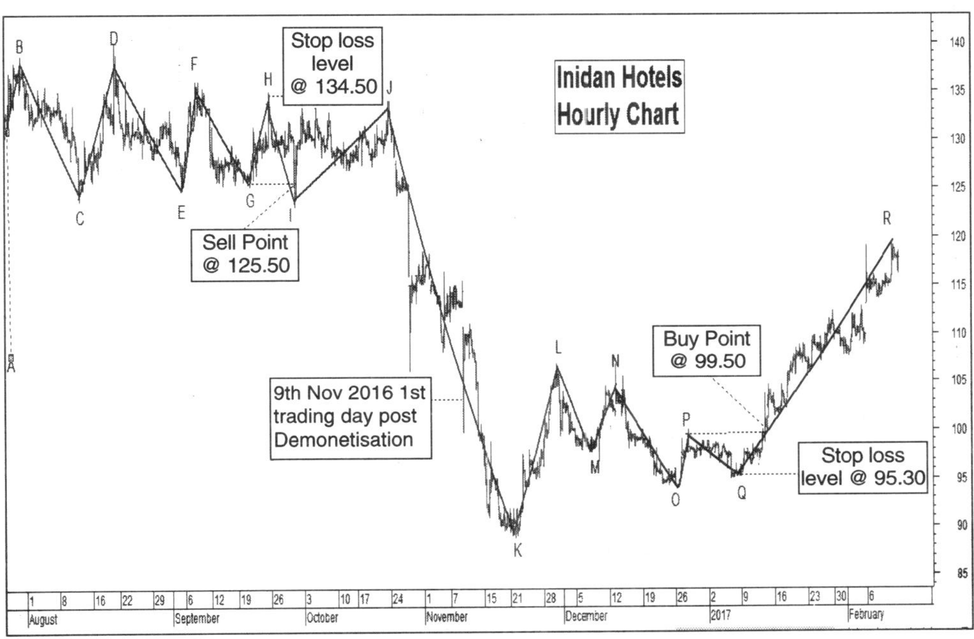

Figure 6.22: **Hourly, i.e. 60-minute, price chart of Indian Hotels with profitable Dow trades highlighted**

~

Higher top, higher bottom and lower top, lower bottom pattern formations in the chart in Figure 6.22 demonstrates Indian Hotel's stock price initially rallying from Point A to Point B, i.e. to around ₹138 levels on the upside, from where it then declined and cracked the earlier Point G levels at ₹125.50 in the down move from Point H to Point I. One should close the buy positions — and instead initiate a fresh sell trade— as and when the Point G level of ₹125.50 is cracked on the downside as at that particular time the stock price enters a lower top, lower bottom pattern regime. At the time of selling, the stop loss can be placed at Point H level, i.e. at around ₹134.60.

Demonetisation was announced after market hours on 8 November 2016 when the stock price was trading significantly below Point I. The next day, i.e. on 9 November 2016, the price opened with a downside gap but closed around the day's high. Thereafter, however, the stock price declined to the lows of around ₹90 levels on the downside, i.e. to around Point K, from where it then rallied strongly upward and cracked the level made earlier by Point P at around ₹99.50 levels in the up move from Point Q to Point R. One should close the sell position — and also initiate a fresh buy trade — as and when the earlier Point P levels of ₹99.50 is cracked on the upside, because as at that particular time, the stock price enters a higher top, higher bottom pattern regime. At the time of buying, the stop loss can be placed at Point Q, i.e. at around ₹95.30 levels.

Thereafter the stock price rallied higher to the highs of around Point P. At the time of this writing, the stock price was trading around ₹116 levels, i.e. around Point R.

Trade Summary

1. Initiating sell trade at ₹123 levels, i.e. after the price closes below Point G at ₹125.50 level.
2. Going long at ₹101 levels, i.e. after the price closes above the Point P level of ₹99.50.
3. At the time of this writing, the stock price of Indian Hotels was trading around ₹116 levels. If the price of ₹116 is taken into account to calculate the mark to market profit / loss account, then trading higher top, higher bottom and lower top, lower bottom pattern formations resulted in a profit of 37 points in the short span of around four months.

~

Example 23: Hero Motor

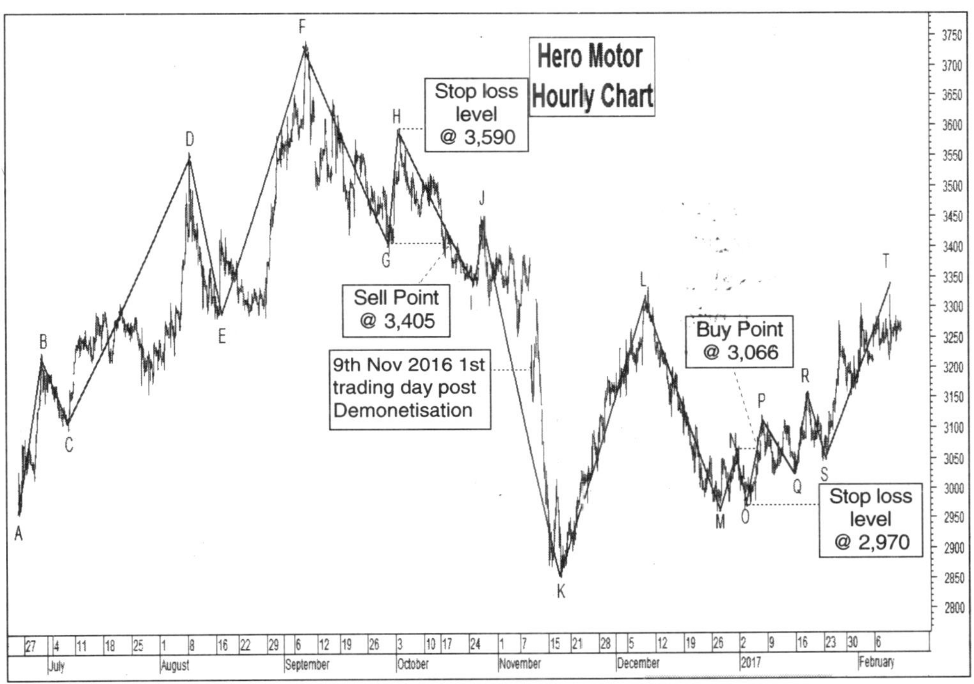

Figure 6.23: **Profitable Dow trades highlighted on the hourly, i.e. 60-minute, price chart of Hero Motor**

~

Higher top, higher bottom and lower top, lower bottom pattern formations in Figure 6.23 highlight that Hero Motors stock price initially rose in a higher top, higher bottom pattern regime, making successive higher tops at points D and F and successive higher bottoms at points C and E. During this up move, the price made a high of around ₹3,725 levels, i.e. at Point F, from where it then declined and cracked the earlier Point G level of ₹3,405 in its down move from Point H to Point I. One should close the buy position — and instead initiate a fresh sell trade position — as and when the Point G level of around ₹3,405 is cracked on the downside as the stock price then enters a lower top, lower bottom pattern regime. At the time of selling, the stop loss can be placed at Point H, i.e. at around ₹3,590 levels.

The stock price then duly declined in a lower top, lower bottom pattern regime and made a lower top at Point J and successive lower bottoms at points I and K.

Demonetisation was announced post market hours on 8 November 2016 when Hero Motor's stock price was trading below Point I. The next day, i.e. on 9 November 2016, the price opened with a downside gap but closed around the day's high. Thereafter the stock price declined to the lows of around ₹2,870, i.e. to around Point K, from where it cracked the level made earlier by Point N at about ₹3,066 levels in the up move from Point O to Point P.

One should close the sell position — and instead initiate a fresh buy position — as and when the earlier Point N level of ₹3,066 is cracked as at that time, the stock price enters a higher top, higher bottom pattern regime. At the time of buying, the stop loss can be placed at Point O, i.e. at around ₹2,970 levels.

The stock price thereafter rallied in a higher top, higher bottom pattern regime and made successive higher tops at points N, P, R and T, and successive higher bottoms at points M, O, Q and S.

At the time of this writing, the stock price was trading around ₹3,250 levels, i.e. around Point T.

Trade Summary

1. Initiating a sell trade at ₹3,399 levels, i.e. after the price closes below the level earlier made by Point G at around ₹3,405.
2. Going long at ₹3,078 levels, i.e. buying after the price closes above the earlier Point N level of ₹3,066.
3. At the time of this writing, the stock price was trading around ₹3,250 levels. If the price of ₹3,250 is taken into account to calculate the mark to market profit / loss account, then trading higher top, higher bottom and lower top, lower bottom pattern formations in this example would have resulted in a profit of 493 points in a short span of only four months.

~

Example 24: HDIL

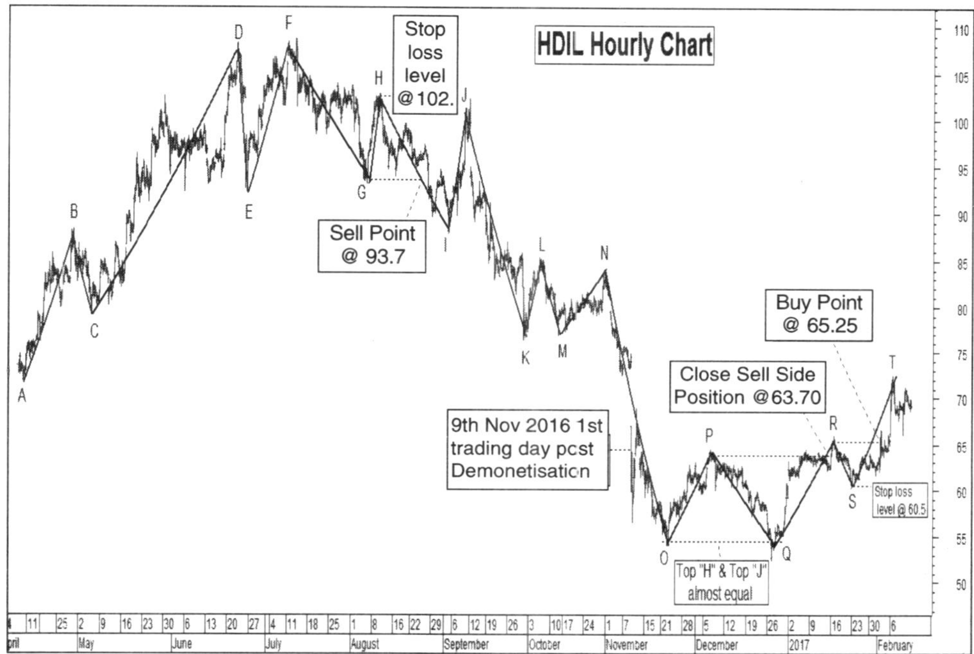

Figure 6.24: **Hourly, i.e. 60-minute, price chart of HDIL with profitable Dow trades highlighted**

~

Higher top, higher bottom and lower top, lower bottom pattern formations in the chart in Figure 6.24 reveal that HDIL's stock price initially rallied in a higher top, higher bottom pattern regime, making successive higher tops at points D and F, and successive higher bottoms at points C and E.

During this up move, the stock price made highs of around ₹107 levels on the upside, i.e. Point F, from where the stock price then declined and cracked the level made earlier by Point G at around ₹93.70 in its down move from Point H to Point I. One should have closed the buy position — and also initiated a fresh sell position, instead as and when the Point G level is cracked on the downside as the stock price then enters a lower top, lower bottom pattern regime. At the time of initiating the sell trade, the stop loss can be placed at the Point H levels, i.e. at about ₹102.50.

The stock price duly declined in a lower top, lower bottom pattern regime and made successive lower tops at points J, L, N and P and successive lower bottoms at points I, K and O.

Demonetisation was announced post market hours on 8 November 2016 when the stock price was trading significantly below Point M. The very next day, i.e. on 9 November 2016, though the price opened with a downside gap but it closed around the day's high. Thereafter, however, the stock price fell to the lows of around ₹55 levels on the downside, i.e. to Point O.

Very soon, thereafter, the stock price rallied strongly from the lows of Point O at around ₹55 levels and cracked the level made earlier by Point P at ₹63.70 in an up move from Point Q to Point R. One should close the sell position as and when the erstwhile Point P levels of ₹63.70 is cracked on the upside as the ongoing lower top, lower bottom pattern formation is then distorted.

Thereafter the stock price rose further and cracked the level made earlier by Point R at ₹65.25 levels in the up move from Point S to Point T. One should initiate a buy trade as and when the Point R level of ₹65.25 is cracked on the upside as the stock price enters a higher top, higher bottom pattern regime at that time. When buying, the stop loss can be placed at Point S, i.e. at ₹60.50 levels. The stock price then duly rallied higher to the highs of around Point T, i.e. around ₹70, where it was trading at the time of this writing.

Trade Summary

1. Initiating a sell trade at ₹92.50 levels, i.e. after the price closes below the Point G level of ₹93.70.
2. Exiting sell positions at ₹64 levels, i.e. exiting after the price closes above the Point P level of ₹63.70.
3. Initiating a buy trade at ₹66.15 levels, i.e. after the price closes above the Point R level of ₹65.25.
4. At the time of this writing, the stock price was trading around ₹70 levels. If the price of ₹70 is taken into account to calculate the mark to market profit / loss account, then trading higher top, higher bottom and lower top, lower bottom pattern formations in this example resulted in a profit of 32.35 points in the short span of around five months.

Example 25: HDFC

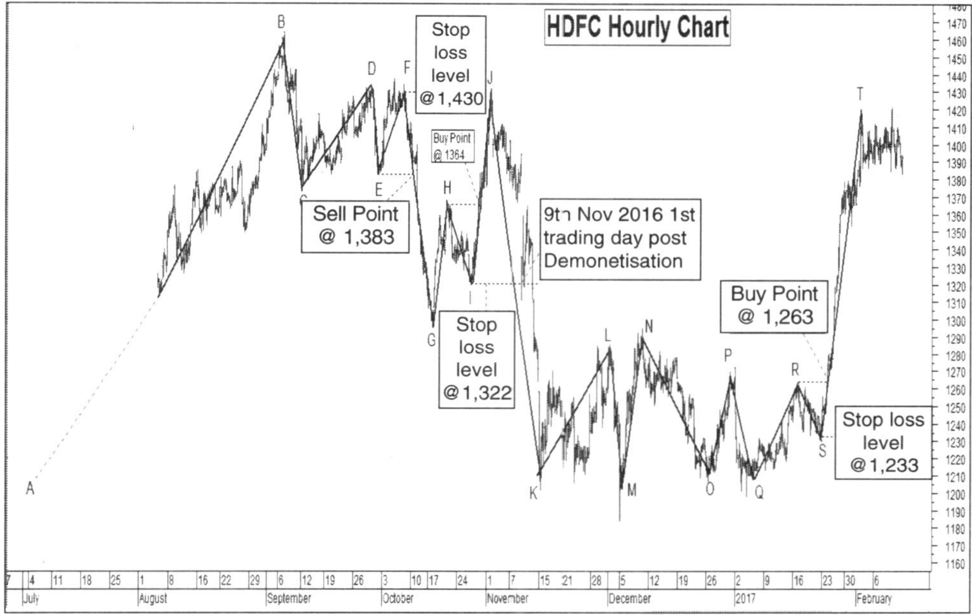

Figure 6.25: **Profitable Dow trades highlighted on the hourly, i.e. 60-minute, price chart of HDFC**

~

Figure 6.25 illustrates that the HDFC stock price initially rallied upward from Point A to Point B levels of about ₹1,460, from where it then declined and cracked the level made earlier by Point E at ₹1,383 levels in its down move from Point F to Point G. One should close the buy position, and initiate instead a fresh sell position as and when the Point E level of ₹1,383 is cracked on the downside as the stock price thereupon enters a lower top, lower bottom pattern regime. At the time of selling, the stop loss can be placed at Point F, i.e. at around ₹1,430 levels.

Thereafter the stock price duly declined to the lows of around ₹1,296 levels, i.e. to Point G, from where it turned and rallied up strongly. It cracked the level made earlier by Point H at around ₹1,364 in its up move from Point I to Point J. One should close the sell trade position — and also initiate instead a fresh buy position — as and when the earlier Point H level of ₹1,364 is cracked because the stock price enters a higher top, higher bottom pattern regime. At the time of buying, the stop loss can be placed at the Point I levels of about ₹1,322.

Thereafter the stock price rallied vertically to the highs of around ₹1,430 levels, i.e. to around Point J, from where it turned and began falling. It cracked the Point I level of ₹1,322 on the downside. One should close the buy side position as and when the Point I level of ₹1,322 is cracked as the stop loss at Point I gets triggered at that particular time.

Demonetisation was announced after market hours on 8 November 2016 when the stock was trading around Point J. The very next day, i.e. on 9 November 2016, the stock price opened with a downside gap but closed around the day's high. The stock price then declined to the lows of around ₹1,200 levels, i.e. to around Point M.

The stock price thereafter rallied strongly from the lows of around ₹1,200 and cracked the level made earlier by Point R at about ₹1,263 in its up move from Point S to Point T. One should initiate a buy trade as and when the Point R level of ₹1,263 is cracked since the stock price then enters a higher top, higher bottom pattern regime. At the time of buying, the stop loss can be placed at the Point S level of around ₹1,233.

Thereafter, the stock price rallied upward to the highs of around Point T, i.e. to around ₹1,400 levels where it was trading at the time of this writing.

Trade Summary

1. Initiating a sell trade at ₹1,367 levels, i.e. after the price closes below the Point E level of ₹1383.
2. Initiating a buy trade at ₹1,364.50 levels, i.e. after the price closes above the Point H level of ₹1,364.
3. Exiting the long positions at ₹1,317 levels, i.e. after the price closes below the Point I level of ₹1,322.
4. Initiating a buy trade at about ₹1,273 levels, i.e. after the price closes above the Point R level of ₹1,263.
5. At the time of this writing, the stock price was trading around ₹1,400 levels. If the price of ₹1,400 is taken into account to calculate the mark to market profit / loss account then trading higher top, higher bottom and lower top, lower bottom pattern formations in this example resulted in a profit of 82 points in the short span of around five months.

Example 26: Oracle Financial Services Software Ltd (OFSS)

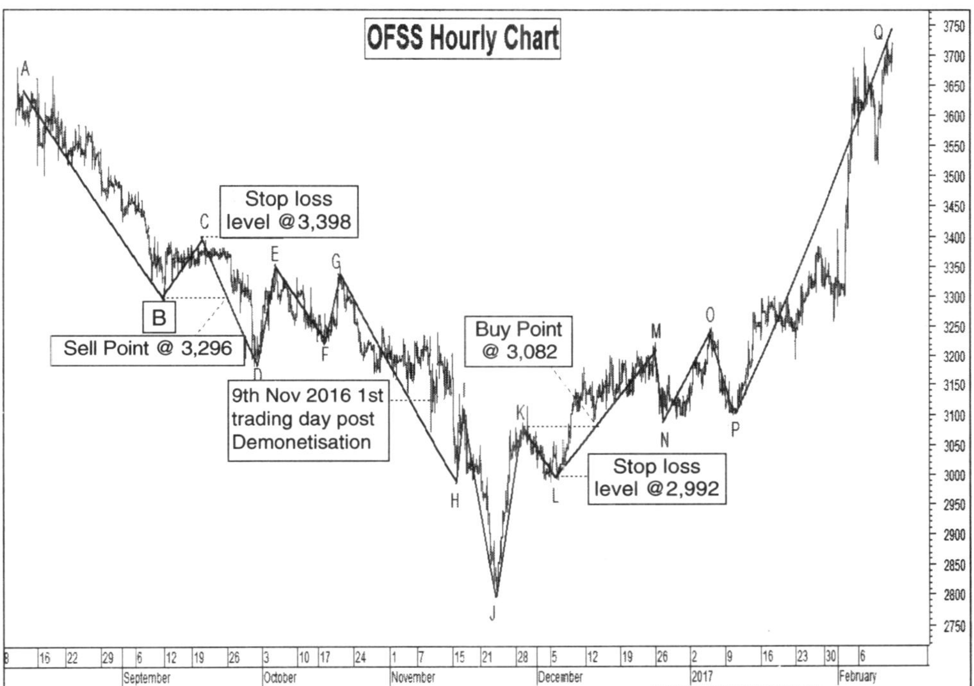

Figure 6.26: **Hourly, i.e. 60-minute, price chart of Oracle Financial Services Software with profitable Dow trades highlighted**

~

Higher top, higher bottom and lower top, lower bottom pattern formations in the case of Figure 6.26 would suggest selling the Oracle stock as and when the level made earlier by Point B at around ₹3,296 cracked in the down move from Point C to Point D since the price then enters a lower top, lower bottom pattern regime. At the time of selling, the stop loss can be placed at Point C, i.e. at around ₹3,398 levels.

Thereafter the stock price declined in a lower top, lower bottom pattern regime and made successive lower tops at points C, E, G and I and successive lower bottoms at points D, H and J.

Demonetisation was announced after market hours on 8 November 2016 when the stock price was trading significantly below Point F. The next day, i.e. on 9 November 2016, though the stock price opened with a downside gap but it closed above the day's low. Thereafter the stock price declined to the lows of around ₹2,800 levels on the downside, i.e. to Point J.

Post demonetisation, the stock price rallied strongly from these lows, i.e. from around Point J and cracked the Point K level of ₹3,082 in its up move from Point L to Point M.

One should close the sell position — and initiate instead a fresh buy position — as and when the Point K level of ₹3,082 is cracked on the upside because at that time the stock price enters a higher top, higher bottom pattern regime. At the time of buying, the stop loss can be placed at the Point L level of ₹2,992.

Thereafter the stock price rallied higher in a higher top, higher bottom pattern regime and made successive higher tops at points M, O and Q and successive higher bottoms at points N and P.

At the time of this writing, the stock price was trading around ₹3,650 levels, i.e. around Point Q.

Trade Summary

1. Initiating a sell trade at ₹3,286 levels, i.e. after the price closes below the Point B level of ₹3,296.
2. Initiating a buy trade at ₹3,102 levels, i.e. buying after the price closes above the Point K level of ₹3,082.
3. At the time of this writing, the stock price was trading around ₹3,650 levels. If this price is taken into account to calculate the mark to market profit / loss account, then trading higher top, higher bottom and lower top, lower bottom pattern formations would have resulted in a profit of 732 points in the short span of around five months.

~

Example 27: Maharashtra Seamless

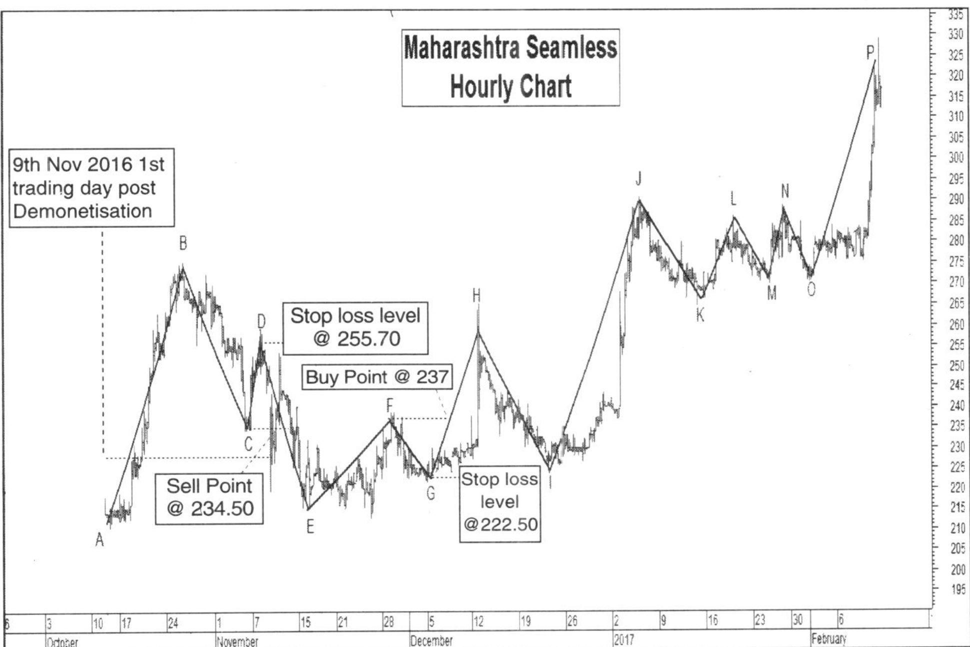

Figure 6.27: **Profitable Dow trades highlighted on the hourly, i.e. 60-minute, price chart of Maharashtra Seamless**

~

In the example in Figure 6.27, the stock price of Maharashtra Seamless initially rallied upward from Point A to Point B at ₹273 levels, from where it then declined and cracked the level made earlier by Point C at around ₹234.50 levels in the down move from Point D to Point E. One should close the buy position — and also initiate a fresh sell position — as and when the Point C level of ₹234.50 is cracked on the downside because at that time, the stock price enters a lower top, lower bottom pattern regime. At the time of selling, the stop loss can be placed at around the Point D level of ₹255.70.

Demonetisation was announced after market hours on 8 November 2016 when the stock price was trading around Point D. The next day, i.e. on 9 November 2016, though the stock price opened with a downside gap it closed around the day's high. Thereafter, the stock price fell to the lows of around ₹215 levels, i.e. to Point E, from where it rallied strongly upward and cracked the level made earlier by Point F at around ₹237 in its up move from Point G to Point H.

One should close the sell position — and also initiate a fresh buy position instead — as and when the Point F level of ₹237 is cracked on the upside as since the stock price then enters a higher top, higher bottom pattern regime. At the time of buying, the stop loss can be placed at Point G, i.e. at about ₹222.60 levels.

Thereafter the stock price rallied upward in a higher top, higher bottom pattern and made successive higher tops at points J and M and successive higher bottoms at points I, K, M and O.

At the time of this writing, the stock price was trading around ₹312 levels, i.e. at around Point P.

Trade Summary

1. Initiating a sell trade at ₹230 levels, i.e. after the price closes below the Point C level of ₹234.50.
2. Initiating a buy trade at ₹260 levels, i.e. after the price closes above the Point F level of ₹237.
3. At the time of this writing, the stock price was trading around ₹312 levels. If the price of ₹312 is taken into account to calculate the mark to market profit / loss account, then trading higher top, higher bottom and lower top, lower bottom pattern formations in this example would have resulted in a profit of 22 points in the short span of around four months.

~

Example 28: L&T

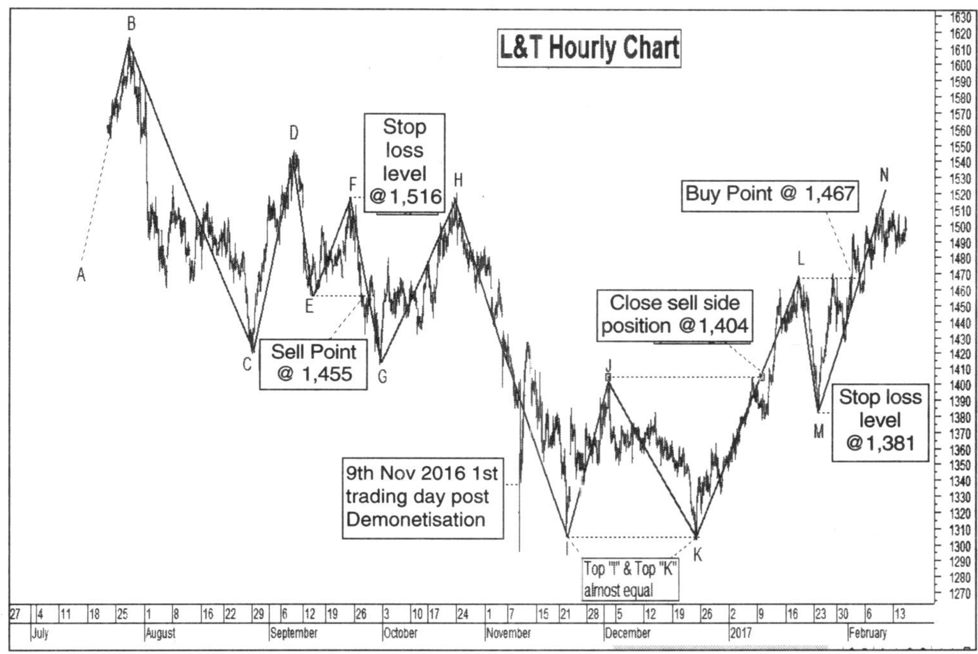

Figure 6.28: **Hourly, i.e. 60-minute, price chart of L&T with profitable Dow trades highlighted**

~

In Figure 6.28, the L&T stock price initially rose from Point A to Point B, i.e. to ₹1,611 levels on the upside, from where it then declined and cracked the level made earlier by Point E at around ₹1,455 in its down move from Point F to Point G. One should close the long position — and initiate instead a fresh sell position — as and when the Point E level of ₹1,455 is cracked on the downside as the stock price then enters a lower top, lower bottom pattern regime. At the time of selling, the stop loss could be placed at the Point F level of about ₹1,516.

Demonetisation was announced after market hours on 8 November 2016 when the L&T stock price was trading significantly below the Point G levels. The very next day, i.e. on 9 November 2016, though the stock price opened with a downside gap but it closed around the day's high.

Thereafter the stock price declined to the lows of around ₹1,309 levels, i.e. to Point I.

Demonetisation resulted in massive price volatility.

Post demonetisation, the stock price rallied strongly from the lows of around ₹1,309 levels, i.e. from around Point K, and cracked the earlier Point J level of ₹1,404 in its up move from Point K to Point L. One should close the sell trade as and when this occurs since the ongoing lower top, lower bottom pattern formation gets distorted at that time.

The stock price then rallied higher and cracked the level made earlier by Point L at about ₹1,467 in the up move from Point M to Point N. One should initiate a buy as and when the Point L level of ₹1,467 is cracked on the upside because the stock price then enters a higher top, higher bottom pattern regime. At the time of buying, the stop loss can be placed at Point M, i.e. at around ₹1,381 levels.

The stock price then rallied further to the higher to around Point L.

At the time of this writing, the stock price was trading around ₹1,497 levels, i.e. around Point N.

Trade Summary

1. Initiating a sell trade at ₹1,453 levels, i.e. selling after the price closes below the Point E level of ₹1,455.
2. Exiting sell side positions at ₹1,412 levels, i.e. after the price closes above the Point J level of ₹1,404.
3. Initiating a buy trade at ₹1,487 levels, i.e. after the price closes above the Point L level of ₹1,467,
4. At the time of this writing, the stock price trading around ₹1,497 levels. If the price of ₹1,497 is taken into account to calculate the mark to market profit / loss account, then trading higher top, higher bottom and lower top, lower bottom pattern formations in this example resulted in a profit of 51 points in the short span of around five months.

~

Example 29: Kalpataru Power

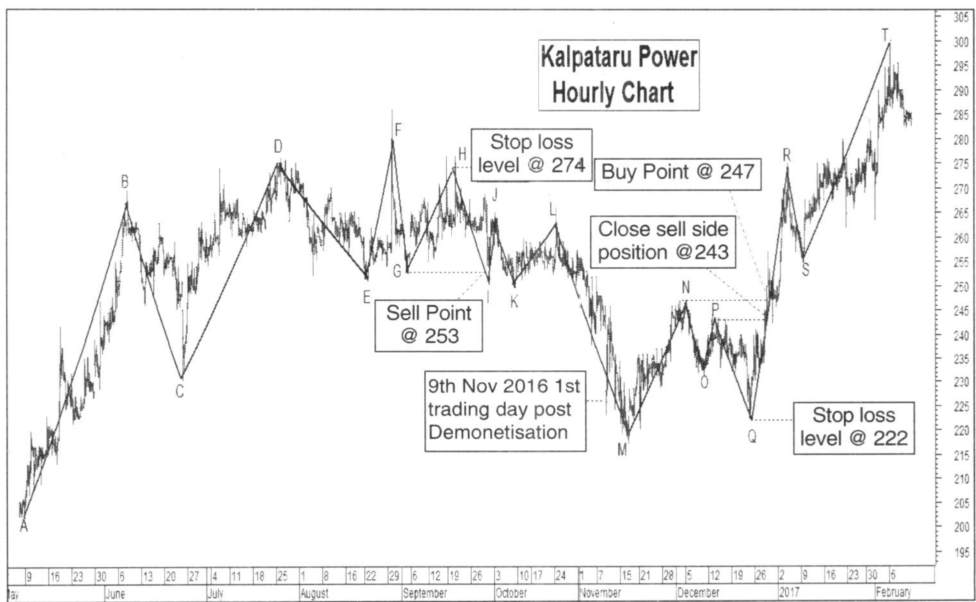

Figure 6.29: **Profitable Dow trades highlighted on the hourly, i.e. 60-minute, price chart of Kalpataru Power**

~

In Figure 6.29, the stock price of Kalpataru is seen initially rallying in a higher top, higher bottom pattern and making successive higher tops at points B, D and F, and successive higher bottoms at points C, E and G.

In this up move, the stock price made the highest high of around ₹280 levels at Point F, from where it then declined and cracked the level made earlier by Point G at around ₹254 levels in the down move from Point H to Point I. One should close the buy position — and also initiate instead a fresh sell position — as and when the earlier Point G level of around ₹254 is cracked on the downside. When this occurs, the stock price enters a lower top, lower bottom pattern regime. At the time of selling, the stop loss can be placed at about the Point H level of ₹274.

The stock price thereafter declined in a lower top, lower bottom pattern regime and made successive lower tops at points J and L and successive lower bottoms at points I, K and M.

Demonetisation was announced after market hours on 8 November 2016 when the Kalpataru stock price was trading significantly below Point K. The very next day, i.e. on 9 November 2016, the price opened with a downside gap but closed around the day's high. Thereafter, however, the stock price declined to the lows of around ₹220 levels, i.e. to Point M.

Demonetisation resulted in massive price volatility. Turning around from Point M, the price rose and cracked the Point P levels of ₹243 in its up move from Point Q to Point R. One should close the sell position as and when this occurs because ongoing lower top, lower bottom pattern formation gets distorted at this point.

The stock price thereafter rose further and cracked the level made earlier by Point N at around ₹247 levels in the up move from Point Q to Point R. One should initiate a buy trade as and when the ₹247 is cracked on the upside because the stock price thereupon enters a higher top, higher bottom pattern regime. At the time of buying, the stop loss can be placed at the Point Q level of about ₹222.

Thereafter the stock price rose in a higher top, higher bottom pattern and made successive higher tops at points R and T, and a successive higher bottom at Point S.

At the time of this writing, the stock price was trading around ₹287 levels, i.e. around Point T.

Trade Summary

1. Initiating a sell trade at ₹251.50 levels, i.e. after the price closes below the Point G level of around ₹253.
2. Exiting the sell positions at ₹244.50 levels, i.e. after the price closes above Point P level of ₹243.
3. Going long at ₹251 levels, i.e. after the price closes above the Point N level of around ₹247.
4. At the time of this writing, the stock price was trading around ₹287 levels. If the price of ₹287 is taken into account to calculate the mark to market profit / loss account, then trading higher top, higher bottom and lower top, lower bottom pattern formations in this study resulted in a profit of 43 points in the short span of around four months.

Example 30: JSW Steel

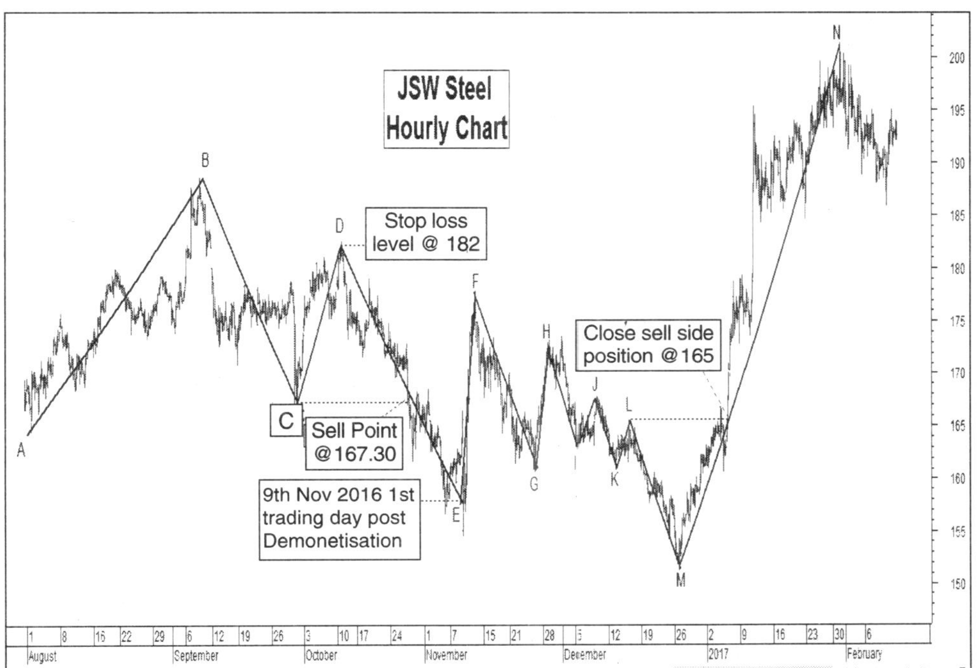

Figure 6.30: **Hourly, i.e. 60-minute, price chart of JSW Steel with profitable Dow trades highlighted**

~

Trading higher top, higher bottom and lower top, lower bottom pattern formations in the case of JSW Steel chart in Figure 6.30 suggests selling as and when the level made earlier by Point C at around ₹167.30 levels is cracked in the down move from Point D to Point E. This is because the stock price thereupon enters a lower top, lower bottom pattern regime. At the time of selling, the stop loss can be placed at the Point D levels around ₹182.

The stock price then duly declined in a lower top, lower bottom pattern and made successive lower tops at points F, H, J and L, and successive lower bottoms at points E and M.

Demonetisation was announced post market hours on 8 November 2016 when the stock price was trading a little above Point E. The next day, i.e. on 9 November 2016, the stock price opened with a downside gap but closed around the day's high. Thereafter, it declined to the lows of around ₹151 levels, i.e. to Point M.

The stock price then rallied strongly back up from the lows of around ₹151 levels, and cracked the level made earlier by Point L at around ₹165 levels in its up move from Point M to Point N.

One should close the sell / short position as and when the Point L level at ₹165 is cracked on the upside as the ongoing lower top, lower bottom pattern formation then gets distorted.

Thereafter the stock price rose to the highs of around Point N in a pattern which does not comply with the higher top, higher bottom pattern regime. As a result, Dow Theory practitioners would not have been able to buy in this up move.

Trade Summary

1. Initiating a sell trade at ₹167 levels, i.e. selling after the price closes below Point C at around ₹167.30 level.
2. Exiting all short positions at ₹167 levels, i.e. after the price closes above the Point N level of around ₹165.
3. Trading higher top, higher bottom and lower top, lower bottom pattern formations in this example would have resulted in a profit of zero points, i.e. basically no profit, no loss.

~

Example 31: Jindal Steel and Power

Figure 6.31: **Profitable Dow trades highlighted on the hourly, i.e. 60-minute, price chart of Jindal Steel and Power**

~

In Figure 6.31, the stock price initially rose from Point A to Point B, i.e. to about ₹91 levels. It then declined and cracked the level made earlier by Point C at ₹77.50 levels in the down move from Point D to Point E. One should close the long position — and instead initiate a fresh sell position as and when the Point C level of ₹77.50 is cracked on the downside. The stock price enters a lower top, lower bottom pattern regime when this occurs. At the time of selling, the stop loss can be placed at Point D, i.e. at around ₹89.40 levels.

Demonetisation was announced after market hours on 8 November 2016 when JSP's stock price was trading significantly below Point E. The next day, i.e. on 9 November 2016, the price opened with a downside gap but closed around the day's high. Thereafter, it declined further to the lows of around ₹65 levels, i.e. to Point I.

Post demonetisation, the stock price rallied strongly upward from the lows of around ₹65 levels, i.e. from around Point I and cracked the level made earlier by Point J at around ₹76.70 in an up move from Point K to Point L. One should close the sell position — and initiate instead a fresh buy position — as and when the Point J level of ₹76.70 is cracked on the upside because the stock price then enters a higher top, higher bottom pattern regime. At the time of buying, the stop loss can be placed at Point K, i.e. at about ₹65.20 levels.

Thereafter the stock price rallied to the highs of around ₹93 levels, i.e. to around Point L, where it was trading at the time of this writing.

Trade Summary

1. Initiating a sell trade at ₹75.55 levels, i.e. after the price closes below the Point E level of ₹77.50.
2. Buying at ₹78 levels, i.e. buying after the price closes above Point J at ₹76.70 levels.
3. At the time of this writing, the stock price was trading around ₹92 levels. If the price of ₹92 is taken into account to calculate the mark to market profit / loss account, then trading higher top, higher bottom and lower top, lower bottom pattern formations in this example resulted in a profit of 11.55 points in the short span of around five months.

~

Example 32: NOCIL

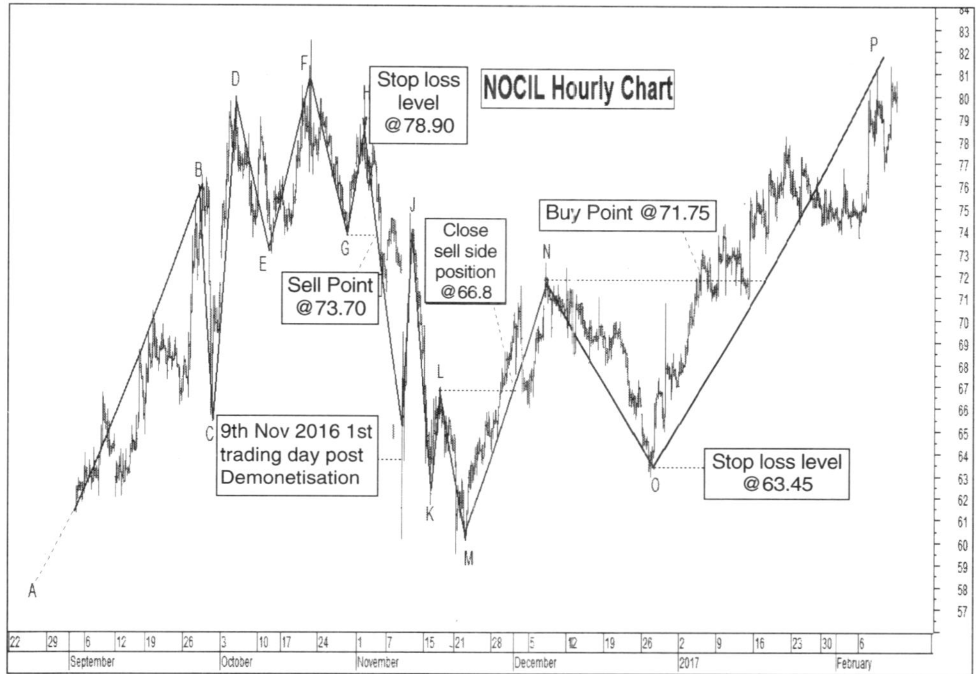

Figure 6.32: **Hourly, i.e. 60-minute, price chart of NOCIL with profitable Dow trades highlighted**

~

Higher top, higher bottom and lower top, lower bottom patterns in Figure 6.32 confirm that NOCIL stock price was rallying higher, making successive higher tops at points B, D and F, and successive higher bottoms at points C, E and G. During this up move, the stock price made a high of around ₹80 levels at Point F.

The stock price then declined and cracked the level made earlier by Point G at around ₹73.70 in its down move from Point H to Point I. One should close any open buy positions — and instead initiate a fresh short position as and when the Point G level of around ₹73.70 is cracked on the downside because the stock price thereupon enters a lower top, lower bottom pattern regime. At the time of selling, the stop loss can be placed at the Point H level of ₹78.90.

The stock price thereafter declined to the lows of around ₹60 in a lower top, lower bottom pattern regime and made successive lower tops at points J and L, and successive lower bottoms at points I, K and M.

Demonetisation was announced after market hours on 8 November 2016. At that time, the stock price was trading below Point G. The next day, i.e. on 9 November 2016, though the stock price opened with a downside gap but it closed around the day's high. Thereafter the stock price fell to the lows of around ₹60 levels, i.e. to Point M.

Demonetisation resulted in massive price volatility.

Post demonetisation, the stock price rallied strongly from the lows of around ₹60 levels, i.e. from Point M, and cracked the level made earlier by Point L at about ₹66.80 in the up move from Point M to Point N. One should close the sell position as and when the crack occurs on the upside because the ongoing lower top, lower bottom pattern formation is distorted when that occurs.

Thereafter the stock price rallied higher and cracked the earlier Point N levels of about ₹71.75 in the up move from Point O to Point P. One should buy as and when this happens because the stock price then enters a higher top, higher bottom pattern regime. At the time of buying, the stop loss can be placed at Point O, i.e. at about ₹63.45 levels. Thereafter the stock price rallied higher to the highs of around Point P.

At the time of this writing, the stock price was trading around ₹79 levels, i.e. around Point P.

Trade Summary

1. Initiating a sell trade at ₹72.70 levels, i.e. after the price closes below the Point G level of ₹73.70.
2. Exiting sell side positions at ₹67.60 levels, i.e. after the price closes above the Point L level of around ₹66.80.
3. Initiating a buy at ₹72.30 levels, i.e. after the price closes above the Point N level of about ₹71.75,
4. At the time of this writing, NOCIL's stock price was trading around ₹79 levels. If the price of ₹79 is taken into account to calculate the mark to market profit / loss account, then trading higher top, higher bottom and lower top, lower bottom pattern formations in this case resulted in a profit of 11.80 points in the short span of around four months.

Example 33: Maruti

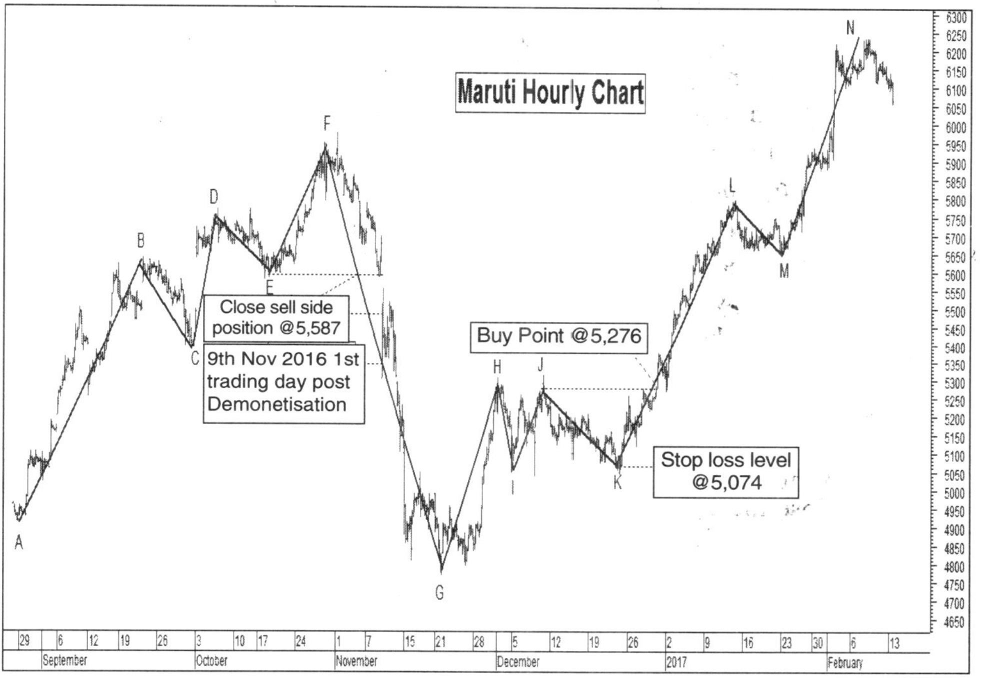

Figure 6.33: **Profitable Dow trades highlighted on the hourly, i.e. 60-minute, price chart of Maruti**

~

In Figure 6.33, the Maruti stock price is seen initially rallying in a higher top, higher bottom pattern regime, making successive higher tops at points B, D and F, and successive higher bottoms at points C and E.

Then, from the highs of Point F at around ₹5,930 levels, the stock price declined and cracked the level made earlier by Point E at ₹5,587 in the down move from Point F to Point G. One should close any open long side positions as and when this happens because the ongoing higher top, higher bottom pattern formation gets distorted at that time.

Thereafter, the stock price fell vertically to the lows of around ₹4,800 levels in a pattern which does not comply with the lower top, lower bottom pattern regime. As a result, Dow Theory practitioners would not have been able to sell in this down move.

Demonetisation was announced after market hours on 8 November 2016. At that time the stock price was trading significantly below Point E. The next day, i.e. on 9 November 2016, though the stock price opened with a downside gap, it closed around the day's high. Thereafter the stock price fell to the lows of around ₹4,800 levels, i.e. to Point G, from where it then rallied upward strongly and cracked the level made earlier by Point J at around ₹5,276 in the up move from Point K to Point L. One should buy as and when the Point J level at around ₹5,276 is cracked on the upside since the stock price then starts a higher top, higher bottom pattern. At the time of buying, the stop loss can be placed at Point K, i.e. at about ₹5,074 levels.

The price then duly rallied in a higher top, higher bottom pattern regime and made successive higher tops at points L and N, and a higher bottom at Point M.

At the time of this writing, the stock price was trading at around ₹6,150 levels, i.e. around Point N.

Trade Summary

1. Initiating a buy at ₹5,349 levels, i.e. buying after the price closes above Point J at ₹5,276 levels.
2. At the time of this writing, Maruti's stock price was trading around ₹6,150 levels. If the price of ₹6,150 is taken into account to calculate the mark to market profit / loss account, then trading higher top, higher bottom and lower top, lower bottom pattern formations in this example resulted in a profit of 801 points in the short span of around three months.

~

Example 34: JP Power

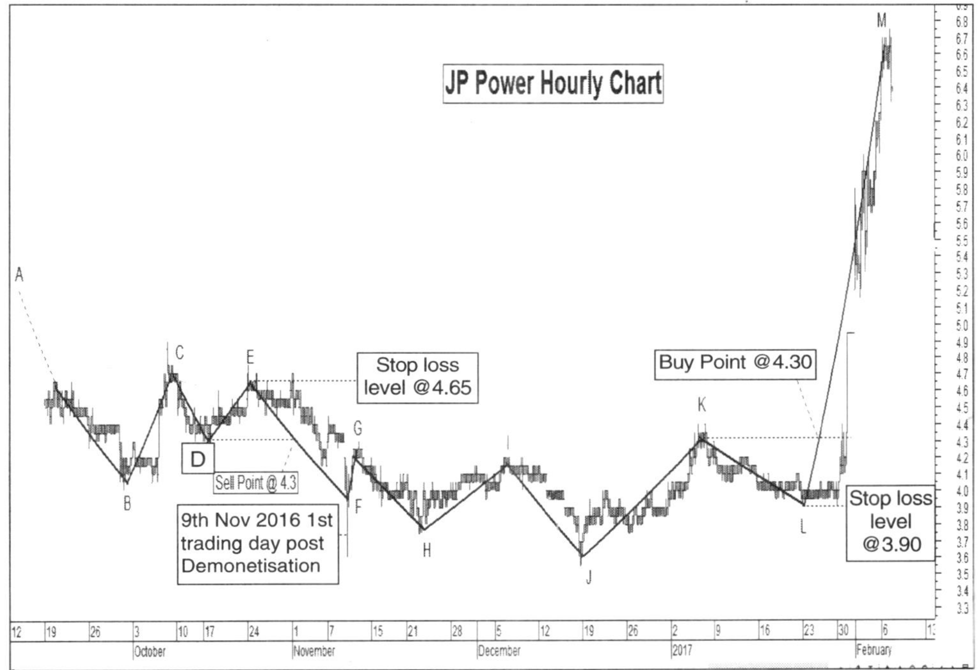

Figure 6.34: **Hourly, i.e. 60-minute, price chart of JP Power with profitable Dow trades highlighted**

~

Trading higher top, higher bottom and lower top, lower bottom pattern formations in the case of JP Power's chart in Figure 6.34 would suggest initiating a sell trade as and when the Point D level of ₹4.30 is cracked in the down move from Point E to Point F. At that time, the stock price enters a lower top, lower bottom pattern regime. The stop loss can be placed at Point E, i.e. at around ₹4.65 levels.

The stock price duly fell in a lower top, lower bottom pattern regime and made successive lower tops at points G and I, and successive lower bottoms at points H and J.

Demonetisation was announced after market hours on 8 November 2016. At that time, the stock price was trading significantly below Point D. The next day, i.e. on 9 November 2016, though the stock price opened with a downside gap it closed around the day's high but subsequently it declined to the lows of around ₹3.60 levels, i.e. to Point J.

Demonetisation resulted in massive price volatility.

From the lows of around ₹3.60 levels, i.e. from around Point J levels, the price rose strongly and cracked the Point K levels of about ₹4.30 in its up move from Point L to Point M.

One should close the short positions — and instead initiate a fresh buy position — when the Point K level of about ₹4.30 is cracked on the upside as the stock price then enters a higher top, higher bottom pattern regime. At the time of buying, the stop loss can be placed at around the Point L levels of ₹3.90.

The stock price then rallied further upward strongly to the highs of around Point M. At the time of this writing, the stock price was trading around ₹6.40 levels, i.e. around Point M.

Trade Summary

1. Initiating a sell trade at ₹4.25 levels, i.e. after the price closes below the Point D level of ₹4.30.
2. Initiating a buy trade at ₹4.95 levels, i.e. after the price closes above the Point K level of ₹4.30.
3. At the time of this writing, the stock price was trading around ₹6.40 levels. If the price of ₹6.40 is taken into account to calculate the mark to market profit / loss account, then trading higher top, higher bottom and lower top, lower bottom pattern formations in this example would have resulted in a profit of 0.75 points.

~

Example 35: Jindal Stainless

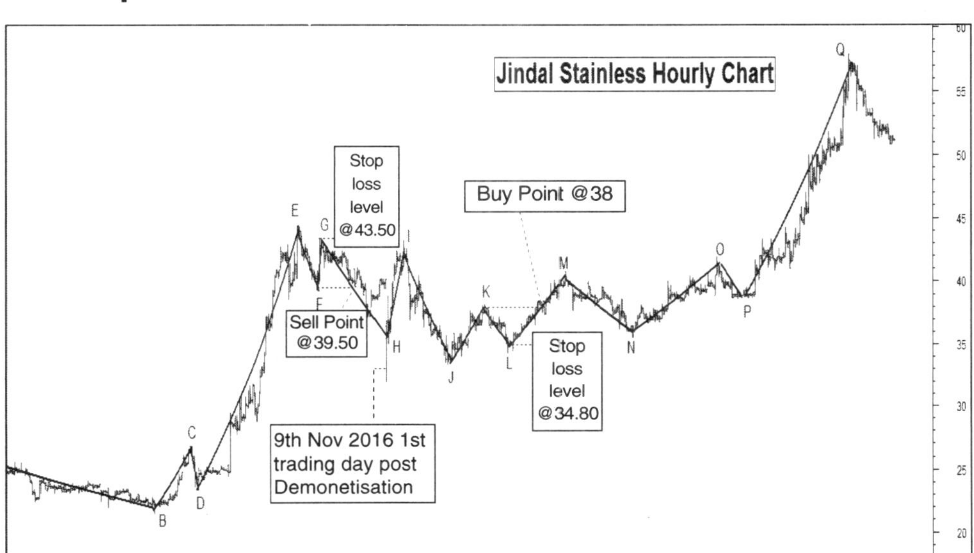

Figure 6.35: **Profitable Dow trades highlighted on the hourly, i.e. 60-minute, price chart of Jindal Stainless**

~

Figure 6.35 illustrates that the Jindal Stainless stock price was initially rising in a higher top, higher bottom pattern regime and made successive higher tops at points C and E, and successive higher bottoms at points D and F.

During this up move, the stock price made the high of around ₹44 levels at Point E, from where it then declined and cracked the level made earlier by Point F at around ₹39.50 in the down move from Point G to Point H. One should close the long positions — and initiate instead a fresh sell position as and when the Point F level at ₹39.50 is cracked on the downside. At that time, the stock price enters a lower top, lower bottom pattern regime. At the time of selling, the stop loss can be placed at the Point G levels around ₹43.50.

Thereafter the stock price declined in a lower top, lower bottom pattern regime and made a lower top at Point I and successive lower bottoms at points H and J.

Demonetisation was announced after market hours on 8 November 2016. At that time the Jindal Stainless stock was trading below Point F. The very next day, i.e. on 9 November 2016, the stock price opened with a downside gap but it finally closed around the day's high. The stock price thereafter declined to the lows of around ₹34 levels, i.e. to Point J.

Demonetisations resulted in massive price volatility. Post demonetisation, the stock price rallied upward strongly from the lows of around ₹34 levels, i.e. from around Point J, and cracked the level made earlier by Point K at about ₹38 levels in its up move from Point L to Point M. One should close the short positions — and instead initiate a fresh buy position — as and when the Point K level of around ₹38 is cracked on the upside. At that point, the stock price enters a higher top, higher bottom pattern regime. At the time of buying, the stop loss can be placed at the Point L levels of ₹34.80.

Thereafter the stock price rallied in a higher top, higher bottom pattern regime and made successive higher tops at points K, M, O, and Q, and successive higher bottoms at points N and P.

At the time of this writing, the stock price was trading around ₹54 levels, i.e. around Point Q.

Trade Summary

1. Initiating a sell trade at about ₹38.95 levels, i.e. after the price closes below Point F at ₹39.50 level.
2. Entering a buy trade at ₹38.45 levels, i.e. after the price closes above the Point K levels of ₹38.
3. At the time of this writing, the stock price was trading around ₹54 levels. If the price of ₹54 is taken into account to calculate the mark to market profit / loss account, then trading higher top, higher bottom and lower top, lower bottom pattern formations in this example would have resulted in a profit of 16.05 points in the short span of around four months.

~

Example 36: Tata Chemicals

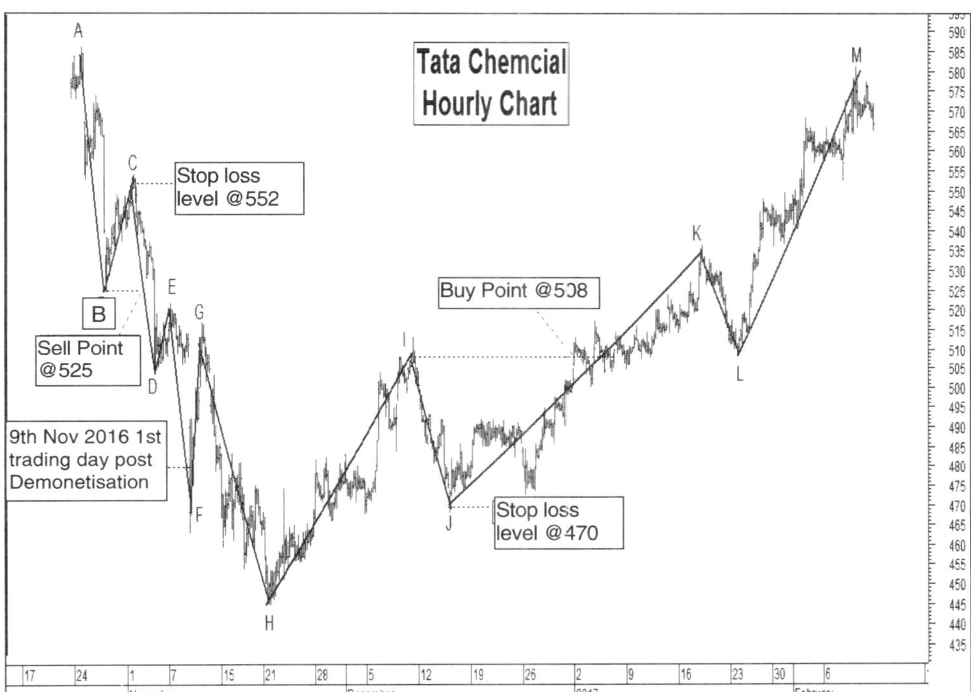

Figure 6.36: **Hourly, i.e. 60-minute, price chart of Tata Chemicals with profitable Dow trades highlighted**

~

Trading higher top, higher bottom and lower top, lower bottom pattern formations in the case of the chart of Tata Chemical in Figure 6.36 would suggest selling as and when the level made earlier by Point B at about ₹525 is cracked in the down move from Point C to Point D because the stock price subsequently enters a lower top, lower bottom pattern regime. At the time of selling, the stop loss can be placed at Point C, namely at around ₹552 levels.

The stock price then dutifully declined in a lower top, lower bottom pattern regime and made successive lower tops at points E and G, and successive lower bottoms points at D, F and H.

Demonetisation was announced after market hours on 8 November 2016 and resulted in massive price volatility. At that time the stock price was trading around Point E. The next day, i.e. on 9 November 2016, the stock price opened with a downside gap but finally closed around the day's high. The stock price thereafter fell to the lows of around ₹447 levels, i.e. to around Point H.

Post demonetisation, the stock price rallied upward strongly from the lows of around ₹447 levels, i.e. from Point H and cracked the level made earlier by Point I at around ₹508 in the up move from Point J to Point K. One should close one's short positions — and instead initiate a fresh buy position — as and when the Point I level of ₹508 is cracked on the upside as the stock price subsequently enters a higher top, higher bottom pattern regime. At the time of buying, the stop loss can be placed at the Point J level of around ₹470.

The stock price thereafter duly rose in a higher top, higher bottom pattern regime and made successive higher tops at points K and M and a higher bottom at Point L.

At the time of this writing, the stock price was trading around ₹570, i.e. around the Point M levels.

Trade Summary

1. Initiating a sell trade at ₹504 levels, i.e. after the price closes below the Point B level of around ₹525.
2. Going long at ₹510 levels, i.e. after the price closes above the Point I level of ₹508.
3. At the time of this writing, the stock price was trading around ₹570 levels. If the price of ₹570 is taken into account to calculate the mark to market profit / loss account, then trading higher top, higher bottom and lower top, lower bottom pattern formations in this example resulted in a profit of 54 points in the short span of around five months.

~

Example 37: SRF

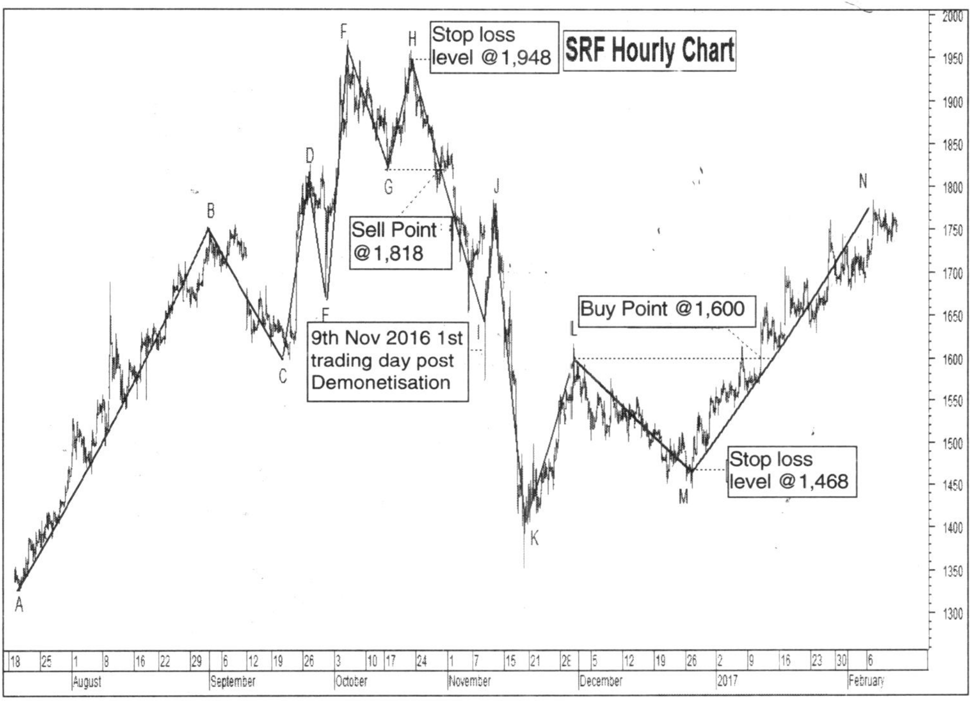

Figure 6.37: **Profitable Dow trades highlighted on the hourly, i.e. 60-minute, price chart of SRF**

~

In Figure 6.37, the stock price of SRF can initially be seen rallying in a higher top, higher bottom pattern regime, making successive higher tops at points B, D and F, and successive higher bottoms at points C, E and G.

From the highs of at around ₹1,960 levels, the stock price then declined and cracked the level made earlier by Point G at about ₹1,818 levels in its down move from Point H to Point I. One should close the buy side position — and instead initiate a fresh sell position — as and when the crack occurs on the downside because the stock thereupon enters a lower top, lower bottom pattern regime. At the time of selling, the stop loss can be placed at the Point H level of around ₹1,948.

The stock price thereafter declined in a lower top, lower bottom pattern regime and made successive lower tops at points J and L, and successive lower bottoms at points I and K.

Demonetisation was announced after market hours on 8 November 2016. The stock price was then trading significantly below Point G.

Demonetisation resulted in massive price volatility. The next day, i.e. 9 November 2016, the stock price opened with a downside gap but finally closed around the day's high. Thereafter the stock price fell to the lows of around ₹1,413 levels, i.e. to Point K.

Post demonetisation, the stock price rallied strongly from the lows of around ₹1,413 levels and cracked the level made earlier by Point L at about ₹1,600 levels in an up move from Point M to Point N.

One should close the short position — and instead initiate a fresh buy trade — as and when the Point L level of ₹1,600 is cracked on the upside because the stock thereafter price enters a higher top, higher bottom pattern regime. At the time of buying, the buy side stop loss can be placed at Point M, i.e. at about ₹1,468 levels.

The stock price thereafter rallied to the highs of around Point N at ₹1,735 levels, where it stood at the time of this writing.

Trade Summary

1. Initiating a sell trade at ₹1,803 levels, i.e. after the price closes below the Point G level of ₹1,818.
2. Going long at ₹1,612 levels, i.e. after the price closes above the Point L levels of ₹1,600.
3. At the time of this writing, the stock price was trading around ₹1,735 levels. If this price is taken into account to calculate the mark to market profit / loss account, then trading higher top, higher bottom and lower top, lower bottom pattern formations in this example resulted in a profit of 314 points in the short span of around four months.

~

Example 38: Sobha Developer

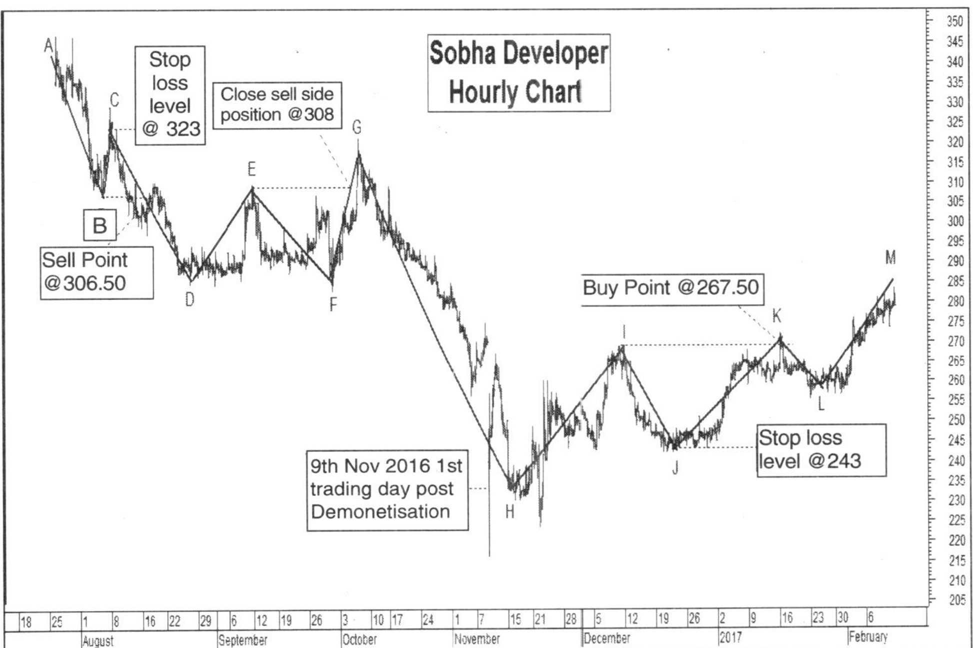

Figure 6.38: **Hourly, i.e. 60-minute, price chart of Sobha Developer with profitable Dow trades highlighted**

~

Trading higher top, higher bottom and lower top, lower bottom pattern formations in the case of the Sobha Developer chart in Figure 6.38 suggests selling as and when the level made earlier by Point B at around ₹306.50 is cracked in the down move from Point C to Point D. When this occurs, the stock price enters a lower top, lower bottom pattern regime. At the time of selling, the stop loss can be placed at Point C, i.e. at about ₹323 levels.

The stock price thereafter declined to the lows of around ₹285 levels, i.e. to Point D, from where it then rallied upward strongly and cracked the ₹308 levels made earlier by Point E in the up move from Point F to Point G. One should close the short position as and when this crack occurs as the ongoing lower top, lower bottom pattern formation then gets distorted.

From the highs of around ₹316 levels, i.e. from around Point G, the stock price fell to the lows of around ₹232 levels, i.e. to Point H in a pattern that does not comply with the lower top, lower bottom pattern regime. As a result, the Dow Theory practitioners would not have been able to sell in this down move.

Demonetisation was announced post market hours on 8 November 2016. At that time, the Sobha Developer price was trading significantly below Point F. The very next day, i.e. on 9 November 2016, it opened with a downside gap but closed around the day's high. Thereafter the stock price declined to the lows of around ₹232 levels, i.e. to Point H, from where it rallied strongly upward and cracked the level made earlier by Point I at about ₹267.50 levels in the up move from Point J to about Point K. One should buy as and when the ₹267.50 level is cracked on the upside because the stock price then enters a higher top, higher bottom pattern regime. At the time of buying, the stop loss was placed at the Point J level of about ₹243.

The stock price thereafter rallied in a higher top, higher bottom pattern regime and made successive higher tops at points K and M, and a higher bottom at Point L.

At the time of this writing, the stock price was trading at around ₹285 levels, i.e. at around Point M.

Trade Summary

1. Selling at ₹305.75 levels, i.e. after the price closes below the Point B level of ₹306.50.
2. Exiting sell positions at ₹312 levels, i.e. after the price closes above the Point E levels of ₹308.
3. Initiating a buy trade at ₹270 levels, i.e. after the price closes above the Point I level of ₹267.50.
4. At the time of this writing, the stock price was trading around ₹285 levels. If this price is taken into account to calculate the mark to market profit / loss account, then trading higher top, higher bottom and lower top, lower bottom pattern formations in this example resulted in a profit of 8.75 points in the short span of around four months.

Example 39: Siemens

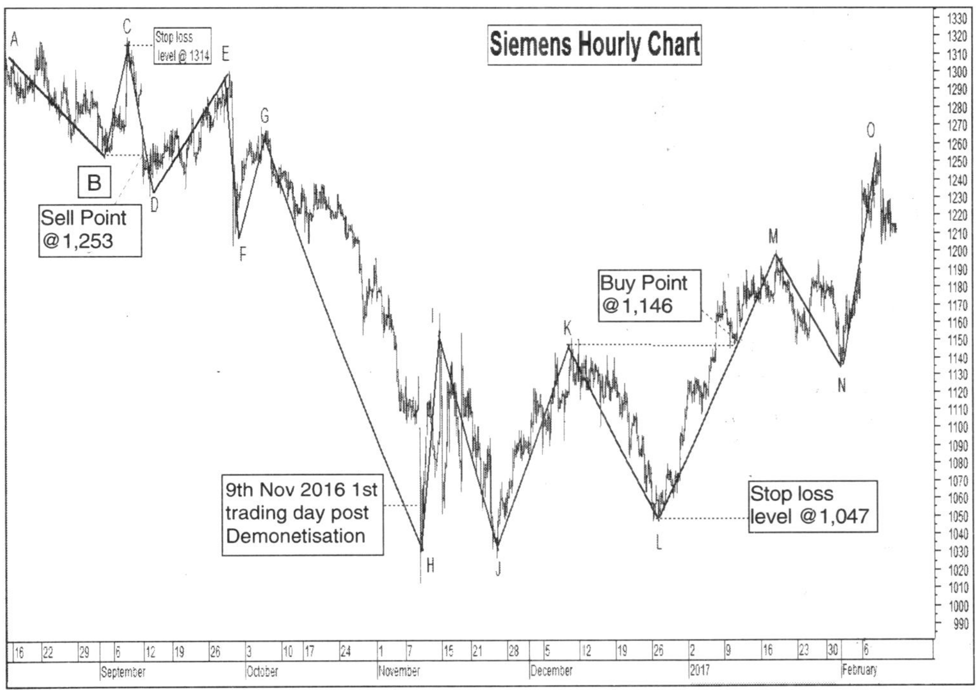

Figure 6.39: **Profitable Dow trades highlighted on the hourly, i.e. 60-minute, price chart of Siemens**

~

Trading higher top, higher bottom and lower top, lower bottom pattern formations in the case of Siemens' hourly chart in Figure 6.39 suggests selling as and when the level made earlier by Point B at about ₹1,243 levels is cracked in the down move from Point C to Point D. This is because the stock price then enters a lower top, lower bottom pattern regime. At the time of selling, the stop loss can be placed at Point C, i.e. at around ₹1,314 levels.

Thereafter the stock price declined in a lower top, lower bottom pattern regime and made successive lower tops at points E and G, and successive lower bottoms at points D, F and H.

Demonetisation was announced after market hours on 8 November 2016. At that time the price of Siemens was trading significantly below Point F. Demonetisation resulted in massive price volatility. The very next day, i.e. on 9 November 2016, the price opened with a downside gap but finally closed around the day's high. Thereafter, the stock price declined to the lows of around ₹1,035 levels, i.e. to around Point H, from where it rallied strongly upward and cracked the level made earlier by Point K at around ₹1,146 levels in the up move from Point L to Point M.

One should close the sell position — and instead initiate a fresh buy position as and when the level made earlier by Point K at around ₹1,146 is cracked on the upside since the stock price thereupon enters a higher top, higher bottom pattern regime. At the time of buying, the stop loss can be placed at Point L, i.e. at around ₹1,047 levels.

The stock price thereafter rallied in a higher top, higher bottom pattern regime and made successive higher tops at points M and O, and a higher bottom at Point N.

At the time of this writing, the stock price was trading around Point O, i.e. at around ₹1,225 levels.

Trade Summary

1. Selling at ₹1,246 levels, i.e. after the price closes below the Point B level of ₹1,253.
2. Initiating a buy trade at ₹1,163 levels, i.e. after the price closes above Point K level of around ₹1,146.
3. At the time of this writing, the stock price was trading around ₹1,225 levels. If this price is taken into account to calculate the mark to market profit / loss account, then trading higher top, higher bottom and lower top, lower bottom pattern formations in this case would have resulted in a profit of 145 points in the short span of around five months.

~

Example 40: Reliance Infrastructure

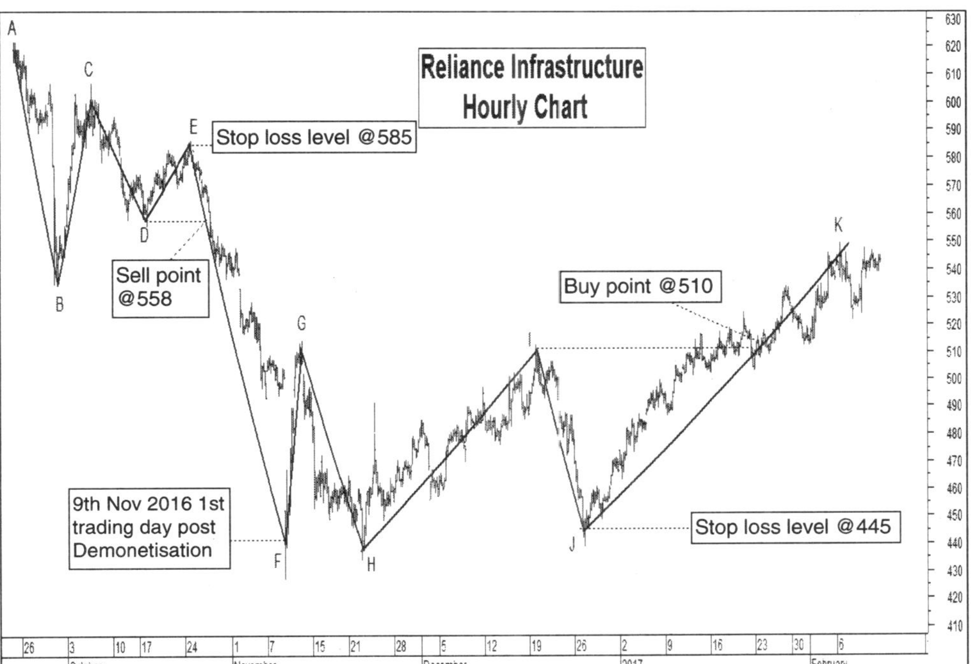

Figure 6.40: **Hourly, i.e. 60-minute, price chart of Reliance Infrastructure with profitable Dow trades highlighted**

~

Trading higher top, higher bottom and lower top, lower bottom pattern formations in the case of the Reliance Infrastructure chart in Figure 6.40 suggests selling as and when the level made earlier by Point D at around ₹558 levels is cracked in the down move from Point E to Point F. When this occurs, the stock price enters a lower top, lower bottom pattern regime. At the time of selling, the stop loss can be placed at Point E levels around ₹585.

Thereafter the stock price declined in a lower top, lower bottom pattern regime and made a lower top at Point G and a lower bottom at Point F.

Demonetisation was announced after market hours on 8 November 2016. At that time the stock price was trading significantly below Point D. Demonetisation resulted in massive price volatility. The very next day, i.e. on 9 November 2016, the stock price opened with a downside gap but closed around the day's high. Thereafter the stock price declined to the lows of around ₹440 levels, i.e. to around Point H, from where it rallied strongly upward and cracked the earlier Point I levels of ₹510 in its up move from Point J to Point K. One should close the short position, and instead initiate a fresh buy trade as and when the Point I level is cracked on the upside as the stock price then enters a higher top, higher bottom pattern regime. At the time of buying, the stop loss can be placed at Point J, i.e. at about ₹445 levels.

Thereafter, the stock price rose to the highs of around Point K on the upside, where it was trading at the time of this writing,

Trade Summary

1. Selling at ₹556 levels, i.e. after the price closes below the Point D levels of ₹558.
2. Buying at ₹512 levels, i.e. after the price closes above the Point I levels of ₹510.
3. At the time of this writing, the stock price was trading around ₹543. If this price is taken into account to calculate the mark to market profit / loss account, then trading higher top, higher bottom and lower top, lower bottom pattern formations in this example resulted in a profit of 75 points in the short span of around four months.

~

Example 41: Reliance Industries

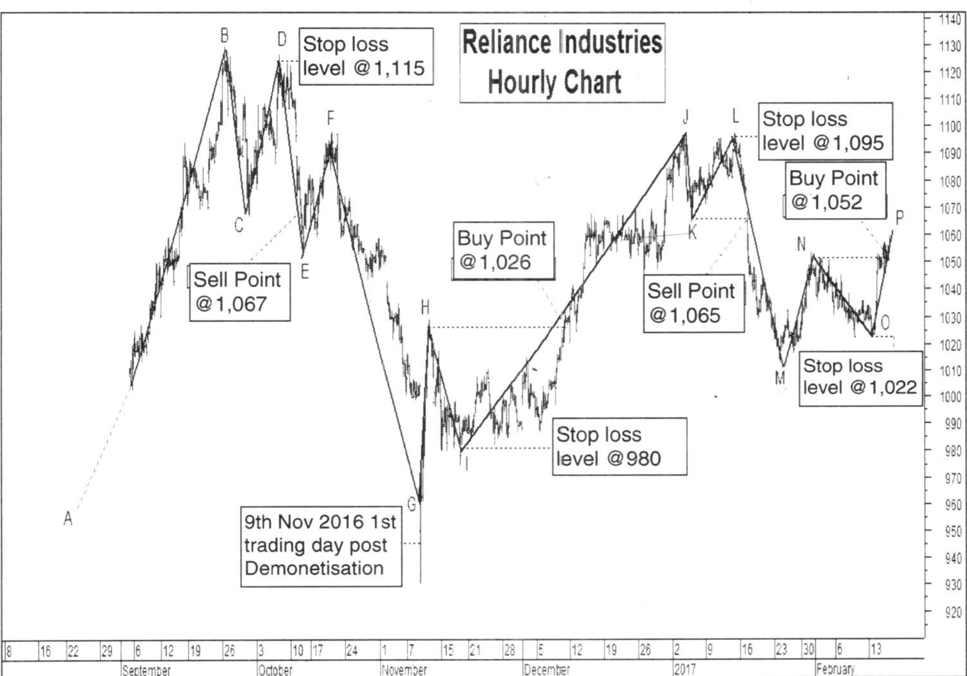

Figure 6.41: **Profitable Dow trades highlighted on the hourly, i.e. 60-minute, price chart of Reliance Industries**

~

Higher top, higher bottom and lower top, lower bottom pattern formations in Figure 6.41 illustrate how the Reliance stock price initially from Point A to Point B. Then, from the highs of around Point B the stock price declined and cracked the Point C levels made earlier at ₹1,067 in the down move from Point D to Point E. One should close the buy position — and instead initiate a fresh sell trade as and when this crack occurs on the downside because the stock price thereupon enters a lower top, lower bottom pattern regime. At the time of initiating the sell trade, the stop loss can be placed at Point D at ₹1,115 levels.

The stock price thereafter declined in a lower top, lower bottom pattern regime and made a lower top at Point F, and successive lower bottoms at points E and G.

Demonetisation was announced after market hours on 8 November 2016, when the Reliance stock price was trading significantly below the level of the earlier bottom at Point E. Demonetisation resulted in massive price volatility. The next day, i.e. on 9 November 2016, the stock price opened with a downside gap but closed around the day's high. Thereafter the stock price fell to the lows of around ₹975 levels, i.e. to Point I, from where it rose strongly upward and cracked the level made earlier by Point H at around ₹1,027 levels in the up move from Point I to Point J. When this crack occurs, one should close the sell position — and instead initiate a fresh buy position because the stock price thereupon enters a higher top, higher bottom pattern regime. At the time of buying, the stop loss can be placed at the Point I levels of about ₹980.

The stock price climbed to the highs of around ₹1,097 levels, i.e. to around Point J, from where it declined and cracked the level made earlier by Point K at ₹1,065 levels in the down move from Point L to Point M. One should close the buy trade — and instead initiate a fresh sell position because the stock price thereupon enters a lower top, lower bottom pattern regime. At the time of selling, the stop loss can be placed at Point L, i.e. at ₹1,095 levels.

The stock price declined further to the lows of around ₹1,010 levels, i.e. to around Point M, but from there it rallied upward strongly and cracked the level made earlier by Point N at about ₹1,052 in the up move from Point O to Point P. One should close one's sell position — and instead initiate a fresh buy position — as and when the ₹1,052 level is cracked on the upside because the stock price thereupon enters a higher top, higher bottom pattern regime. At the time of buying, the stop loss can be placed at Point O, i.e. at about ₹1,022 levels.

At the time of this writing, the stock price was trading around ₹1,060 levels.

Trade Summary

1. Selling at ₹1,066 levels, i.e. after the price closes below the Point C level of ₹1,067.
2. Buying at ₹1,027 levels, i.e. after the price closes above the Point H level of ₹1,026.

3. Selling at ₹1,058 levels, i.e. after the price closes below the Point K level of ₹1,065.
4. Buying at ₹1,055 levels, i.e. after the price closes (above the Point N levels of ₹1,052.
5. At the time of this writing, the stock price of Reliance Industries was trading around ₹1,060 levels. If the price of ₹1,060 is taken into account to calculate the mark to market profit / loss account, then trading higher top, higher bottom and lower top, lower bottom pattern formations in this example resulted in a profit of 78 points in the short span of around four months.

~

Example 42: Reliance Capital

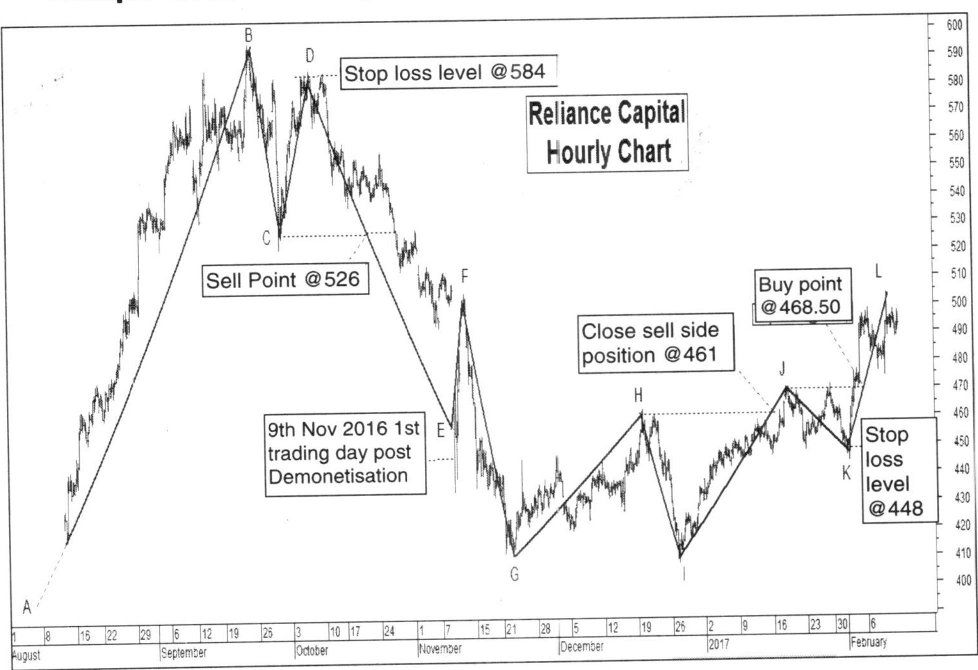

Figure 6.42: **Hourly, i.e. 60-minute, price chart of Reliance Capital with profitable Dow trades highlighted**

~

Higher top, higher bottom and lower top, lower bottom pattern formations in Figure 6.42 demonstrate that Reliance Capital's stock price initially rallied from Point A to Point B.

From the highs of around Point B, the stock price then declined and cracked the level made earlier by Point C at around ₹526 in the down move from Point D to Point E. When this occurs, one should close the buy position and initiate a fresh sell trade instead because the stock price thereupon enters a lower top, lower bottom pattern regime. At the time of selling, the stop loss can be placed at the Point D level of around ₹584.

The stock price thereafter duly declined in a lower top, lower bottom pattern regime and made successive lower tops at points F and H, and successive lower bottoms at points E, G and I.

Demonetisation was announced after market hours on 8 November 2016. At that time, the stock price was trading significantly below the level earlier made by Point C. Demonetisation resulted in massive price volatility. The next day, i.e. on 9 November 2016, the stock price opened with a downside gap but closed around the day's high. The price thereafter declined to the lows of around ₹410 levels, i.e. to around Point I, from where it rallied strongly upward and cracked the level made earlier by Point H at around ₹461 levels in the up move from Point I to Point J. One should close the sell trade position as and when the Point H levels of around ₹461 made earlier is cracked on the upside because at that time, the ongoing lower top, lower bottom pattern formation gets distorted.

The stock price thereafter rallied higher and cracked the level made earlier by Point J at ₹468.50 levels in its up move from Point K to Point L. One should initiate a buy trade as and when the level made earlier by Point J at about ₹468.50 levels is cracked on the upside because the stock price thereupon enters a higher top, higher bottom pattern regime. At the time of buying, the stop loss can be placed at the Point K levels, i.e. at about ₹448. The stock price thereafter rallied to the highs of around Point L.

At the time of this writing, the stock price was trading around ₹495 levels, around Point L.

Trade Summary

1. Initiating a sell trade at ₹524 levels, i.e. after the price closes below the Point C level of ₹526.

2. Exiting sell positions at ₹464 levels, i.e. after the price closes above the Point H level of ₹461.
3. Buying at ₹472 levels, i.e. buying after the price closes above the Point T levels of ₹468.50.
4. At the time of this writing, the stock price was trading around ₹495 levels. If the price of ₹495 is taken into account to calculate the mark to market profit / loss account, then trading higher top, higher bottom and lower top, lower bottom pattern formations in this study resulted in a profit of 83 points in the short span of around four months.

~

Example 43: PTC India

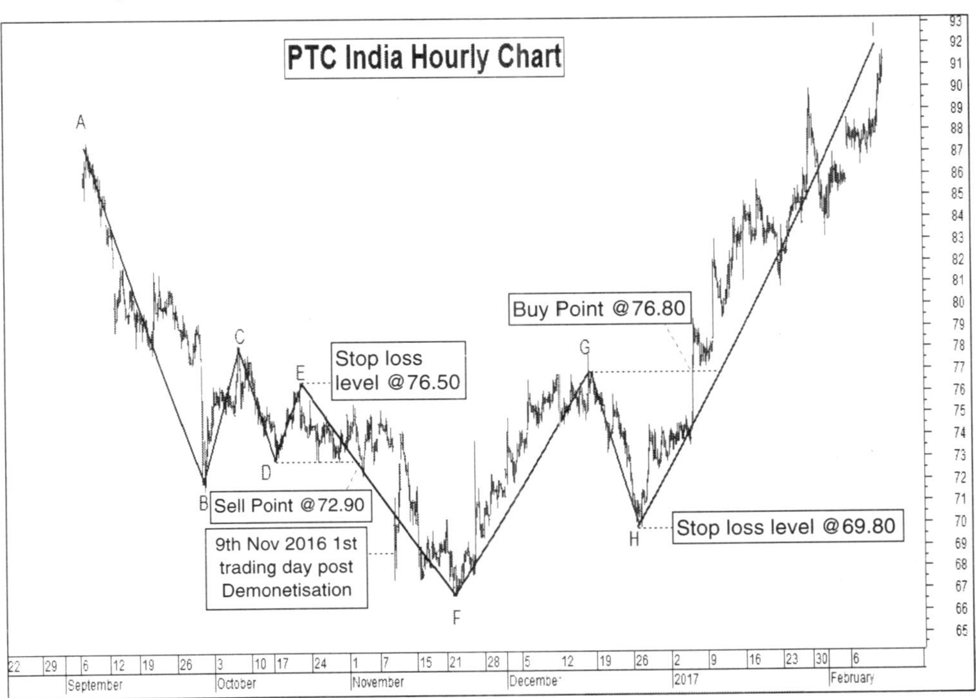

Figure 6.43: **Profitable Dow trades highlighted on the hourly, i.e. 60-minute, price chart of PTC India**

~

Trading higher top, higher bottom and lower top, lower bottom pattern formations in the case of PTC India's chart in Figure 6.43 would suggest selling as and when the level made earlier by Point D at ₹72.90 levels is cracked in the down move from Point E to Point F, whereupon the stock price enters a lower top, lower bottom pattern regime. At the time of selling, the stop loss can be placed at near the Point E levels of about ₹76.50.

The stock price thereafter declined in a lower top, lower bottom pattern regime and made successive lower tops at points C and E, and successive lower bottoms at points D and F.

Demonetisation was announced after market hours on 8 November 2016, when the stock price was trading around Point D. Demonetisation resulted in massive price volatility. The very next day, i.e. on 9 November 2016, the stock price opened with a downside gap but closed around the day's high. Thereafter the stock price declined to the lows of around ₹67 levels on the downside, i.e. to around Point F, from where the stock price rallied upward strongly and cracked the level made earlier by Point G in its up move from Point H to Point I. One should close the sell trade position — and instead initiate a fresh buy position as and when the level made earlier by Point G at around ₹76.80 levels is cracked on the upside whereupon the stock price, enters a higher top, higher bottom pattern regime. At the time of buying, the stop loss can be placed at the Point H levels of ₹69.80.

Thereafter the stock price rallied to the highs of around Point I on the upside. At the time of this writing, the stock price was trading around ₹90 levels, i.e. around Point I.

Trade Summary

1. Initiating a sell trade at ₹72.50 levels, i.e. selling after the price closes below the Point D levels of ₹72.90.
2. Buying at ₹77 levels i.e. after the price closes above Point G at ₹76.80 levels.
3. At the time of this writing, the stock price was trading around ₹90 levels. If the price of ₹90 is taken into account to calculate the mark to market profit / loss account, then trading higher top, higher bottom and lower top, lower bottom pattern formations in this study resulted in a profit of ₹8.50 points in the short span of around five months.

Example 44: Sterlite Technologies

Figure 6.44: **Hourly, i.e. 60-minute, price chart of Sterlite Technologies with profitable Dow trades highlighted**

~

Higher top, higher bottom and lower top, lower bottom pattern formations in Figure 6.44 reveal that the stock price of Sterlite Technologies initially rallied from Point A to Point B. Then, from the highs of around Point B, the price declined almost vertically to Point C on the downside, from where the price then rallied to Point D on the upside.

Demonetisation was announced after market hours on 8 November 2016 when the stock price was trading around Point D. The very next day, i.e. on 9 November 2016, the stock price opened with a downside gap but eventually closed around the day's high.

Thereafter the stock price rallied strongly from the lows of around ₹95 levels, i.e. from around Point G, and cracked the level made earlier by Point F at ₹99.95 levels in the up move from Point G to Point K. One should initiate a buy trade as and when the Point F level of ₹99.95 is cracked on the upside. The stock price thereupon enters a higher top, higher bottom pattern regime. At the time of buying, the stop loss can be placed at about Point G levels around ₹95 levels.

Thereafter, the stock price rose to the highs of around Point K on the upside. At the time of this writing, the stock price was trading around ₹134 levels, i.e. around Point K.

Trade Summary

1. Buying at ₹101.30 levels, i.e. after the price closes above Point F at ₹99.95 levels.
2. At the time of this writing, the stock price was trading around ₹134 levels. If the price of ₹134 is taken into account to calculate the mark to market profit / loss account, then trading higher top, higher bottom and lower top, lower bottom pattern formations in this case resulted in a profit of 32.70 points in the short span of around two months.

~

Example 45: Zee Entertainment

Figure 6.45: **Profitable Dow trades highlighted on the hourly, i.e. 60-minute, price chart of Zee Entertainment**

~

Trading higher top, higher bottom and lower top, lower bottom pattern formations in Figure 6.45 suggests selling Zee Entertainment as and when the level made earlier by Point D at about ₹500.40 levels is cracked in the down move from Point E to Point F. At that time, the stock price enters a lower top, lower bottom pattern regime. At the time of selling, the stop loss can be placed at Point E, i.e. at around ₹523.60 levels.

Thereafter the stock price declined in a lower top, lower bottom pattern regime and made a lower top at Point G and successive lower bottoms at points F and H.

Demonetisation was announced after market hours on 8 November 2016 when the stock price was trading around Point D. Demonetisation resulted in massive price volatility. The very next day, i.e. on 9 November 2016, the stock price opened with a downside gap but eventually closed around the day's high. Thereafter the stock price declined to the lows of around ₹430 levels on the downside, i.e. to around Point L.

Post demonetisation, the stock price rallied upward strongly from the lows of around ₹430 levels, i.e. from around Point L, and cracked the level made earlier by Point K at around ₹463.85 levels in the up move from Point L to Point M. One should close the sell / short position as and when the Point K level is cracked on the upside because the ongoing lower top, lower bottom pattern formation gets distorted at that point.

Thereafter the stock price rallied higher to the highs of around Point N in a pattern which does not comply with the higher top, higher bottom regime. As a result, Dow Theory practitioners were not able to buy during this up move.

Trade Summary

1. Selling at ₹497.40 levels, i.e. after the price closes below the Point D levels of ₹500.40.

2. Closing the sell side trades at ₹471.50 levels, i.e. exiting after the price closes above the Point K level at ₹465.35.

3. Trading higher top, higher bottom and lower top, lower bottom pattern formations in this study resulted in a profit of 25.90 points in the short span of around two months.

~

Example 46: United Spirits

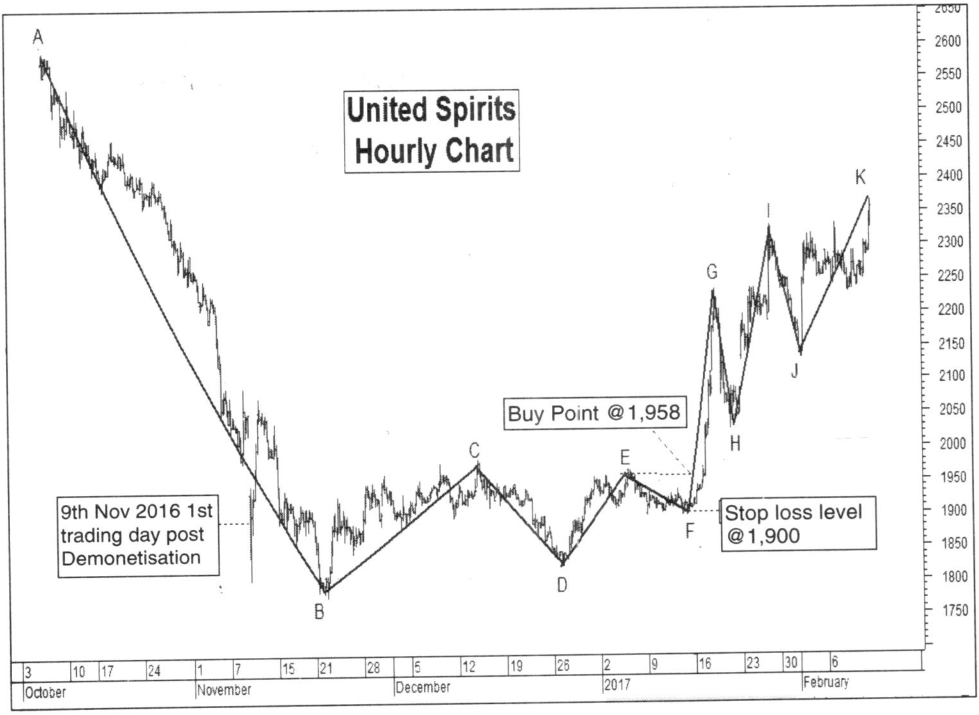

Figure 6.46: **Hourly, i.e. 60-minute, stock price chart of United Spirits with profitable Dow trades highlighted**

~

In Figure 6.46, the stock price of United Spirits initially declined from Point A to Point B in a pattern which does not comply with the lower top, lower bottom pattern regime. As a result, Dow Theory practitioners would not have been able to sell short during this down move.

Demonetisation was announced post market hours on 8 November 2016 when the stock price was trading significantly below Point A. The very next day, i.e. on 9 November 2016, the stock price opened with a downside gap but ultimately closed around the day's high, from where it then declined to the lows of around ₹1,788 levels on the downside, i.e. to around Point B.

The price then turned around and rallied strongly upward from the lows of around Point B and cracked the level made earlier by Point E at ₹1,958 levels in its up move from Point F to Point G. One should buy as and when the Point E level of ₹1,958 is cracked on the upside as the price thereupon enters a higher top, higher bottom pattern regime. At the time of buying, the stop loss can be placed at Point F, i.e. at about ₹1,900 levels.

Thereafter the stock price rallied in a higher top, higher bottom pattern regime and made successive higher tops at points G, I and K, and successive higher bottoms at points H and J.

At the time of this writing, the stock price was trading around ₹2,350 levels, i.e. around Point K.

Trade Summary

1. Buying at ₹1,962 levels, i.e. after the price closes above the Point E level of ₹1,958.
2. At the time of this writing, the stock price was trading around ₹2,350 levels. If this price of ₹2,350 is taken into account to calculate the mark to market profit / loss account, then trading higher top, higher bottom and lower top, lower bottom pattern formations in this example resulted in a profit of 388 points in the short span of around one month.

~

Example 47: Titan

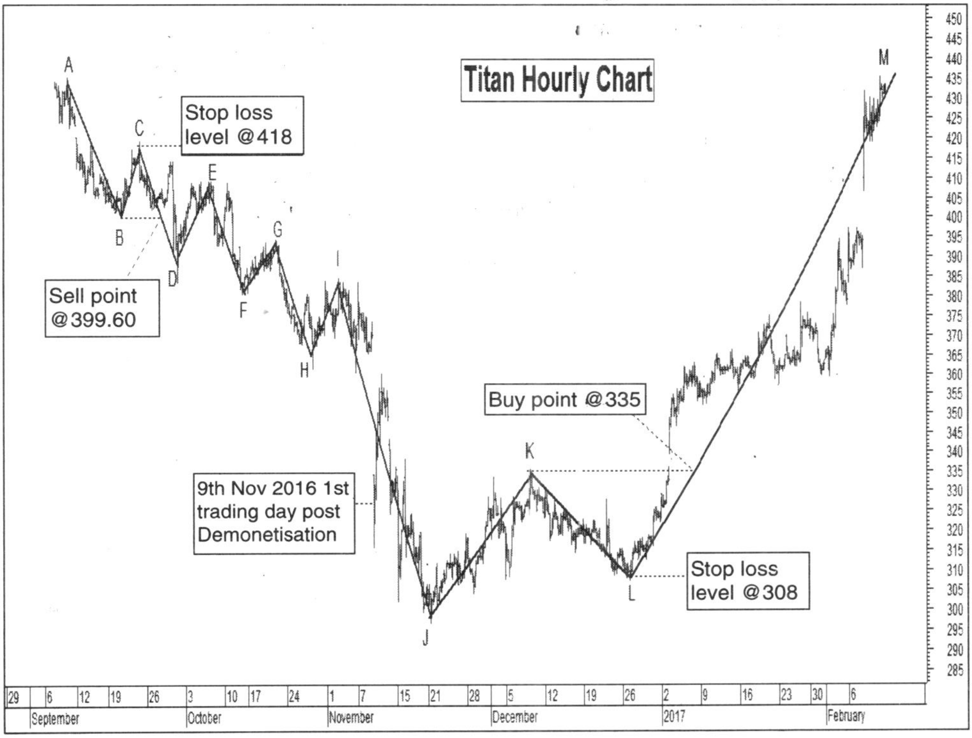

Figure 6.47: **Profitable Dow trades highlighted on the hourly, i.e. 60-minute, price chart of Titan**

~

Trading higher top, higher bottom and lower top, lower bottom pattern formations in the case of Titan's 60-minute chart in Figure 6.47 suggests initiating a sell trade as and when the level made earlier by Point B at around ₹399.60 levels is cracked in the down move from Point C to Point D. Since the stock price thereupon enters a lower top, lower bottom pattern regime. At the time of selling, the stop loss can be placed at Point C, i.e. at about ₹418 levels.

Thereafter the stock price duly declined in a lower top, lower bottom pattern regime and made successive lower tops at points E, G, I, K and successive lower bottoms at points D, F, H, J.

Demonetisation was announced after market hours on 8 November 2016 when the stock price was trading around Point H. Demonetisation resulted in massive price volatility. The very next day, i.e. on 9 November 2016, the stock price opened with a downside gap but closed eventually around the day's high. Thereafter the stock price declined to the lows of around ₹300 levels on the downside, i.e. to around Point J.

Post demonetisation, the stock price rallied strongly from the lows of around ₹300 levels, i.e. from around Point J, and cracked the earlier Point K levels of ₹335 in its up move from Point L to Point M. One should close the sell trade — and instead initiate a fresh buy position — as and when this level cracks on the upside because the stock price thereupon enters a higher top, higher bottom pattern regime. At the time of buying, the stop loss can be placed at Point L at ₹308 levels.

Thereafter the stock price rallied upward to the highs of Point M. At the time of this writing, the stock price was trading around ₹432 levels, i.e. around Point M.

Trade Summary

1. Initiating a sell trade at ₹395 levels, i.e. selling after the price closes below Point D at ₹399.60 level.
2. Buying at ₹347 levels, i.e. after the price closes above the Point K level of ₹335.
3. At the time of this writing, the stock price was trading around ₹432 levels. If the price of ₹432 is taken into account to calculate the mark to market profit / loss account, then trading higher top, higher bottom and lower top, lower bottom pattern formations in this study resulted in a profit of 133 points in the short span of around five months.

~

Example 48: Tata Global Beverages

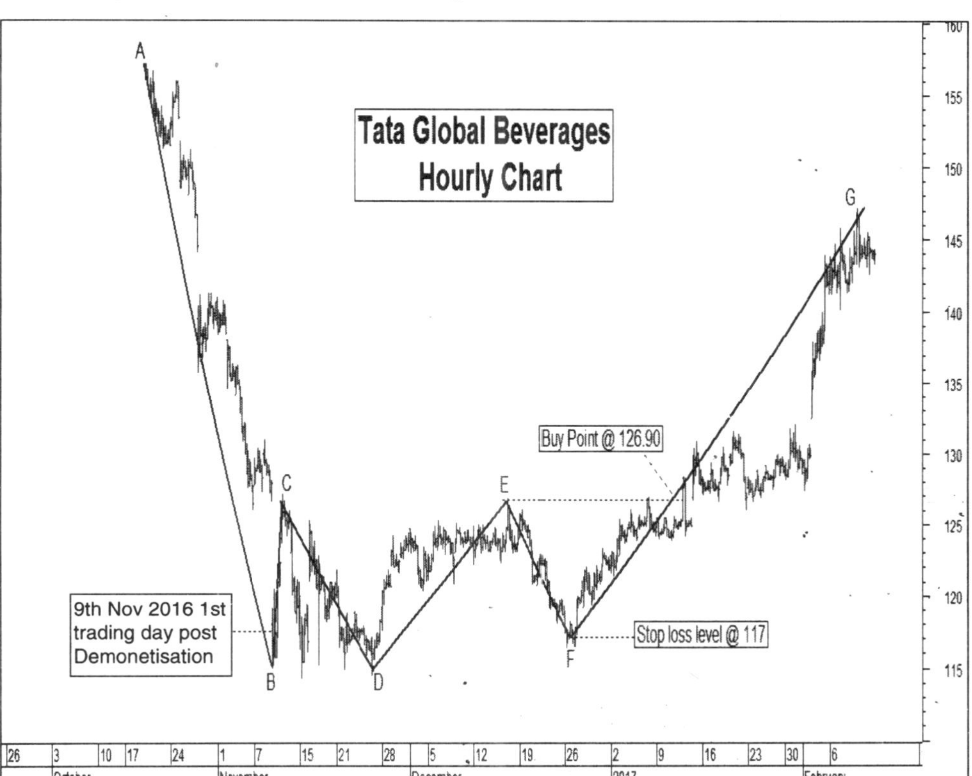

Figure 6.48: **Hourly, i.e. 60-minute, stock price chart of Tata Global Beverages with profitable Dow trades highlighted**

~

In Figure 6.48 the stock price of Tata Global Beverages initially declined from Point A to Point B in a pattern which does not comply with the lower top, lower bottom pattern regime. As a result, Dow Theory practitioners were not able to sell in this down move.

Demonetisation was announced after market hours on 8 November 2016 when the stock price was trading significantly below Point A. The very next day, i.e. on 9 November 2016, the stock price opened with a downside gap but closed around the day's high. The stock price thereafter declined to the lows of around ₹115 levels on the downside, i.e. to around Point D.

Post demonetisation, the stock price rallied upward strongly from around Point D and reached Point E at ₹126.90 levels in the up move from Point F to Point G. One should buy as and when the level made earlier by Point E at around ₹126.90 levels is cracked on the upside whereupon the stock price enters a higher top, higher bottom pattern regime. At the time of buying, the stop loss can be placed at the Point F level at around 1,900 levels. Thereafter the stock price rallied to the highs of around Point G on the upside.

At the time of this writing, the stock price was trading around ₹145 levels, i.e. around Point G.

Trade Summary

1. Buying at ₹127.65 levels, i.e. after the price closes above Point E at ₹126.90 levels.
2. At the time of this writing, the stock price was trading around ₹145 levels. If the market price of ₹145 is taken into account to calculate up to date mark to market profit / loss account then trading higher top, higher bottom and lower top, lower bottom pattern formations would have resulted in a profit of 17.35 points in the short span of around one month.

~

Example 49: Adani Power

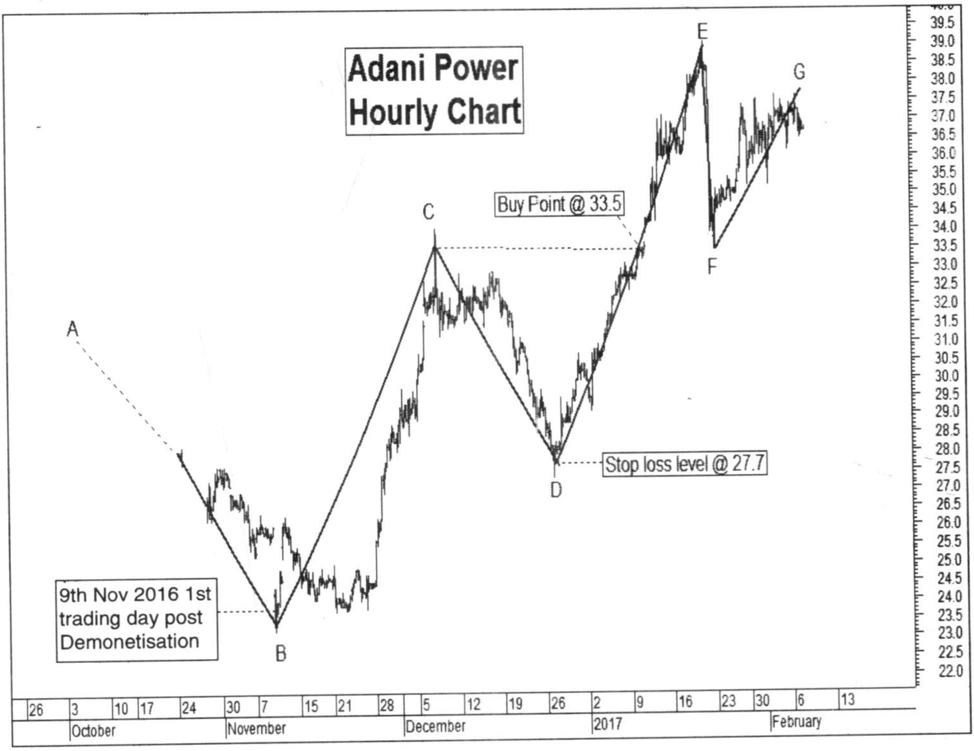

Figure 6.49: **Profitable Dow trades highlighted on the hourly, i.e. 60-minute, price chart of Adani Power**

~

In Figure 6.49, the stock price of Adani Power is seen originally declining from Point A to Point B in a pattern which does not comply with the lower top, lower bottom pattern regime. As a result, Dow Theory practitioners would not have been able to sell in this down move.

Demonetisation was announced after market hours on 8 November 2016 night, when the stock price was trading significantly below Point A. The very next day, i.e. on 9 November 2016, the stock price opened with a downside gap but eventually closed around the day's high. Thereafter the stock price declined to the lows of around ₹115 levels, i.e. to around Point D.

Post demonetisation, the stock price rallied upward strongly from the lows of around ₹23.70 levels and cracked the level made earlier by Point E at around ₹33.50 in the up move from Point F to Point G. One should buy as and when the Point E level of ₹33.50 is cracked on the upside because the stock price then enters a higher top, higher bottom pattern regime. At the time of buying, the stop loss can be placed at the Point F level of ₹27.70.

Thereafter the stock price rallied in a higher top, higher bottom pattern regime and made a higher top at Point G and a higher bottom at Point H.

At the time of this writing, the stock price was trading around ₹37 levels, i.e. around Point I.

Trade Summary

1. Buying at ₹33.55 levels, i.e. after the price closes above Point E level of about ₹33.50.
2. At the time of this writing, the stock price was trading around ₹37 levels. If the price of ₹37 is taken into account to calculate the mark to market profit / loss account, then trading higher top, higher bottom and lower top, lower bottom pattern formations in this case resulted in a profit of 3.45 points in the short span of around one month.

~

Example 50: Allahabad Bank

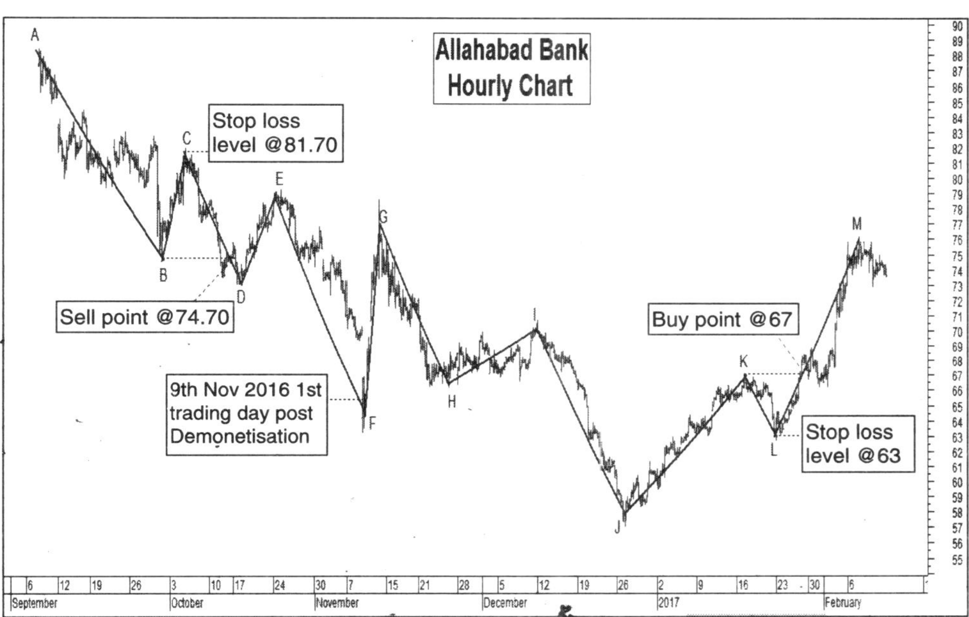

Figure 6.50: **Hourly, i.e. 60-minute, price chart of Allahabad Bank with profitable Dow trades highlighted**

Trading higher top higher bottom and lower top, lower bottom pattern formations in the case of the chart in Figure 6.50 would suggest selling as and when the level made earlier by Point B at ₹74.70 levels is cracked in the down move from Point C to Point D. This is because the stock price thereupon enters a lower top, lower bottom pattern regime. At the time of selling, the sell trade stop loss can be placed at Point C, i.e. at ₹81.70 levels.

Thereafter the stock price declined in a lower top, lower bottom pattern regime and made successive lower tops at points E, G and I, and successive lower bottoms at points D, F and J.

Demonetisation was announced after market hours on 8 November 2016 night when the stock price was trading significantly below Point D. Demonetisation resulted in massive price volatility. The very next day, i.e. on 9 November 2016, the stock price opened with a downside gap but eventually closed around the day's high. The stock price thereafter declined to the lows of around ₹58 levels to Point J, from where it rallied strongly upward and cracked Point K at ₹67 levels on the upside, in the up move from Point L to Point M. One should close the sell position — and instead initiate a fresh buy trade— as and when the level made earlier by Point K at ₹67 levels is cracked on the upside as the stock price thereupon enters a higher top, higher bottom pattern regime. At the time of buying, the stop loss can be placed at the Point L level around ₹63.

Thereafter, the stock price rallied higher to the highs of Point M.

At the time of this writing, the stock price was trading around ₹74 levels, i.e. around Point M.

Trade Summary

1. Initiate a sell trade at ₹74.45 levels, i.e. after the price closes below the Point B level of ₹74.70.
2. Buying at ₹67.75 levels, i.e. buying after the price closes above the Point K level of around ₹67.
3. At the time of this writing, the stock price was trading around ₹74 levels. If the price of ₹74 is taken into account to calculate the mark to market profit / loss account, then trading higher top, higher bottom and lower top, lower bottom pattern formations resulted in a profit of 12.95 points in the short span of around five months in this case.

~

Chapter 7

~

Rebutting Dow Theory Critics

- **Critics** hold that trading higher top, higher bottom and lower top, lower bottom pattern formations is not profitable. They assert that trading higher top, higher bottom pattern formations comprises buying as and when the first higher top, higher bottom pattern formation occurs and thereafter one holds the buy side / long position until either the ongoing higher top, higher bottom pattern formation gets distorted or the stock price enters the lower top, lower bottom pattern regime. One therefore tends to miss out on substantial gains from the upside by the time the ongoing higher top, higher bottom pattern formation gets distorted, or the price enters the lower top, lower bottom pattern regime.

  I believe that nobody can buy at the very bottom and sell at the very top: Hence, instead of focussing on the proportion of profit being missed out, one should consider the profit proportion being garnered.

- **Critics** point out that the stop loss is very deep at the time of initiating a Dow trade.

  While it is true that the stop loss is deep but it is deep only at the time of initiating the trade, i.e. the risk of loss is maximum only at the start of initiating the trade. Thereafter, as the stock price moves in the favourable direction, the stop loss also gets tighter, or one gets a new, comfortable exit point. Yes, I do agree that the stop loss placed at the time of initiating the trade gets triggered, too, without narrowing down or without facilitating a new comfortable exit point, but such instances are fewer in number. One can easily reckon the number of such instances from the one hundred real examples given in this book where the initial stop loss placed at the time of initiating the trade actually got triggered.

To conclude, both evidence and experience suggest that trading higher top, higher bottom and lower top, lower bottom Dow patterns can be consistently profitable.

~